The Shakespeare
Revolution

The Shakespeare Revolution

Criticism and Performance in the Twentieth Century

J. L. STYAN

Andrew Mellon Professor of English
University of Pittsburgh

Cambridge University Press

CAMBRIDGE
LONDON · NEW YORK · MELBOURNE

Published by the Syndics of the Cambridge University Press
The Pitt Building, Trumpington Street, Cambridge CB2 1RP
Bentley House, 200 Euston Road, London NW1 2DB
32 East 57th Street, New York, NY 10022, USA
296 Beaconsfield Parade, Middle Park, Melbourne 3206, Australia

First published 1977

Printed in the United States of America
Typeset by Interprint, Ltd., Malta
Printed and bound by R. R. Donnelley & Sons Company,
Crawfordsville, Indiana

Library of Congress Cataloguing in Publication Data

Styan, J. L.

The Shakespeare Revolution.

Bibliography: p.

Includes index.

1. Shakespeare, William, 1564–1616 – Criticism
and interpretation – History.   2. Shakespeare,
William, 1564–1616 – Dramatic production.

I. Title. PR2969.S85   822.3′3   76 3043
ISBN 0 521 21193 X

36,359

Contents

v

Illustrations

Illustrations

It has proved impossible to locate the copyright owners of
some of the illustrations, but if the author or publisher is
informed, details will be added at the earliest opportunity.

Acknowledgements

Part of the preparation of this book was made possible by a Rackham Research Grant from the University of Michigan, and I wish to express gratitude to the many librarians who have given generous assistance, especially the Librarians of the Shakespeare Centre, Stratford-upon-Avon (Miss Eileen Robinson), the British Theatre Association (formerly the British Drama League), the British Library and its Colindale Newspaper Collection. Some of my material appeared in another form in *Modern Language Quarterly* with the title 'Elizabethan Open Staging: William Poel to Tyrone Guthrie' and I wish to thank the Editor for his kind permission to reprint. My sincere thanks also go to particular colleagues and friends who in various capacities have assisted with contributions or comments or both: Claribel Baird, Michael Black, B. G. Cross, Attilio Favorini, Miriam Gilbert, G. B. Harrison, W. P. Halstead and Rita Huber. My debt to the many excellent accounts of modern Shakespeare production by distinguished playgoers like A. C. Sprague, J. C. Trewin and Norman Marshall will be apparent. The fundamental debt is to all those amateur and professional players who have, for whatever reason and however well or badly, made their contribution to the total of our experience of Shakespeare over the years.

J. L. S.

Introductory

This is a history which tries to trace a revolution in Shakespeare's
fortunes both on the stage and in the study during this century. 'Revolution' seems to be the appropriate word for an unusual turn-about in
both criticism and performance. One grand discovery of the twentieth
century is that Shakespeare knew his business as a playwright. On the
one hand, this century has seen directors turn a complete somersault
in their approach to the production of his plays. The stage has moved
from the elaborate decoration of Beerbohm Tree to the austerities of
Peter Hall, from the illusory realism of Henry Irving to the non-illusory
statements of Peter Brook. Through this development some have felt
that our generation knows more of the genuine Shakespeare experience
than our grandfathers did.[1] On the other hand, the new academia has
encouraged a phenomenal growth in Shakespeare scholarship and
criticism, and this has ranged from the circumstantial character
analysis of Bradley, through digressive studies in imagery and word
patterns after Spurgeon, to the inspirational, impulsive visions of
Wilson Knight. Harley Granville-Barker's verdict was:

His plays have had every sort of treatment. Actors have twisted them up into
swagger shapes, scholars have rolled them flat, producers have immured them
in scenery.[2]

He went on to say that the one tribute still to be paid to them was to
discover what, as plays, they essentially are.

Could the Shakespeare of the stage and the study have been the
same man, the plays the same plays? The Shakespeare industry
branched in such different directions that it scarcely seemed to have
the same root. This is a sad reflection on how our first of playwrights
has been regarded by those who teach and play him, and a worse
reflection on our general failure to see the drama as requiring a mutual
discipline of study and performance.

A few warning voices were heard in the early years. William Poel

1

and the Elizabethan Stage Society must take the credit for trying as practically as possible to show that Shakespeare should be understood in his own medium. Before he became professor of English literature at Oxford, Sir Walter Raleigh had written to Poel, 'I am sure the only thing for Shakespeare critics is to go back to the Globe and Fortune and understand them.'[3] In the correspondence surrounding Percy Simpson's work on the punctuation of the original text[4] Granville-Barker threw in his weight with

It is unwise to decide upon any disputed passage without seeing it in *action*, without canvassing all its dramatic possibilities. For a definitive text, we need first a Shakespeare Theatre in which a generation of scholars may be as used to seeing as to reading the play.[5]

Addressing the Royal Society of Literature, Granville-Barker drew attention to the fact that an overwhelming proportion of dramatic criticism 'is written by people who, you might suppose, could never have been inside a theatre in their lives'. His plea was for a new school of Shakespeare criticism based upon experiment with the plays in the theatre.[6]

From another quarter at about this time, there were signs that the drama was being regarded with less of the Puritan prejudice that for so long banished it to academic limbo. In 1919 Geoffrey Whitworth founded the British Drama League to encourage the art of the theatre both amateur and professional, and to urge the material establishment of such fantasies as a national theatre, drama departments in universities and a drama curriculum in the schools. The bigger American universities began the practical study of drama, generating some of the impulse to create community theatre in the USA. Recognizing the close relationship between the theatre and social life, a correspondent to *The Times* was found writing,

We are apt to think of the drama, in its lower reaches, as mere tomfoolery, in its higher as a Cinderella-sister to literature.... But, however natural an upgrowth from the soil drama may be, it needs no less than other such products its refinery of thought, which it should find, surely, in our universities. Here what is needed is something like a Faculty of Personal Expression. . . .[7]

The writer dared to advocate that 'certain aspects' of music and 'even' of dancing constitute part of the study.

Introductory

It is hard to believe how few were willing to acknowledge that the actor and director of a play, not to mention its spectators, acquire special insights which can only develop in the actual presentation of a play, tested by a live audience. The first and last values of drama are revealed in the response of an audience in a theatre, and all else must be secondary and speculative. Nor does an actor's best thinking about his part emerge in some vacuum of novelty: he is the closest student of a play who offers himself in it, as if naked, to the public view. At the same time, what serious director dare ignore the best kind of dramatic scholarship?

The record of any direct indebtedness of criticism to practice, or of practice to criticism, is ridiculously sparse. Hazlitt and Leigh Hunt gave the impression that John Philip Kemble at Drury Lane and Covent Garden 'had succeeded in stamping his own image of Macbeth on the imagination of a whole generation of critics'.[8] Goethe's notion of Hamlet as a pale and melancholy romantic finally emerged as Henry Irving's gentle, lovesick Prince, imitated by a score of others in this vein.[9] Beerbohm Tree's programme note to his Macbeth at the Haymarket in 1911 acknowledged the 'inspiring' study of the character by Bradley.[10] Dover Wilson believed that our understanding of *Love's Labour's Lost* was completely changed by Guthrie's production at the Old Vic in 1936.[11] In his work on the production of *King Lear* at Stratford in 1962, Peter Brook was excited by Jan Kott's *Shakespeare Our Contemporary*, which had just appeared in its French edition. All of this, however, is ephemeral and a matter of chance: any true interaction between study and stage runs deeper, and points as much to the history of taste as of perception.

In spite of the chasm between acting and criticism, Shakespeare production since Irving and Beerbohm Tree has undergone something of a revolution, comparable and in parallel with a less apparent, but no less profound, change in criticism. Certain productions beginning with the courageous attacks on tradition by William Poel and Granville-Barker have marked the progress of the change. The work of these men did echo contemporary scholarship, though it owed less than is thought to that psychological speculation about character which any good actor had always regarded as his personal prerogative, or to the literary interest in word and image patterns, which often requires that a play be read backwards to arrive at the point.[12] The former assumed the play to be a realistic novel, the latter a metaphysical poem. As men of the theatre, the best practitioners accepted that an actor's and director's first duty was to be loyal to their author by first making him acceptable to their audience, but the finest directors of the twentieth century sought to interpret Shakespeare's meaning by looking increasingly to his own stage practice. The secret of what he intended lies in how he worked.

It is questionable whether the real advances in Shakespeare scholarship in this century have come through verbal and thematic studies. A stronger claim can be made for another line of scholarship more directly related to the practical business of staging a play, research which can be traced from the new interest in the Elizabethan playhouse and its conventions after the discovery of the Swan drawing in 1888 and W. W. Greg's publication of Henslowe's *Diary* and *Papers* between 1904 and 1908. The interest in the playhouse was a first sign of an even more important concern with Elizabethan playing conditions, the form these imposed on the playwriting and thence the nature of the Elizabethan dramatic experience. The new direction for study is early seen in the work on the playhouses by the Malone Society after 1906, and by scholars like J. Q. Adams, A. H. Thorndike, W. J. Lawrence and E. K. Chambers in the first years of this century. This in turn is to be linked with what has been called the 'workshop' approach to the plays, associated at first with such names as R. G. Moulton, George Pierce Baker and Arthur Quiller-Couch.[13]

Yet the matter is not simple, since theatrical sensibility is hardly confined to the study. While Poel and the Elizabethan Stage Society were rediscovering their Shakespeare by testing him in a mock-up of his own conditions, European theatre at large was already reacting against the realism of the proscenium arch. Men of immense theatrical influence – Adolphe Appia, Meyerhold, Gordon Craig, Georg Fuchs, Max Reinhardt and others – were bent on demolishing the concept of theatre-as-illusion. By the time Granville Barker set up his daring impressionist productions of the comedies at the Savoy in 1912 and 1914, the notion that theatre had to reproduce life by verisimilitude was already succumbing to the non-illusory assaults of the theatre men. Had they known, the students of Elizabethan dramatic convention might eventually have found themselves marching in step with such

4

scandalous avant-gardists as Pirandello, Cocteau, Brecht, Genêt and others who have returned its former elasticity to the stage.

The new Shakespeare, often bitterly derided by the traditionalists, did not, however, make his appearance on any make-shift Elizabethan stage. The real sense of change came when such apparent eccentrics as Nigel Playfair, Barry Jackson and Tyrone Guthrie sought repeatedly to give their audiences what they took to be the stuff of the Shakespeare experience. As far as it could be reclaimed three centuries later, they tried to capture and translate the temper of the original. Each man's search was for an authentic balance between the freedom a Shakespeare script grants the actor and the responsibility of recharging the play's first meaning. Where Granville-Barker had aimed at a new unity of tone and effect by returning to Shakespeare's text and structural continuity, the new men aimed at hitting a modern approximation to the Elizabethan *mode* of performance.

While a few brilliant directors pursued their Elizabethan Shakespeare on the stage, at the same time a few scholars were looking more closely at Elizabethan dramatic conventions. E. E. Stoll, Levin Schücking and, later, M. C. Bradbrook pursued a more objective, less impressionistic criticism; they hoped to blow away what Granville-Barker called the transcendental fog of nineteenth-century thinking about Shakespeare. Characters were to be understood in period, and not in terms of modern realistic motivation. This development of historical criticism was soon matched by an increasing interest in the thrust stage as a practical medium for production. A surprising post-Second World War spurt in scholarship on the Elizabethan playhouse is associated with a much longer list of distinguished names: G. F. Reynolds, G. R. Kernodle, G. E. Bentley, Cranford Adams, Walter Hodges, Leslie Hotson, Glynne Wickham, Richard Southern, Bernard Beckerman and Richard Hosley. Although most of these would not claim to be dramatic critics, it is clear that each shares the idea of non-illusory Elizabethan performance, controlled by the medium of the playhouse. The flexible Elizabethan mode of performance, playing to the house, stepping in and out of character, generating a stage action allegorical and symbolic, making no pretence at the trappings of realism, encouraged a verbally acute, sensory and participatory, multi-levelled and fully aware mode of experience for an audience.

Meanwhile Tyrone Guthrie was working on his plans for his first festival theatre with projecting stage at Stratford in Ontario (1953). Designed by Tanya Moiseiwitsch, it was based on Guthrie's conviction that 'a play can be best presented by getting as near as possible to the manner in which the author envisaged its performance'. Its success was another new departure, and the Stratford, Ontario stage became the pattern for new theatre-building throughout America and England.

There is no question but that the actors spurned most of the scholarship and criticism which seemed to lead readers away from the aural and visual heart of the play experience. The schoolroom lacks the corrective aura of the theatre, and, for students, criticism which is not stage-centred has been the source of much enervating treatment of Shakespeare, the liveliest of playwrights. However, some of the more fruitful research of recent years has been in the history of performance, reconstructed through promptbooks and contemporary reports.[14] Such work recognized directions for future Shakespeare studies, and brought practice and criticism into a healthier alliance for the benefit of both the stage and the study.

In retrospect, it seems no coincidence that the new direction and focus of scholarly thinking about Shakespeare, together with the new freedom from the constrictions of realism and the proscenium arch, should culminate in Peter Brook's landmark production of *A Midsummer Night's Dream* at Stratford in England in 1970. This performance fittingly brings the first phase of the story to a close. It is easy to be deceived by Brook's apparently non-Elizabethan devices. The plays of Shakespeare, although the most familiar in the classical repertory, remain the most subject to variation in performance: the mode of non-illusory theatre is still remote and elusive for modern actors and spectators. What may at first seem outrageous in a production —fairies in gold paint, a Hamlet in plus-fours, the Athenian lovers in a gymnasium — may actually be urging upon the audience the true substance of the make-believe.

The call for a stage-centred study of Shakespeare is not new, nor has it been fully answered. William Poel is the father of this history, but his voice was eccentric in his time. Granville-Barker lent his greater authority to the movement, and in *The Exemplary Theatre*,[15] his manifesto of principles for a national theatre, he wrote a seminal essay which must have seemed out of key with the profession and its ways:

Introductory

The matured actor's best chance of developing his art and observing his progress lies less in the performances he gives than in his opportunities for study, and especially for the co-operative study (the only valid kind, as we have seen and must further see) involved in the rehearsing of a play.

To ask the actor to study more and perform less was hardly realistic in 1922, but is now the established policy of the Royal Shakespeare Company since Peter Hall's administration. We note, incidentally, the link between better stage practice and a subsidized repertory system.

With the fearlessness of youth Muriel Bradbrook put the case for a stage-centred understanding of Shakespeare in her prize essay of 1931, *Elizabethan Stage Conditions: A Study of their Place in the Interpretation of Shakespeare's Plays.*[16] It was an outright attack upon the academic Shakespeare industry.

It is a curious fact that [the study of stage conditions], the latest to be studied, should be the most indisputably direct influence upon the plays ... but it is only during the last thirty years that a detailed investigation of stage conditions has been carried out.

She pointed out that Malone's scholarly pioneer work on the stage conditions[18] had been ignored for a hundred years. Why did this matter? Because critics who forget the stage can get their premises wrong:

Writers of appreciative criticism who neglect the historic approach are liable to blunder on questions of tone; to mistake conventions for faults, to rationalise an illogical custom of the theatre, or to miss the point of a device.... But perhaps the chief value of the knowledge of stage conditions is a negative one. It prevents wrong assumptions, or the laying of emphasis in the wrong place. This unobtrusive correcting of the critical focus is almost impossible to define or describe, like the change of vision produced by wearing glasses.[19]

Reviewing the critical record, Dr Bradbrook remarked the dislike shared by Coleridge, Lamb and Hazlitt of their own representational stage, and their 'inability to conceive of any other'. Coleridge, for example, condemned Shakespeare's 'naked room, a blanket for a curtain', and Dr Bradbrook aptly commented, 'It apparently never occurred to him that a naked room might make a suitable background for Shakespeare.'[20]

The inability to conceive of some other mode of theatre is the trouble still, and, in the second impression of her book in 1962, Dr Bradbrook rather flattered the modern theatre by suggesting that the twentieth century had abolished the picture stage,[21] coming closer to its Elizabethan forerunner than any other. She was too optimistic in believing that we had at last learned to recognize and respect the dramatic conventions of the Elizabethans.[22] But she smelt the wind. A practical knowledge of the living theatre has enriched scholarship, and on all sides there are signs of fresh thinking.

At random: Bernard Grebanier believes that the simplicity of *Hamlet* on the stage has been distorted by academic criticism.[23] Harry Levin has remarked the 'renewed concentration on [Shakespeare] in his natural habitat, the theatre', and believes that 'the next generation — not without gratitude — could undertake to synthesize and interpret with more freedom and more security'.[24] John Russell Brown believes that the shocking gap between the actor and the academic could be bridged by keeping a scene-by-scene record of every major production.[25] Maurice Charney cuts new ground in the study of the character of Hamlet by recognizing the self-conscious artifice of Elizabethan stage illusion and the play's obsession with acting *per se*.[26] Stanley Wells, commenting on the 'discovery' by the R.S.C. in 1964 that Marlowe's *The Jew of Malta* was a viable play in the theatre, raises another issue: 'The reading of plays in an untheatrical way can help to contribute to their neglect in the professional theatre and to their under-valuation.'[27] While he believes that the writings of Shakespeare critics can perform a valuable service to the theatre,[28] Wells conversely insists that 'theatrical experience of the plays is necessary for a Shakespeare critic'.[29]

Performance-experiment and performance-analysis have at least this claim to validity, that those devices of Elizabethan origin which can be made to work, those rhythms of speech, the flexing of character, illusion and the structural orchestration of the play, when tried upon a live audience assembled in conditions of theatre, are less open to the irrelevancies of impressionistic criticism for which the writer need consult no one other than himself. Norman Rabkin may summarize the matter for us. The English Institute Essays he recently collected[30] provoked a foreword in which he marked a distinct shift in approach to the criticism of Shakespeare and his contemporaries. All the collected papers discuss drama 'as earlier critics neither could nor wanted to:

Introductory

the play as it impinges on its audience, as it is experienced'. The acknowledged debt is to the stage itself. His authors

seem to agree also that the new concern is best served by a new kind of scrutiny of the play itself. In the view which I believe they hold in common of the work of art as a complex and highly determined shaping of an audience's responses, the writers are freed from the increasingly deadening obligation to an old paradigm to reduce works to meanings.[31]

The search is on, for the theatrical effect and experience of the original performance, in the belief that the meaning is in the experience.

It is probably too soon to tell whether the critic's sense of the new Shakespeare has moved closer to the actor's, or vice versa. Nevertheless, in tracing the development of our understanding of Shakespeare as it reveals itself in and out of the theatre and in its progress from Victorian illusion to Elizabethan non-illusion over the last hundred years, the present investigation will find that actor and critic often have more in common than would at first appear.

1

Victorian Shakespeare

When individuals walk about the stage with measured steps, stand in symmetrical positions, raising their hands first to their breasts, then towards the heavens, then towards the earth, making recitals of every speech they utter, I feel sure it is fatal to all interpretation of character. . . . A man, when he tells his friends he hopes to go to heaven, does not point towards the sky to demonstrate his meaning. Why, then, should it be done on the stage? [1]

William Poel wrote this in response to an average Drury Lane production of *Hamlet* in 1874. It is salutary to be reminded of how playgoers saw Shakespeare a hundred years ago. [2] Playgoers who today are more accustomed to bare boards and a symbolic spotlight against a non-representational skeleton set may find it hard to understand the satisfaction with which our predecessors viewed the spectacular realism of Kemble and the Keans, Macready, Phelps, Irving and Tree while still accepting the declamatory school of acting. [3] Theirs was satisfaction indeed, with rarely a doubt. Moreover, the mid-Victorians were hearing more of Shakespeare's words. The insistent criticism of men of letters like Coleridge, Lamb and Hazlitt had taken effect, and enthusiasts congratulated themselves on a steady return to Shakespeare's text under Robert Elliston, Edmund Kean, William Macready and Samuel Phelps.

For in spite of the new bardolatry at the end of the eighteenth century, in the early years of the nineteenth the hacking and plastering of Shakespeare for the stage was still normal practice. *Henry IV, Part I* lost its mock trial because the scene was too long, although, like its sequel *Henry IV, Part II*, it was rarely played because of 'the want of ladies' in the cast. *Measure for Measure* was purged of its 'bawdy' scenes for the sake of propriety, and *The Merchant of Venice* lost much of Bassanio for the sake of convenience. *Twelfth Night* sacrificed 'O mistress mine' and 'Come away, death' because Feste was played by a woman. Polonius was always played for a buffoon, and so Laertes had to manage without his father's words of wisdom. Hamlet did not give his reasons for sparing Claudius at prayer, because they were thought unnecessarily weakening to the character of the Prince. Lear had to manage without the Fool, who was taken to be too low for high tragedy, like Bianca the harlot in *Othello*. Decorum also dictated the excision of the scene of Cassio and the handkerchief (which in any case was too much for the Moor to bear) and of Desdemona's preparation for bed— she expected to die by the dagger, not by a pillow.[4]

The London stage at the beginning of the nineteenth century was still dominated by John Philip Kemble, and remained so until his retirement in 1817. He used Cibber's *Richard III* unquestioningly,[5] and returned to the vandalism of Tate's *Lear*, introducing his own mutilations by omitting the blinding of Gloucester and his 'fall' from Dover Cliff.[6] At this time it was evident that there was little feeling in the theatre for Shakespeare's structural rhythms and ordering of emphasis. Kemble's *Tempest* still included Dryden's gay Restoration couple Dorinda and Hippolyto, and since Dorinda rather outshone Miranda as a pert innocent, her part was usually played by the better actress. Hippolyto was in any case a breeches part, always given to a woman the better to show her legs. Of such kind was the interest in Shakespeare's mature comedy in 1806 (see Plate 1).

It is easy to ridicule this sort of cobbling, but Odell reminds us that Kemble had first to ensure the paying presence of an audience:

Without some such tempering mercy, we shall hardly know how to deal with a manager whose King Lear is Tate's, whose Richard III is Cibber's, whose Comedy of Errors is Hull's, who uses Garrick's Romeo and Juliet, and goes out of his way to engraft on Coriolanus large bits of Thomson [James, author of *The Seasons*], and on The Tempest larger masses of Dryden and Davenant.[7]

However, by the middle of the century, the 'judicious' additions of the eighteenth century had vanished. Gone were Davenant's jolly songs and dances for *Macbeth*,[8] with the stage filled with a host of witches singing and dancing to make an operatic pantomime; Pyramus and Thisbe no longer appeared in *As You Like It*,[9] nor Beatrice and Benedick in *Measure for Measure*; the Cordelia of Nahum Tate was never again expected to survive Edmund's writ upon her life in order to wed Edgar; Colley Cibber no longer shared the honour of being part-author with Shakespeare of *Richard III*; lacking James Howard's judicious sense of timing, Juliet failed to wake from her drugged sleep just in time to stop Romeo's fatal draught and bring the curtain down on a happy marriage.

Amid the self-congratulation, however, other problems arose less easy of solution. After the fires of 1808 and 1809, Covent Garden and

1   The height of fashion for Ferdinand and Miranda in *The Tempest*, Theatre Royal, Drury Lane, 1777

2   The Drury Lane Theatre, Drury Lane, in 1808

Drury Lane had been rebuilt as temples to Thespis, worthy of the national poet. If the new Drury Lane had a proscenium opening of 33 feet, that at Covent Garden extended to 42 feet 6 inches with wings of 20 feet. 300 lamps lit the stage. Covent Garden seated 3,044 persons, and Drury Lane 3,611. Magnificence knew no bounds.[10] But, sitting in the upper gallery, a playgoer could find himself 100 feet from the stage. This immense size of the playhouse should be held in mind when we judge a Victorian actor–manager's failure to capture Shakespeare's intention behind a scene of domestic intimacy, or the rapport between an Elizabethan clown and his audience, or the pace of the repartee in one of the comedies. Both great patent theatres were not good for much more than bellowing if Shakespeare's words were to be heard at all. Certainly, there could have been no thought of approximating the working conditions of an Elizabethan playwright and his actors (see Plate 2).

In the chapters that follow we shall be looking closely at *A Midsummer Night's Dream* as seen through the eyes of Granville-Barker and Peter Brook. In the time of Kemble the comedies had almost been transmuted into musicals, their music and lyrics pillaged from every source and freely exchanged from play to play. *The Dream* put on at Covent Garden by Frederick Reynolds in 1816 was proudly embellished with a host of songs, duets, glees and dances. Pyramus and Thisbe found themselves transposed to allow the triumphs of Theseus to conclude the play in music and pageantry, while their scene was watched by Theseus from behind a convenient tree in the wood. The lovers had their lines drastically reduced in order to make room for pretty jingles like this of Demetrius as he runs from Helena:

> Recall the minutes that are fled,
>   Forbid fleet time to move;
> To new life wake the sleeping dead,
>   But ne'er recall my love.
> Forbid the stormy waves to roar,
>   The playful winds to rove,
> Revive the sun at midnight hour,
>   But ne'er recall my love.

The urge towards comic operetta at least acknowledged that Shakespeare's romantic comedy was none too realistic.

Another, almost uncontrollable, force began to overwhelm Shakespeare on the stage and to dog the actors. The theatres of the mid-century became magic boxes, and their audiences were at once enthralled by the arts of the new scenic machinery. Kemble and Mrs Siddons were particularly pleased to play the Roman and the history plays in more authentic and splendid costume and stage décor. They made spectacular use of processions and dances wherever the play lent itself to them, and decorated the stage with marble architecture, painted palaces and imposing cathedrals and streets. *Richard III* had on stage the Tower of London itself. None of this was 'authentic' by the standards of the modern cinema, and Hamlet could appear as a courtier wearing the Orders of the Garter and Elephant, Othello could assume the scarlet uniform of a British general and Lear might rave in a flowered satin night-gown.

The new Shakespearian spectacular arrived at Covent Garden in the season of 1811–12 with Kemble's *Henry VIII*. *The Times* provided an awestruck description of the lavish display without which, the correspondent believed, the audience could not sustain the play's 'accumulated *ennui*':

In its five acts it has, as distinctly as we can remember, three processions, two trials before the king, a banquet, and a royal christening. The banquet deserved all the praise that can be given to costly elegance. It was the most dazzling stage exhibition that we have ever seen. The tables were continued round the stage, covered with golden ornaments, and the whole pomp of princely feasting. As the scene receded, it was filled with attendants and guards in their glittering 'coats of livery'. The Gothic pillars – the rich tracery of the architecture – the various and shifting splendour that fell from the chandeliers – the glittering company of 'courtly dames and barons bold' . . . gave as many images to the eye and the mind, as perhaps could be given by the highest combination of theatric ornament and theatric taste.

This kind of indulgence served as a challenge to subsequent actor—managers, and panoramic forum scenes appeared in *Julius Caesar*, an overwhelming storm in *The Tempest*, magnificent sea-fights in *Antony and Cleopatra* and an unending procession to match the glories of the coronation in *Henry IV, Part II*. By 1859, a line from the Chorus in *Henry V*, 'How London doth pour out her citizens', could prompt an actual mob of 300 extras to welcome Henry back to London after Agincourt.

The playbills began to announce the names of armies of decorators and to sell their wares in detail. In 1814 Edmund Kean proudly announced the following new 'scenes' for *Macbeth*:

Romantic Landscape — Rocky Pass and Bridge — Gothic Screen — Gallery in Macbeth's Castle — Banquet Hall — Cavern and Car of Clouds — Hecate's Cave — Castle Gate and Courtyard — Exterior of the Castle.

In his *A Midsummer Night's Dream* of 1816, Frederick Reynolds graced Theseus's palace with 'a Grand Doric Colonnade'; Oberon and Titania made their entrance riding in cars with their trains of fairies in procession; from time to time clouds descended and opened to discover singing fairies before they ascended again; and it seems that Titania's fairy province was not only bosky but pelagic, since she also had a fleet of galleys on the sea. Confirming the impression that spectators had begun to rate a play by its ostentation before its matter, Macready in 1841 finally instituted the practice of distributing descriptive lists of the scenes on handbills, adding historical notes where necessary. The general feeling at this time was that Shakespeare wrote magnificent poetry, but not good plays. Therefore, the actor—manager's aim was to produce memorable 'illustrations' of Shakespeare.

Historiography became fashionable after Kemble's younger brother Charles mounted a *King John* which set a new standard for scenic scholarship, and advertized its pedantry on the playbill:

This present Monday, January 19, 1824,
Will be revived Shakespeare's Tragedy of
KING JOHN
With an attention to Costume
Never equalled on the English stage. Every Character will
appear in the precise
HABIT OF THE PERIOD
The whole of the Dresses and Decorations being executed
from indisputable Authorities, such as
Monumental Effigies, Seals, Illumined MSS., &c.

The poster continued with a most convincing list of such authorities, from King John's effigy in Worcester Cathedral to his silver cup 'in the Possession of the Corporation of King's Lynn, Norfolk'. This suggests not only a characteristically misplaced ingenuity in the interpretation of poetic drama, but also a donnish appeal to a new kind of playgoer. It was a curious antiquarianism which thrived on *Antony and Cleopatra* for its opportunity to display the splendours of Alexandria and the Roman capitol, or revelled in *Cymbeline* for its mixture of artifacts suggested by collections of ancient British weapons, the Welsh Triads and the literature of Augustan Rome. What is in worse taste than to pursue authenticity blind to all but a false ideal of erudition?

After about 1817 the new world of gas-light emerged (and twenty years later, lime-light), providing a new incentive for the painters and carpenters, costume designers and machinists. Not only could *Twelfth Night* offer the public a 'grand masque' of Juno and Ceres with which to embellish the original, and not only could Cleopatra's galley sail again on the River Cydnus after two thousand years, but it was now possible to supply a moonlit garden for *The Merchant of Venice* and the moonlit wood for *A Midsummer Night's Dream*. When electricity arrived in the time of Irving and Beerbohm Tree, enthusiasm for illusion knew no bounds.[11]

Following Lamb, the critics of misplaced illusion soon made a swelling chorus. Ariel of *The Tempest* had become, according to one critic, 'a robust young lady with a pair of painted gauze wings stuck to her shoulders', and on Prospero's 'to the elements/Be free', her last song was usually embellished with a glee sung by 'half a dozen fat chorus-singers, let down from the ceiling in a clumsy creaking piece of machinery'. The point was then made: 'The whole affair is a futile attempt to embody beings who can have no existence but in the imagination'[12] — or, we might add, only in a theatre of a non-illusory kind. In 1820, Kean contrived so fine a storm for his *Lear* that the effects of trees bending and wind roaring stole applause from the actor, who could not be heard above the din. *The Times* quipped, 'He should have recollected that it is the bending of Lear's mind under his wrongs that is the object of interest, and not that of a forest beneath the hurricane.' *John Bull* had misgivings about Macready's spectacularly beautiful *Tempest* of 1838, but argued that scenic resources could aid the dramatic illusion 'provided they are made subservient to the higher purposes of the scene'. Those higher purposes remained obscured for many years.

At Covent Garden in 1838, Macready's *Henry V* went so far as to illustrate the words of the Chorus with 'Pictorial Illustrations from the Pencil of Mr Stanfield', and amazed its audience with a machine to provide a moving diorama of the siege of Harfleur in which the pictorial melted into the action of the play itself. *The Times*'s critic, impressed like everyone else, nevertheless cautioned

Excessive pageantry is no sign of a revival of the drama.... However great the attempt to represent closely an army on a battle field, still the obviousness of the attempt can only render its fruitlessness more apparent. . . . The discrepancy between the stage and reality still remains.

John Bull said of Mme Vestris's *Dream* of 1840, 'An occasional preference of the suggestive to the actual would be more in keeping with the fairy texture of the drama and would take greater hold of the fancy.' The voice was still timid, but such hints that some of the Victorian public were sensible of a contradiction between intention and execution would grow stronger.

In 1838, Macready had the honour of eliminating Tate's sorry love affair between Cordelia and Edgar, and of recovering the Fool in *King Lear*. Even then, lacking confidence that the Fool could ever be played by a man, he settled for a woman in the part and turned the character for pathos as a 'fragile, hectic, beautiful-faced, half-idiot-looking boy', according to the *Diary*.[13] There was more Shakespeare in Macready's production than at any time since Burbage, but speeches were still cut and rearranged to give Lear, played of course by Macready, stronger exits. Here now began that nineteenth-century phenomenon of running scenes together out of order, so contrived as to ease the burden on the scene-changers. Odell described a medley of mad scenes from the third act:

The fourth scene begins with Shakespeare's fourth — part of the heath, with a hovel — into which is injected, much curtailed, Shakespeare's Scene 6 — the farmhouse, with the entry of Gloster, Lear's imagined trial of Goneril, etc. — and then ends with the last part of the original Scene 4![14]

Worse could happen. Beerbohm Tree's garden set for *Twelfth Night* in 1901 was so sumptuous that it could not be struck, and Odell reports that it was perforce used for many episodes for which it was absurdly inappropriate: 'all evening this lovely garden appeared and reappeared, always, I think, to the delight of the audience'.[15] Unhappily, Norman Marshall reminded us that the transposition of scenes to fit the scenery was still the practice not long ago:

Imagine a conductor beginning his performance of a Beethoven symphony by transposing the first and second subjects of the opening movement. Yet this seems to me no worse than what was done to *Twelfth Night* when it was produced at Stratford in 1948 with the first and second scenes transposed. The opening lines of Scene One ('If music be the food of love, play on') announce the theme of the play. Musically the verse is exquisitely attuned to its purpose, which is to establish a mood. Begin instead with the deliberately utilitarian verse of the second scene and the musical structure is at once shattered.[16]

After the Act of 1843 repealed the monopoly of Covent Garden and Drury Lane, legitimate Shakespeare could be played anywhere. Covent Garden became an opera house in 1847 and Drury Lane sank temporarily under a popular load of opera and circus, but the shrewd Samuel Phelps at Sadler's Wells and the scholarly Charles Kean at the Princess's supplied new homes for Shakespeare in their very different ways. To these theatres should be added the Haymarket, where Benjamin Webster's unusual revival of *The Shrew* in 1844 was played with two screens and two curtains designed by J. R. Planché, that is, it was played without scenery, and advertised 'as acted divers times at the Globe and Blackfriars Playhouses'. However, before reformists claim a founding father, it should be remembered that, to add to the number of orchestra stalls, Webster had the year before boasted 'a curtailment of the useless portion of the Stage in front of the Curtain'. Shakespeare's stagecraft remained a secondary consideration — if it was considered at all.

Phelps's purist approach to the text could not be sustained in 1849 for *Antony and Cleopatra*, in which 42 scene changes prompted every kind of scene juggling. But Phelps pleased for other reasons than the attraction of the spectacular. Henry Morley commented,

A main cause of the success of Mr Phelps in his Shakespearean revivals is, that he shows in his author above all things the poet. Shakespeare's plays are always poems, as performed at Sadler's Wells. The scenery is always beautiful, but it is not allowed to draw attention from the poet, with whose whole conception it is made to blend in the most perfect harmony. The actors are content also to be subordinated to the play, learn doubtless at rehearsals how to subdue excesses of expression that by giving undue force to one part would destroy the balance of the whole, and blend their work in such a way as to produce everywhere the right emphasis.... We have perceived something like the entire sense of one of Shakespeare's plays, and have been raised above ourselves by the perception.[17]

We perceive a new, Coleridgean standard implicit in these remarks: a requirement of something like 'poetic unity' such as is not fully satisfied until the twentieth century. Stage presentation may have been thoroughly Victorian, localizing every scene as nearly as possible, but in Phelps's Shakespeare the dramatic poet was allowed to speak.

With his passion for archaeology, Charles Kean diligently sought out the minutiae of history for every detail of his décor, calling in experts, studying documents, writing his programmes like textbooks. If he thought the histories were intended to educate the Elizabethans, he proceeded to go lavishly to work on schooling the Victorians, as much by his endless programme notes as by the plays themselves. Behind this feverish activity lay another misplaced belief, that to eliminate anachronism was to return dramatic unity to Shakespeare. Unfortunately Kean employed nearly 550 hands to mount his spectacles, and with every new extravagance of scenic accuracy, some new piece of the text had to go. Yet the conflict between author and authenticity, poetry and pageantry, was accepted almost without demur.

It is amusing to find Kean in 1856 grievously troubled in *The Winter's Tale* by the treacherous and elusive sea-coast of Bohemia: he set these scenes in 'Bithynia' and dressed the Bohemian characters in the costumes of Asia Minor. It did not bother him that Autolycus and the English shepherds were omitted. Kean settled for the barest bones of dialogue in order to furnish *Richard II* (1857) with a spectacular entry into London and *The Tempest* of the same year with a sumptuous masque to defy description. Bigger and better facilities promoted a dogged but mistaken realism. Macbeth's Witches seemed more and more supernatural, materializing and vanishing behind green gauzes; battles and processions recruited veritable armies of supers; Phelps's transparencies dissolved the fairies of *A Midsummer Night's Dream* into a dream indeed; the shipwreck in *The Tempest* was contrived to make the spectators actually feel seasick. Trees were never more verdant, palaces never more palatial, the magic island never more magical. The Venice of *The Merchant* so bustled with life and carnival that a mere pound of flesh dwindled in importance (see Plate 3). Squeezing Shakespeare into the scenery rather than the scenery into Shakespeare did not offend those who equated the Shakespeare experience with conspicuous consumption.

The actor sought complete impersonation, and the *Illustrated London News* reported with satisfaction on Phelps's realistic skills as Antony drunk on Pompey's galley, 'The illusion was almost perfect; the actor could scarcely be recognized through the disguise.' No comment, how-

3   Spectacle in Charles Kean's *The Merchant of Venice* at the Princess's Theatre, 1858

ever, on a Cleopatra in crinolines. And speeches had still to be projected as into a deep cave, more sung than spoken, with 'claptraps' designed to prompt a burst of applause. Kean worked especially on the pause, during which his face would reproduce 'a rapid succession of expressions fluently melting into each other'[18] and when as Shylock he spoke the line 'I am a Jew', the drop in his voice from the declamatory manner produced a storm of applause.

Henry Morley's was a dissenting voice. He poured scorn on Kean's attempt at a shadow dance for Titania in 1856 (see Plate 4):

Elaborately to produce and present, as an especial attraction, fairies of large size, casting shadows made as black and distinct as possible, and offering in dance to pick them up, as if even they also were solid, is as great a sacrifice of Shakespeare to the purposes of the ballet-master, as the view of Athens in its glory was a sacrifice of poetry to the scene-painter.[19]

At all events, mid-Victorian academia rewarded Charles Kean's historical efforts by making him a Fellow of the Society of Antiquaries. Beerbohm Tree at Her Majesty's was Kean's true heir as a magnificent decorator. Every play a feast for the eye — the clichés abounded in the reviews. In *The Tempest*, an Ariel darting among rock-pools and sea-nymphs; in *Twelfth Night*, a garden for Olivia adorned with cypresses, a graceful bridge and flights of steps mounting up and up to a blue sky. In January of 1900, as if to mark the end of an era, Tree mounted *A Midsummer Night's Dream* to surpass everything. *The Times*'s correspondent was ecstatic:

No scene has ever been put upon the stage more beautiful than the wood near Athens in which the fairies revel and the lovers play their game of hide-and-seek. With a carpet of thyme and wild flowers, brakes and thickets full of blossom, and a background seen through the tall trees, of the pearly dawn or the deep hues of the night sky — the picture is one of real charm and restfulness.[20]

Not that this reviewer liked the play, since he could not regard the lovers as 'offering any real interest' and 'the goings to and fro of the lovers soon becomes tedious': its only recommendation was the opportunity it offered for spectacle. However:

The fairies by whom this sweet solitude is peopled are so dainty and fairylike that they seem quite in place as its nightly inhabitants. They are played by troops of graceful children, who go through their dances and gambols with pretty enjoyment.

4   A dance of Victorian fairies in Charles Kean's *A Midsummer Night's Dream* at the Princess's Theatre, 1856

'O.P.C.', writing in *The Outlook*, dared to add that the fairies, 'being mostly children', were 'bound to succeed'.[21]

The climax came in act five when the mortals left Theseus's splendid palace to the fairy throng:

> There they dance, and, as they wind in and out, gradually the pillared hall glows with mysterious light, every pillar a shaft of fire, with little points of light starting out here and there at the touch of Oberon's wand. . . . Slowly the hall darkens again. The glow dies away, the stage is swallowed up in gloom, the lights in the house are suddenly turned up, and the play is over. It is as if the audience were rudely awakened from a pleasing vision . . . and they find themselves blinking at the curtain, wondering whether it has not really all been a dream.

Brecht would have heaped scorn on such theatre of witchcraft and trance, lasting till midnight, sweetly accompanied by Mendelssohn's *Sommernachstraum* music. Tree played Bottom with 'the bibulous visage of a confirmed toper and a voice thickened with indulgence in liquor', but it was essentially ladies' night at Her Majesty's: Oberon and Puck were played by actresses, and Mrs Tree as Titania had 'O.P.C.' confessing that she 'set most of us to envying the long-eared Bottom', bibulosity and all. When Benson risked a revival of his less spectacular *Dream* at the Lyceum two months later, 'Y.B.' of *The Outlook* believed that you got 'far more Shakespeare for your money in the more modest production'.[22]

Persuading an audience to higher standards of appreciation is a far harder business than educating a stubborn schoolboy. The nineteenth-century actor–manager's work must be seen against the inadequate state of scholarship, the imperious demands of the proscenium-arch stage, the recalcitrant traditions of the theatre and his primary loyalty to his audience. Beerbohm Tree's claim at the end of the century might have been made by any Victorian actor–manager:

> I am at least entitled to maintain that I have done my best to present the works of Shakespeare in the manner which I consider most worthy, and I feel a certain pride in remembering that, be our method right or wrong, we are enabled to give Shakespeare a wider appeal and a larger franchise — surely no mean achievement. Thousands witness him instead of hundreds. His works are not only, or primarily, for the literary student, they are for the world at large. Indeed, there should be more joy over ninety-nine Philistines that are gained than over one elect that is preserved.[23]

We may pass over the huge *non sequitur* implicit in this common argument. More see Shakespeare, but was more of Shakespeare seen?

However, the last quarter of the century belonged to Henry Irving, whose tenure at the Lyceum from 1878 to 1902 marked the triumph and the decline of the old order. What Odell called Irving's 'dreadful voice' and 'ungraceful figure', which denied his tragic character-acting its full expression, mattered less than the fact that the Lyceum began to drift with the contemporary European movement towards stage naturalism.[24] The Company of Saxe-Meiningen had played Shakespeare in London in 1881, and their work had set new standards in the detail and accuracy of rehearsal, especially of living crowd and other ensemble effects. Charles Shattuck offers a list:

About the turn of the century, too, incidental local-color effects – street musicians, flirtatious sailors lounging along wharves, old crones telling fortunes beside wishing wells, maids a-spinning, children bobbing for apples, ambulating monks doling out their *benedicites* – proliferate oppressively, teaching us of the double drive inherent in the theatre of the time: toward the cinema, which would discard language entirely and tell the whole story in pictures; toward the new art of theatre, which would clear the stage of such irrelevant detail and try once more to 'get back to Shakespeare'.[25]

Doubtless, the Saxe-Meiningen productions were something too literal. When the clouds drifting across the Forum scene in *Julius Caesar* hovered only a foot or two from the ground and concealed the Capitol from view, one critic believed them out of control. Not so, explained Kroneg the director,

It must be borne in mind that the Forum Romano, or Campo Vuecino as it is now called, is situated at a considerable elevation and that, therefore, the clouds which lowered and frowned upon Rome on the night preceding the death of Caesar must have been at a very low altitude to obscure the Capitol and the higher buildings of the city from view.[26]

Nevertheless, the attempt to place on the stage a photographic reproduction of real life was widely respected.

All this, of course, was yet another distraction from the real Shakespeare. Overburdened with scenery set in a stereoscopic picture-frame, the text continued to be mutilated and the scenes transposed to accommodate the designer: Shaw called it 'butchering Shakespeare to make a stage-carpenter's holiday'. When the actress Mary Anderson wrote the preface to an acting edition of *The Winter's Tale* in 1887, she made the general position quite clear: 'No audience of these days would desire to have the "Winter's Tale" produced in its entirety. A literal adhesion to the text as it has been handed down to us would in any case savour of superstition.' Superstition indeed: critics displayed alarm at the unnatural academicism of F. R. Benson when he presented a complete *Hamlet* in a five-and-a-half hour treatment in 1900, on which *The Times* commented, 'Greatly daring, he has set himself to undo the work of time. He has put the clock back three centuries. He has walked, like a crab, backwards. He has reconverted the manufactured article into the raw material.' [27] The argument was that 'the plain man' was puzzled by the foreign policy of Denmark, the interminable homilies and digressions: 'Why does Hamlet fill up the interval of waiting for the Ghost with a sermon on intemperance? Why does Laertes lecture his sister at such length on lovers' lightness and maidens' modesty?' The answer was that the art of drama in Shakespeare's time was 'an art of rhetoric rather than an art of realistic imitation' and 'concentrated action', and the plain man did not know these things, and would not much care if he did. Few were troubled when Irving lopped the first act of *Coriolanus* to avoid playing the soldier, and the last act of *The Merchant of Venice* after the final exit of his Shylock. Tyrone Guthrie summarized:

Irving's productions were based on a realistic formula. There would be three or four splendid, elaborate 'stage-pictures', and into these would be crammed as much of the action as possible. The scenes which simply could not be expressed realistically in these three or four environments were either cut or played as 'front scenes'. [28]

The drive towards realism was powerful. Irving still strove for tableaux, [29] made his points and pranced out of the scene to accept applause in the old spirit of the melodrama, but the actor at this time was set far apart from his audience and the lines were not spoken to the spectators. Naturalism increasingly demanded that the actor pretend that the audience was not there. *The Athenaeum* of 1895–6 steadily deplored the loss of the tragic tone, the underplaying of the new realism, and declared that realism had 'conquered convention'. Of Forbes Robertson's Romeo, for example: 'Never more shall we, apparently, hear the representative of Macbeth or Othello strive with swelling breast to "out-roar the lion-throated seas".' [30] And of Irving's Richard III:

Where, however, is tragedy? It is gone. Richard III is not now a tragic *role*. It is what is conventionally called 'a character part'. . . . We are gratified, tickled, amused. . . . Once and again a ripple of merriment passed over the house as Richard announced his intentions or uttered his asides.[31]

The critic was not gripped. Worse, he failed to see that the new element of ambiguity possible in underplaying, and the new response of ambivalence suggested by the ripple of merriment, might produce a new Shakespeare experience.

In his productions Irving essayed his own beautiful vraisemblance: bridges for Venice, grass for Arden, fountains for Illyria, moonlight as never before. But he was intelligently and tastefully aware of his age's scenic excesses, and in the preface to the acting version of his *Hamlet* in 1879 he implied a modern caution:

Shakespeare, if well acted on a bare stage, would certainly afford great intellectual pleasure; but that pleasure will be all the greater if the eye be charmed, at the same time, by scenic illustrations in harmony with the poet's ideas.

In his preface to *The Merchant of Venice* in that year he made much the same point about the desirability of balance:

In producing 'The Merchant of Venice' I have endeavoured to avoid hampering the natural action of the piece with any unnecessary embellishment; but have tried not to omit any accessory which might heighten the effects.

He kept the expected Venetian carnival crowds for Jessica's elopement, but juxtaposed them with a pathetic Shylock returning to an empty house across a silent stage.[32] Art was superseding archaeology, but the idea of Shakespeare as a realist was still omnipotent.

The innovations of Granville-Barker and Peter Brook were undreamed of. By the turn of the century, essentially Victorian conventions had been substituted for Elizabethan ones. Since it seemed incredible by realistic standards that in *Twelfth Night* Olivia should not see that Sebastian was not Cesario, it became fashionable to play the scene of his return in dim moonlight. Forbes Robertson brought Fortinbras back to Elsinore for the first time in 1897, not to complete the structure and meaning of the play, but merely to mount a tableau in which the Prince could be borne aloft on Swedish shields. Beerbohm Tree's most magnificent scene in his *King John* of 1899 was that of the Magna Carta done in pantomime, a scene which Shakespeare had omitted to include in the original.

Nevertheless, when *The Times* reviewed Irving's *Cymbeline* in 1896, it was clear that the rethinking of first principles had begun:

> It is obvious that any attempt to obtain archaeological consistency in such a hotch-potch of history, fiction and period must fail, and the question suggests itself whether . . . for such plays as *Cymbeline* . . . it would not be well to adopt on the stage a more or less fantastic setting, with something of that indefiniteness of place, period, and costume, which the modern stage-manager for some reason will only allow to comic opera. Perhaps after all there is not much more reality in these picturesque kilted Britons who fill the Lyceum picture.

In any case the kind of magnificent production associated with Beerbohm Tree was soon to be killed by the cinema, which really could mount a cast of thousands whenever necessary. The theatre was ripe for Gordon Craig's theories of stage impressionism, for Poel's search for a modern equivalent to Elizabethan playing conditions and for Granville-Barker's first steps towards non-illusory Shakespeare.

It could have done with some help from the scholars.

2

Scholars and actors

The title of this chapter echoes that of a clarion call of an article by Richard David, who presented himself, not as an actor or a scholar, but as an informed playgoer. He wrote, 'It is the first article of my belief that outside the theatre Shakespeare can have only the thinnest and most unsubstantial of existences.'[1] He sought, as we all do, the essential Shakespeare, and his theme was that the actor and the scholar needed each other:

> In truth the actor's and the scholar's gifts must help each other out where Shakespeare is concerned, and both are essential if the plays are to be so presented as to reveal the true 'form and pressure' of Shakespeare's intention. Except in and through the actor the scholar cannot properly 'realize' Shakespeare, any more than even the best musician can judge the full impact of a symphony from reading the score. . . . But the scholar is equally indispensable to the actor, for however unchanging the essential quality of 'theatre', the theatrical modes that Shakespeare employs, and especially that of language, are over three hundred years old.

David cited as a prime example the 'subtle and all-pervading distortion' that ruined most modern productions: realism. It was chiefly about the mode of communication, the rules of the Shakespeare game, that scholar and actor must collaborate: the one to check the rules, the other to test them in play. That this need to reconsider the realism in Shakespeare is now widely recognized adds to the claim that in this century our understanding has undergone a radical change.

Such a position as Richard David's is now, if not exactly commonplace, almost respectable. Our progress to the point where the theatre itself can be considered the appropriate place for the study of Shakespeare's purpose and style implies not only that we see drama as a mode of communication different from other literary forms, but also that the name Shakespeare today suggests a kind of artistic endeavour not previously acknowledged.

At the first annual conference of the British Drama League in Stratford, 1919, the new attitude to Shakespeare was publicly proclaimed. In the chair at one session sat no less a man than Ben Greet, a Stratfordian of boundless enthusiasm,[2] who announced that Shakespeare was 'the greatest manager of his time'. He was echoed by Norman Wilkinson, Granville-Barker's designer, who declared Shakespeare 'the supreme practical dramatist, the technician of all time'.[3] The Bard a manager, a technician? Whatever next! But at the same conference Elsie Fogerty, who founded the Central School of Speech and Drama, also submitted that the study of dramatic art belonged in a university, rather than an academy for drama. She envisaged 'a great workshop of theatrical production . . . taught and modelled not upon the tradition of study, but upon the art of the theatre'.[4] She was to become a member of the Advisory Committee for the first Diploma in Dramatic Art established in 1923 by the University of London.

Support for the stage-centred study of Shakespeare increased rapidly between the wars. Granville-Barker had presided at another session of the first B.D.L. conference when it addressed itself to 'Dramatic Art in National Life'. At this Ellen Terry, London's leading actress, found herself on the platform alongside Gilbert Murray, Professor of Greek at Oxford. For his part, Granville-Barker pursued his new role as mediator between the stage and the study by lecturing throughout the country. His *Players' Shakespeare Prefaces* began to appear in a limited edition by Ernest Benn in 1923, and then were expanded and published in book form by Sidgwick and Jackson between 1927 and 1947. Their uniqueness as perceptual criticism was recognized immediately. To John Dover Wilson, the Cambridge scholar who was to become Professor of English at Edinburgh in 1936, the *Lear Preface* was a revelation, and in his British Academy Lecture of 1929 he praised the *Prefaces* as 'essays towards the new critical method'.[5]

The new critical method was as yet undefined, but Wilson's rather rambling paper sparkled with those elementary practical insights which are now familiar: that Hamlet was 18 when he saw the Ghost and 30 at Ophelia's graveside hardly worried an audience who was watching the same actor throughout; that Desdemona's suspected adultery may have been impossible in real time, but it was technically perfect in the tempo of the theatre; that Emilia failed to tell her mistress about the handkerchief may have been her 'gross stupidity' according to Bradley,[6] but it added wonderfully to the tension in the theatre;

and only in performance is it possible to know that the virility of Mercutio helps us accept the raptures of Romeo. Finally, John Dover Wilson astonished his distinguished audience by confessing that 'however wooden the company or slipshod the production, I never come away without fresh light, new hints'.[7]

J. W. Mackail, who succeeded Bradley as Professor of Poetry at Oxford in 1906, offered this interim report on the state of Shakespeare in his Lord Northcliffe Lectures in Literature delivered at University College, London in 1930:

A generation ago it might have been thought, indeed it was, that Shakespearian study was exhausted. Nothing short of a revolution has since taken place. New lines of criticism, new methods of analysis, new fields of inquiry have multiplied. . . . The Elizabethan stage, and all that that phrase in its widest sense implies, has taken fresh life. . . . Its dramatic quality, needless to say, can hardly be grasped by mere reading. The dramatic structure and movement can only be very imperfectly apprehended at second hand; unacted action comes rather near to being a contradiction in terms. From any faithful stage-production these become visible in quite a new way. We realize what a master of stagecraft Shakespeare was, and how to stagecraft, to action, which is what stagecraft embodies, everything else in him is subordinated.[8]

Mackail's lectures were general, but at that time they characteristically disparaged puling controversies like those of the *Othello* time-scheme, the previous relations of Hamlet and Ophelia, and the possible married life of Sir Toby and Lady Belch. Shakespeare was careless of what was not essential, and in the last scene of *A Midsummer Night's Dream* told us so: Hippolyta asks, on our behalf, 'How chance Moonshine is gone before Thisbe comes back and finds her lover?', and she gets the obvious answer, 'She will find him by starlight'. In his introduction to the British Academy Lectures, Mackail's was a stern and powerful voice warning against the perils of aesthetic comment and the dangers of the theoretic reconstitution of Shakespeare's views and doctrines. The real problems in the appreciation of Shakespeare as an artist were to be faced by a better acquaintance with the theatre and drama at the time when Shakespeare was actor, producer and playwright.[9]

But this part of the story belongs to John Dover Wilson and Harley Granville-Barker. In his Inaugural Lecture of 17 January 1936 as Professor of Rhetoric and English Literature at the University of Edinburgh, Dover Wilson returned to his favourite theme:

Scholars and actors

It is one of the most important literary discoveries of our age that Shakespeare wrote, not to be read, but to be acted, that his plays are not books but, as it were, libretti for stage-performances. It is amazing that so obvious a fact should so late have come to recognition. The truth is that critics writing when the English theatre was at its nadir could not bring themselves to believe that Shakespeare had ever served so shabby an art.[10]

Again praising Granville-Barker's *Prefaces* for having begun a fresh epoch in Shakespeare criticism, he linked them with the study of the Elizabethan stage:

He has shown us that no school of dramatic criticism is — I will not say valueless but — safe, which is divorced from theatrical experience. . . . We students of Shakespeare must try out his effects in action upon a stage, if we are to understand them.[11]

Thinking of Caldwell Cook's famous lower-school 'Mummery' at the Perse School, Cambridge, and echoing an earlier plea by Granville-Barker,[12] Wilson went so far as to propose a school of practical dramatic criticism which would use an actual stage upon which the problems of a play could be tackled as they arose in discussion. He did not ask for an auditorium, so, clearly, his notion of dramatic criticism did not yet embrace audience-reaction or drama as communication. Nevertheless, although his aim was strictly academic, to study the principles and practice of Shakespeare's art, he declared that this work 'would, no doubt, exert an influence upon the theatrical world'.

Dover Wilson had spent two years editing the obscure jests and allusions in *Love's Labour's Lost*,[13] but it was not until he saw Tyrone Guthrie's production at the Old Vic in 1936 that he 'caught sight of the play as a whole . . . so full of fun and *permanent* wit'.[14] In his B.B.C. broadcast of 1937, he offered his listening audience this: 'Let a professor begin by giving you a piece of advice. *Never believe what the scholars and professors tell you about a Shakespeare play until you have seen it on the stage for yourself.*' He was not speaking merely out of his own enthusiasm when he asserted that scholars had never before been so interested in the theatre, and that never had men of the theatre been so ready to read the books of the scholars. 'And some of them, like Mr Granville-Barker,' he added, 'write books which outdo the scholars at their own game.'

The extreme position in this vein is now John Russell Brown's: 'I am presupposing that scholars should work with, and in, the professional theatre; that they should be familiar with the problems of production involving mature actors, a professional rigour, and an ordinary audience.'[15] Brown wrote this as the first Professor of Drama at the University of Birmingham. His requirement would have been unimaginable a hundred years ago, and some sense of how the nineteenth-century critic viewed the activities of the playhouse is necessary for an appreciation of the change in attitude that has occurred. We return, then, to the place in the story where no respectable critic believed that Shakespeare would be other than diminished by his association with the stage.

Goethe believed in the power of the imagination first and last, and that Shakespeare as a poet spoke always to the 'inner sense'. The stage was unworthy of him, especially in its 'primitive' Elizabethan state, and Shakespeare must have tolerated the theatre like an alien world. These sentiments were universal in the early nineteenth century. Coleridge's great contribution to the understanding of Shakespeare lay in his sensitivity to a play's mood and tone – one is tempted to say its 'organic' qualities as dramatic poetry. But in his lectures of 1813–14 he declared that he 'never saw any of Shakespeare's plays acted but with a degree of pain, disgust and indignation'. No wonder Granville-Barker believed that 'our English school of metaphysical closet-criticism'[16] sprang from Coleridge. There was a kind of narcissism in the romantic criticism of Shakespeare: Coleridge's idolizing of Hamlet followed from his provocative suggestion, 'I have a smack of Hamlet'; and yet, technically speaking, such identification of audience with character is what drama is all about.

Coleridge was revered by Charles Lamb, whose notorious contribution at this time (1811) was his essay, 'On the Tragedies of Shakspeare, Considered with Reference to Their Fitness for Stage Representation' – by which he meant their unfitness:

When the novelty is past, we find to our cost that instead of realizing an idea, we have only materialized and brought down a fine vision to the standard of flesh and blood. . . . It may seem a paradox, but I cannot help being of opinion that the plays of Shakspeare are less calculated for performance on a stage, than those of almost any other dramatist whatever.

Lamb was honest, but he was typical. He complained of being shown Macbeth's cumbersome coronation robe, since in the reading we do not see it: we now know how well this visual image fits and enforces the recurring metaphor of borrowed garments. He complained of Mrs Siddons's graceful performance as Lady Macbeth when she dismissed the guests, arguing that in his mind the reader would dismiss them as rapidly as he could; we now know that such an on-stage audience designed to induce the public tensions of the scene must not be forgotten. He found 'something extremely revolting in the courtship and wedded caresses of Othello and Desdemona', preferring to see Othello's colour only in his imagination: such squeamishness denies much of the point and structure of the play, which emerges only when a participating audience is continually aware of black and white skin. He wondered how 'the shy, negligent, retiring Hamlet' could mouth his feelings before an audience and give lectures to the crowd: indeed, why should a character speak at all?

By contrast, Hazlitt enjoyed going to the theatre, and his best insights came from watching a performance, especially by Edmund Kean. He was uncommonly aware of Shakespeare's visual sense. He appreciated the force of Malcolm to Macduff: 'What! man, ne'er pull your hat upon your brows'. He commented with approval on Kean's kissing Ophelia's hand, coming back from 'the extremity of the stage' after his abuse of her in the nunnery scene: 'It had an electrical effect on the house. It was the finest commentary that was ever made on Shakespeare.'[17] He applauded Kean's Richard III for his 'smooth, smiling villainy', and added, 'Richard should woo, not as a lover, but as an actor.'[18] Yet he could criticize Kean as a cold Romeo by an apt comparison between Garrick and Barry in the balcony scene: 'The one acted it as if he would jump up to the lady, and the other as if he would make the lady jump down to him.'[19] Nevertheless, Hazlitt seemed to deny his instincts in approving Lamb's verdict on *Lear* as unactable, in finding *The Dream* 'converted from a delightful fiction into a dull pantomime' on the stage, and finally in believing that 'the boards of a theatre and the regions of fancy are not the same thing'. He dedicated *The Characters of Shakespear's Plays* (1817) to Charles Lamb.[20]

It is true that the critics at the beginning of the nineteenth century saw only Tate's *Lear*, Cibber's *Richard* and outrageously doctored versions of the rest. The new realism was sweeping the London stage, new scenic obstacles between the poetry and the spectator were erected in increasing profusion and the Shakespeare playhouses became vast caves for Victorian spectacle. Any sense of the original conditions of performance was lost, and with it the notion that drama was an expressive form of an order different from the poem or the novel. The direction of critical effort for a hundred years was to be toward the realization of Shakespeare's gift for creating characters.

The creation of characters is not the primary part of playwriting; the Victorians elevated it to pre-eminence. The many studies of Shakespeare's characters culminated in A. C. Bradley's outstanding treatment of the tragic characters in *Shakespearean Tragedy* (1904), which, according to Kenneth Muir, was to be 'for a whole generation the truest and most profound book ever written on Shakespeare'.[21] Earlier, Augustus Ralli in his voluminous survey of Shakespeare criticism had found him 'one of the very greatest' critics in history:

> He convinces because his process of critically re-creating the scenes of the plays is something similar to Shakespeare's imaginative process of creating. Here again — as we said with Coleridge — is absolute critical truth; and those writers should take warning who oppose the requirements of the stage and need to please the audience, against any attempts to know Shakespeare.[22]

All this is now up for question, but at the time Bradley's solemn, confident and straightforward style, pleasantly articulate, with his compelling use of the assumptive 'we' throughout, gave the book a special appeal to the common reader, the kind of reader who naturally finds much of his drama in the characterization. Altogether, the book served as an excellent substitute for going to the theatre — not that Bradley was not himself a keen playgoer: his home was in London, and he missed nothing of importance. The steady sale of the book testifies to the kind of value that has been placed upon it. But, for all that Bradley has been chewed over, plagiarized, worshipped or challenged, a further comment in the present context is needed.

Bradley's process of re-creating Shakespeare's scenes concealed as much as it revealed Shakespeare's way of working, and *Shakespearean Tragedy* remains 'a great monument to the closet Shakespeare'.[23] His ability to combine an Hegelian philosophic breadth with analytic detail, seeming to embrace a whole play while probing a single character, appeared to bring a reassuring 'scientific method' to the study of Shakespeare. His avowed aim was, moreover, to encourage 'dramatic appreciation':

to increase our understanding and enjoyment of these works as dramas; to learn to apprehend the action and some of the personages of each with a somewhat greater truth and intensity, so that they may assume in our imaginations a shape a little less unlike the shape they wore in the imagination of their creator.[24]

and in particular to trace 'the inner movements which produced these words and no other, these deeds and no other, at each particular moment'. In this, he believed himself to be reading a play like an actor 'who had to study all the parts'. And his second lecture seemed to reinforce the scientific approach: the subject here was 'Construction in Shakespeare's Tragedies', as if Shakespeare set himself structural problems to be solved in some imaginative workshop for playwriting. But, notwithstanding Tree's statement of his gratitude for Bradley's piece on Macbeth, Granville-Barker's obvious indebtedness in his *Prefaces*, and no doubt other actors who have been attracted by the 'psychological' treatment of the characters in the age of Freud and Stanislavsky, the great bulk of Bradley's book proposed character-study of a wholly non-theatrical kind, and those actors who turned to him as a guide to working on a role have commonly found themselves in confusion. Was there ever a star bright enough to realize on the stage all of Bradley's closet subtleties?

He offered an attractively simple theory of tragedy, which he found to be the story of a man who faces 'suffering and calamity conducting to death' and 'generally extending far and wide beyond him'.[25] The tragedy happened because of what the hero *does*, rarely because of the work of accident or the supernatural. Hence the keystone of Bradley's idea of tragedy, that it must 'lie in action issuing from character, or in character issuing in action. Shakespeare's main interest lay here. To say that it lay in *mere* character, or was a psychological interest, would be a great mistake, for he was dramatic to the tips of his fingers.'[26] It turned out that Bradley's main interest also lay in those inner movements, the spiritual force driving a man's soul, although it remains to be seen how far his character-in-action included stage action. The ultimate power, the causal law, which took the hero's life was a moral government of the universe which of necessity must punish any moral transgression: the usual pedestrian equation of the Victorians. We record this merely for the record, together with Bradley's need to recognize a so-called Aristotelian 'flaw' or fatal tendency towards a one-sided and irrational passion.

Of primary interest, and of far-reaching consequence, was Bradley's very full discussion of Shakespeare's characters, major and minor, as if they were real people. It was this talent of Bradley's to bring the persons of the play to life, set them in different plays (what would Cordelia have done in Desdemona's place?), enquire about their childhood, their ages (how old was Hamlet or Macbeth?), puzzle out their lives before the action of the play had begun (where was Hamlet at the time of his father's death?), compare fact with fiction (what had Napoleon and Iago in common?), and so forth, which set actor and critic on the wrong path. Bradley's insistent investigation into the motives behind a character's behaviour was quite un-historical and non-Elizabethan, but it placed Shakespeare in the mainstream of new ideas about the Victorian novel, so that a soliloquy need not look quite unlike Jamesian stream-of-consciousness, provided, of course, the reader was not asked to imagine it addressed to some audience in a theatre. Needless to say, the common reader was delighted to have Bradley's immense authority behind what he always wanted to do — talk about the characters, and pass moral verdicts upon each, as if they were the people next door.

No harm in this, one may say, until it is seen what else must be sacrificed to the process. Coleridge's ideas about Shakespeare's plays as organic unities in which the characters were properly the intricate and ideal parts of the whole were not widely available until 1930, and belong to the period of the 'new criticism' and Wilson Knight. F. R. Leavis's attack on Bradley's belief that Othello was Iago's foil, for which he substituted the notion that Iago was merely a 'necessary piece of dramatic mechanism' to split Othello's mind, did not appear until 1937.[27] Meanwhile, the influence of Bradley's book was reflected in the potted 'characters' which were offered in the introductions to school texts, and is still felt strongly in the work of the average theatre reviewers in the newspapers. The best early statement of the danger of the Bradleyan character-study was published as a warning against committing a comparable sin in the criticism of the novel. This was C. H. Rickword's 'A Note on Fiction' in the short-lived *Calendar of Modern Letters*, founded in 1925.[28]

Rickword summarized the concept of 'character' commonly assumed.

In fiction it was regularly taken to be either 'character in repose' or 'character in action', and then either an image of the 'inner man' or the 'outer man'. In whatever aspect that character might be seen, however, it was always regarded as an objective portrait of an imagined human being, there to be judged by moral, social or other standards appropriate to real human beings. It was as if such portraits were not merely composed of responses to their author's verbal arrangements. As with character, so it was also with the plot and form of a novel, which only existed as 'a balance of response on the part of the reader', 'precipitates from the memory'. Each element was part of the work's functional technique and dependent on 'devices of articulation' – dependent, that is, 'as legs are on muscles, for the *how* but not the *why* of movement'. The true values of the work were to be found only in its 'inner necessity', not in such emergent qualities as character and plot.

In this discussion, Rickword was unwittingly formulating the modern notion of the novel as a dramatic poem, with character and plot subordinated to a thematic unity where the work's true vitality was to be found. In mid-century, parallel ideas about the drama increasingly obsessed directors of Shakespeare when they sought to impose a 'theme' or a 'meaning' on a production. Theories of poetic unity will find their richest expression in the criticism of G. Wilson Knight. Meanwhile, Bradley's character-in-action could not avoid carrying all the moral implications accruing to the man-in-the-street who, say, thinks his wife unfaithful, slaps her in public, prepares to revenge himself and finally does so. This kind of thinking was to emasculate *Othello*, and was as sentimental as to see Othello and Desdemona as a happy couple made the unhappy victims of evil (which was what Leavis interpreted as Bradley's reading of the play). For all his science, Bradley was substituting his own play for Shakespeare's, and betraying the shortcomings of his own theatre experience like Charles Lamb before him. Embarrassed and constricted by concepts of illusion and realism, Bradley simply did not acknowledge what was in the play he was reading, and his particular failure lay in his unreadiness to submit himself to the imaginative unrealities of a poetic drama.

He must always be explaining away 'inconsistencies' – those of his own misreading. And at any crucial moment of carefully contrived ambivalence for an audience watching a play in the theatre, he consistently missed the point. Where the audience seeing *Hamlet*'s play scene may not know whether it is Claudius or the Prince who has prematurely sprung the mouse-trap, Bradley found that 'Hamlet's device proves a triumph far more complete than he had dared to expect'. Of the brilliant and decisive eavesdropping scene in *Othello*, the scene in which the Moor reveals all his ignoble weaknesses and on his side of the stage supplies as corrupt an image of Desdemona as Bianca's on the other, Bradley has nothing to say. He has nothing to say, either, on the theatrically daring use of Edgar's role-playing in *King Lear*: he found him merely an admirable young man of confidence and resource, with 'something of that buoyancy of spirit which charms us in Imogen'. Instead, he wondered why Gloucester should 'wander painfully all the way to Dover simply in order to destroy himself' and why Edgar did not reveal himself to his blind father. Of Edgar's acutely ironic 'miracle' on the 'cliff', Bradley must explain that Edgar 'thought it *was* the gods who, through him, had preserved his father', because 'he is the most religious person in the play'. Bradley never once read *King Lear* as performance, never sat himself with an audience as it were, so that it is no surprise that he found the blinding of Gloucester 'a blot upon *King Lear* as a stage-play' and the whole work 'too huge for the stage'.

Leavis accused Bradley of reading Shakespeare's poetic drama as if it were 'a psychological novel written in dramatic form and draped in poetry' and in 1937 thought him to be 'still a very potent and mischievous influence'.[29] No matter that Leavis himself could counter Bradley's analysis of Othello's character only with one in exactly the same kind: he was right to question whether Bradley has been good for Shakespeare. *Shakespearean Tragedy* was also attacked by E. E. Stoll for its disregard of those historical conventions which made the plays work on a stage of non-illusion; by L. C. Knights for its failure to see the characters as part of the total design of a dramatic poem; and by Lily B. Campbell for its unwillingness to admit into a theory of tragedy those elements of fate and the supernatural which were also part of Shakespeare's design. To all this we may add that, published at the very moment when the study of the Elizabethan stage was disclosing new horizons to the understanding, Bradley's great book may in time be seen as a disaster.

Shakespeare scholarship (as opposed to criticism) in the Victorian age was in motley disorder, sometimes devoting itself to the 'beauties of Shakespeare' as typified by *Cupid's Birthday Book: One Thousand Love-Darts from Shakespeare* (1875) and *Sweet Silvery Sayings of Shakespeare on the Softer Sex* (1877).[30] It was also fervently filling out the Bard's scanty biography, though the best in this kind was J. O. Halliwell-Phillipps's *Life* (1848); to this he added more material from the Stratford records for *Outlines of the Life* in 1881, which went through seven editions in his lifetime. It was also concerned with the parallel business, begun by F. J. Furnivall, of tracing Shakespeare's moods in the plays: the 'Sunny-or-Sweet-Time' Group (*Twelfth Night, Much Ado, As You Like It*), the 'Ingratitude-and-Cursing' Group (*Lear, Timon, Coriolanus*), the 'Reunion-or-Reconciliation-and-Forgiveness' Group (*Pericles, The Tempest, Cymbeline*), and so on.[31] Furnivall's New Shakspere Society attempted a scientific ordering of the canon by verse tests, and Edward Dowden in his *Shakspere: A Critical Study of His Mind and Art* (1875) and *Shakspere Primer* (1877) clinched the matter by biographical 'periods': 'In the Workshop', 'In the World', 'Out of the Depths' and 'On the Heights' (one or two people like Appleton Morgan wondered whether Shakespeare would have refused the request for a comedy with the regret that he was currently in the depths). However, the most serious work being done at this time was establishing the text and rediscovering the Elizabethan theatre; of these two, the latter is of paramount importance.

Halliwell-Phillipps is more remarkable in this story for the kind of matter-of-fact attention he devoted to collecting contemporary Elizabethan materials, and in 1874 he began publishing them with his *Illustrations of the Life of Shakespeare*. In an atmosphere of almost universal bardolatry and romanticizing, he asserted that Shakespeare wrote his plays, not for posterity, but 'as a matter of business'.[32] His relentless search for facts ensured that his papers dealt with Shakespeare the professional playwright, and, according to a recent judgment, 'his discourse on the theatres and companies is the soundest up to that time.'[33] He seemed to be unusually aware of the special intimacy of the Elizabethan playhouse at a time when the Victorian theatres which played Shakespeare had grown to be vast emporia for his display. In a paper read to the Elizabethan Literary Society in 1893, William Poel quoted Halliwell-Phillipps with approval for having observed that the Globe was a place 'wherein an actor of genius could satisfactorily develop to every one of the audience not merely the writ-

5 The nineteenth-century idea of the Globe playhouse: painting by George Pycroft

ten, but the unwritten words of the drama, those latter which are expressed by gesture or by the subtle language of the face and eye'.[34] More provocatively,

There can be no doubt that Shakespeare, in the composition of most of his plays, could not have contemplated the introduction of scenic accessories. It is fortunate that this should have been one of the conditions of his work, for otherwise many a speech of power and beauty, many an effective situation, would have been lost. All kinds of elaborate attempts at stage illusion tend, moreover, to divert a careful observance of the acting, while they are of no real service to the imagination of the spectator.[35]

Halliwell-Phillipps here had in mind the Chorus to *Henry V* with its theme 'Piece out our imperfections with your thoughts'. All this is now commonplace, but at that time it reflected a new understanding of the Shakespeare experience: for an exciting event had recently occurred.

In 1888 Dr K. T. Gaedertz, a German scholar, had published *Zur Kenntnis der altenglischen Bühne*, printing for the first time a crude sketch of an Elizabethan playhouse which he had come upon in the library of the University of Utrecht. Johannes de Witt was a Dutch student who came to London in the latter part of the 1590s and wrote an account of his visit to the Swan Theatre; to the account he attached a sketch of what he saw. The originals of the description and the drawing were lost, but a copy had been kept in a commonplace book by his fellow student at Leyden, Arend van Buchell. This rough drawing remains to this day the only eye-witness picture of an Elizabethan playhouse interior, and is worth a thousand conjectures. It shows a great platform with two doors like the screen doors in a Tudor hall; there are no proscenium opening, no borders and no curtain between the pillars, no scenery or properties except for a bench.[36]

A comparable stimulus to fresh thinking came from nearer home. Philip Henslowe was the leading theatre manager of Elizabethan times, building the Rose, owning the Newington Butts playhouse, managing the Fortune and the Hope. His papers had been found in Dulwich College library by Edmond Malone, the great scholar of the eighteenth century. He based his *History of the Stage* on what he found, together with other contemporary records such as the Revels Accounts showing whom the Court dealt with for its entertainment. W. W. Greg edited and published the Henslowe *Diary* and *Papers* between 1904 and 1908,[37] and overnight the whole business of managing a theatre, working for an actors' company and offering a play for performance in the time of Elizabeth became vividly real and practical. Shakespeare was suddenly less of a myth.

The retrospective verdict on these developments has been unanimous. The notion that the Elizabethan theatre and dramaturgy were in some way primitive was dispelled at last, and in its place crept the awful doubt that Victorian practice was not necessarily better. Allardyce Nicoll reported that the discovery of the Swan Theatre sketch produced a flurry of activity: 'Seeing that sketch, scholars eagerly applied themselves to a study of the Elizabethan playhouse structure and, even more importantly, turned to analyze Shakespeare's dramatic method in the light of their findings.'[38] Many others have agreed that the new work on the Elizabethan stage 'profoundly affected our understanding of Shakespeare's own works'.[39] The best single statement of the significance of the research came from a scholar who began to apply the new knowledge of the physical stage to the detail of the plays, W. J. Lawrence:

> We have good reason to rejoice over the establishment and digestion of the remarkable number of new facts evoked by the scientific investigation, so diligently pursued by the scholars of two continents for a score of years past, of the physical conditions of the old platform stage and the dramaturgic laws to which they gave rise. If only because of the readjustment it has brought about of the prescribed attitude towards the entire corpus of Elizabethan drama – an attitude of mild contempt tempered by a narrow admiration – this work, so long looked at askance as mere idle antiquarianism – has triumphantly vindicated itself. Order has been evolved out of seeming chaos. It has at last dawned upon us that dramaturgy actually existed in Shakespeare's day, a dramaturgy, with all its faults, more individual and more racial [sic] than that which rules on the English stage of to-day; and, rebuked by this knowledge, we are ceasing to judge the seventeenth-century playwright by our standards and beginning to rank him by his own. We see now that it is not a question of inferior and superior techniques, but simply of techniques fundamentally different and operating on different planes.[40]

The new interest in the Elizabethan theatre is associated with the mushroom growth of Shakespeare societies at the end of the century. Halliwell-Phillipps had worked for the Shakespeare Society founded in London by J. P. Collier in 1840. When Collier's forgeries were disclosed in 1853, the Society was dissolved. The New Shakspere Society was founded in 1873 by a professional 'society man', F. J.

Furnivall, who founded no less than six societies in his time, in honour of writers from Chaucer to Browning. Before the New Shakspere was disbanded in 1894 Furnivall had established its reputation by 'scientifically' ordering the plays by verse tests published in a series of its *Transactions*. In this activity he was backed up by such scholars as F. G. Fleay, whose inaccuracies and dogmatism troubled the more factual Halliwell-Phillipps. Of Fleay and his prodigious industry, Samuel Schoenbaum has written, 'He is forever discovering the truth, and the truth is always different.'[41]

Another discontented member of the New Shakspere was none other than the actor and producer William Poel. Furnivall had published an edition of Shakespeare in 1877, the *Leopold Shakespeare*, whose introduction was universally praised for its decidedly unscientific pursuit of the 'four periods' theory: Furnivall fallaciously identified character and playwright and pieced together passages from the plays to make a life of sorts. Poel rebelled. The famous introduction, he said, 'has yet one vital defect as dramatic criticism — his comments apply to the art of the novelist, not to that of a playwright'.[42] The papers Poel read to the Society aggressively took his listeners back to the theatre. For he also was a society man, in 1887 becoming Instructor to Shakespeare Reading Society of University College, London, under the presidency of Henry Irving. With Poel, the 'recitals' of the Reading Society offered Shakespeare's text without delay or interruption for setting-changes, and he was able to report 'the interest and breathless attention' aroused among the audience, especially at scenes normally cut for their inconvenience to the carpenters.[43]

At the time of the closing of the New Shakspere Society, Poel was warming to his task. In 1881 he had attempted an Elizabethan production of the First Quarto *Hamlet* (of which more later). After readings of *The Merchant of Venice, Romeo and Juliet, Twelfth Night, Much Ado, Henry V, Measure for Measure* and *The Two Gentlemen of Verona* he began to apply his theories to performance itself. With his founding of the Elizabethan Stage Society in 1894, and its regular productions of Elizabethan plays in the ten years that followed, Poel could give his ideas full rein. Of the Society Poel wrote simply,

The Elizabethan Stage Society was founded with the object of reviving the masterpieces of the Elizabethan drama upon the stage for which they were written, so as to represent them as nearly as possible under the conditions

45

existing at the time of their first production —that is to say, with only those stage appliances and accessories which were usually employed during the Elizabethan period.[44]

The Society was a society of scholars: among its subscribers were Edmund Gosse, Israel Gollancz and Sidney Lee. As its chairman, Lee made this daring pronouncement at the annual meeting of 1899:

Speaking as one who has studied the works of Shakespeare and his contemporaries with some attention, both on and off the stage, I have never witnessed the simple, unpretentious representation of a great play by this Society without realizing more of the dramatic spirit and intention than I found it possible to realize when reading it in the study.[45]

A considerable scholar himself, Poel moved easily in the world of late Victorian Shakespeare research. He could see eye to eye with Halliwell-Phillipps, discuss issues with Dowden, cross swords with Furnivall. He had a warm supporter in Sidney Lee, the biographer and Renaissance scholar. Poel conducted an extensive correspondence with W. J. Lawrence, who became a close friend on the basis of their common interest in the Elizabethan stage, its conventions, its shape and size, and how it was exploited by the actors. But of all these only William Poel was able to test theory by practice. In him scholar and actor came together, and it was he who started the uneasy but passionate marriage of scholarship and the stage.

3

Mr Poel's 'Hamlet'

In London, the business of out-doing Irving and Tree in spectacular Shakespeare continued unabated. Oscar Asche planted his Forest of Arden at His Majesty's Theatre in 1907 with the help of two thousand pots of fern and cartloads of leaves; trampled by the cast, they had to be renewed weekly. For his *Merry Wives* at the Garrick in 1911, he smothered his stage in four inches of salt to simulate snow and dressed a red-nosed cast in mittens and mufflers.[1] But by this time the forces of non-illusion were stirring. Asked for an opinion on Irving, William Poel's celebrated response had been, 'I wouldn't give him five pounds a week. He is wonderful in his way, but it is not my way.'[2] Poel devoted his life to finding the right way with Shakespeare, often in the face of critics who might better have respected his intentions; in him was 'some attribute of sainthood', according to W. Bridges-Adams,[3] director of the Shakespeare Festival at Stratford after 1919; but much of what he discovered by the direct test of performance remains to be documented. In the long view, he can claim to be the father of modern thinking about Shakespeare on the stage and the first to sense that the creation of realistic illusion was not the purpose of Shakespeare's drama. Two testimonials from his brightest pupils suggest that we should look at him again. The first is from Granville-Barker in his address to the Royal Society of Literature:

I should like to register my appreciation of the work of Mr. William Poel, his founding of the Elizabethan Stage Society and his gallant persistence with his experiments in the face of many difficulties .... The value was experimental, and much of it has, I fear, been lost by the lack of any adequate and constructive criticism of the experiments.[4]

The second is a tribute paid to Poel by Tyrone Guthrie near the end of his own life of experiment, when he said simply, 'I believe that he, if anybody, ought to be regarded as the founder of modern Shakespearean production.'[5]

47

The Shakespeare Revolution

The story of Elizabethan staging in modern times goes back to 1811, when Ludwig Tieck, the German romantic and great translator of Shakespeare, pleaded for a reconstructed Globe in which to play Shakespeare as he would have been seen in his own time. In 1844 and 1846, Benjamin Webster and the versatile J. R. Planché, antiquary, playwright, composer and designer, attempted *The Taming of the Shrew* without scenery at the Haymarket, using a backcloth representing a view of London and the Globe. It was a curiosity, and the correspondent for *The Times* observed a different quality in the performance:

> By mere substitution of one curtain for another, change of scene was indicated, and all the exits and entrances are through the centre of the curtain, or round the screens, the place represented being denoted by a printed placard fastened to the curtain. This arrangement, far from being flat and ineffective, tended to give closeness to the action, and by constantly allowing a great deal of stage room, afforded a sort of freedom to all the parties engaged.[6]

There is no telling what was meant by 'closeness to the action', not pace, since the play lasted three and a half hours, but perhaps focus and continuity, since 'the attention of the house never failed'. However, it is 'a sort of freedom' which remains the challenging phrase; more than spatial, it points to the spirit and mode of the playing.

Poel's striking contribution to the discovery of a true Shakespeare is easy to mistake. It lay not in his adoption of Elizabethan dress, but rather in a more authentically Elizabethan regard for the play; not in the new rapid delivery of the verse, but rather in the permanent stage set which revealed the musical structure of the play; not in any return to a full text, but rather in his working towards the original rhythmical continuity of scene upon scene.

He was never the purist in clinging to the text: without hesitation he cut anything bawdy which offended his Victorian sensibility. But he kept all the scenes, however small, which the actor–managers had found inconvenient in the scene-shifting, and he kept them in the correct order, trusting to Shakespeare's own structural intentions. He relentlessly dressed his plays in period, as if a visual reminder of his search for authenticity; nowadays Elizabethan costume at all costs would be thought pedantic. This dogmatism, matched by a respect for the verse at the expense of the acting, encouraged his more sceptical critics to speak of 'Mr Poel's costume recitals'. In the verse-speaking of Shakespeare, Poel rehearsed his players in a fast delivery which was neither slavishly iambic nor the chatty prose familiar today, so that 'the two hours' traffic of our stage' had some basis in fact. But he also sought the musicality of the poetry through what he called 'tuned tones', casting a play as one would opera (with, for example, Viola mezzo soprano, Olivia contralto, Maria high soprano, Orsino tenor, Malvolio baritone, Toby bass, Andrew falsetto), and requiring a vocal range of two octaves from each speaker. The cast would spend two or three weeks learning his tunes, while he lay back listening with his eyes closed.[7] No doubt the visual performance suffered from this tyranny, but the fast pace permitted a new variety in rhythm and emphasis, and the proximity of the audience granted meaning to the faintest of modulations.

Yet it is not in any of this that Poel lays real claim to our attention as scholar–actor. His emphasis on the Elizabethan qualities in Shakespeare derived from his belief that the literary historian could learn from a study of the Elizabethan theatre, and that 'playbooks', or standardized stage-versions, of the plays should be prepared by a joint board of actors and scholars.[8] Doubtless, he was mistaken on a variety of matters: that Shakespeare was anxious to rid his company of extemporizing clowns, because they must be fatal to dramatic unity, as were the groundlings who were 'too busy cracking nuts'; that Lear was lovable, that Lady Macbeth was a devoted mother, that Capulet was imperious and vigorous when he called for his long sword; and he was strangely of his time in questioning how Ophelia could stray beyond the palace to pick wild flowers. But in many things he was asking the right questions: he challenged the pruning of the Porter's scene in *Macbeth*, Lady Macduff's moment with her son and Malcolm's test of Macduff on the ground that they were trifling or tedious. He argued instead that they 'might have some significance in the scheme of the author's drama independently of their individual characteristics':[9] 'The appearance of Lady Macduff on the stage affords opportunity for the reflection that Duncan's murder would never have taken place had she been Macbeth's wife.'[10] A lone voice against a chorus of approval, he dared to question Irving's sympathetic rendering of Shylock at the Lyceum: he was thinking historically of the tradition of Plautus's miser, Marlowe's Barabas, Molière's Harpagon and Sheridan's little Moses. He demanded that actors take seriously their responsibility for interpreting

Shakespeare's characters and not take liberties with their author, claiming his 'shortcomings' as an excuse:

Ask the actress who impersonates Olivia why she is not wearing a black dress, and she replies without a moment's hesitation that black is not becoming to her, as if it were an impertinence on Shakespeare's part to expect her to wear black.[11]

In all this is the refreshing assumption that Shakespeare knew what he was doing.

So Poel's Shylock was comic, his Cressida was an Elizabethan lady, his Claudius a gallant of the time. But nowhere does his sense of the 'new' Shakespeare show itself better than in his search for the proper structure of the plays, and this he rediscovered by his practical experiments with a permanent set. The Elizabethan Stage Society aimed 'to give practical effect to the principle that Shakespeare should be accorded the build of stage for which he designed his plays'.[12] This was to be Poel's greatest step in his pursuit of Elizabethan form, demonstrating his reverence for the poet's 'constructive plan', the unity of design in which each scene is related to the rest of the play. His simple assumption was that 'Shakespeare invented his dramatic construction to suit his own particular stage',[13] that his art was dependent upon the form of his theatre, and that therefore the only place where he could be properly understood was in his own theatre:

Elizabethan players had an advantage over modern actors in that they could more readily appreciate the construction of Shakespeare's plays. They knew that the dramatist's characters mutually supported each other within a definite dramatic structure, and that it was the business of the actor to preserve the author's framework.[14]

And even at this early date Poel recognized that Shakespeare's kind of play did not seek the illusion of realism. What followed from the reclamation of the original action was, in theory at least, a revival of the original experience of the drama, and in explanation Poel cited John Addington Symonds's important comment on the Elizabethan stage. Shakespeare's stage, Symonds had said, brought the action into prominent relief:

It acquired *a special kind of realism* which the vast distance and manifold artifices of our modern theatres have rendered unattainable. This was *the realism of an actual event*, at which the audience assisted; not the realism of a scene in which the actor plays a somewhat subordinate part.[15]

'The realism of an actual event' seems to contradict the concept of non-illusion, but this surely was the true thrust of the experience which followed from the absence of the realistic convention. Careless of time and place, the audience concentrated upon the persons of the play and what they did; there was a single place, which was 'here', and a single time, which was 'now'. Continuity of playing not merely restored the text, but it also restored the authentic experience of a play's form, and allowed the non-illusory mode of the drama to re-assert its control over the audience's self-awareness of its role.

William Poel's process of reclamation began in 1881, when he was quite unknown, with a simple and unheralded production of the First Quarto *Hamlet* played in the unconventional St George's Hall. Hardly a great performance, it was nevertheless a momentous production in this history. Its importance must be measured by the conventional Victorian Hamlets of the autocratic actor—managers with their gorgeous, but cumbersome, trappings, the bric-à-brac of 'illustrated', picture-book Shakespeare.

Irving's great Hamlet of 1874 had interpreted the sweet Prince as a man overpowered by love for Ophelia (played by Ellen Terry). To guarantee this focus of interest, the soliloquy on revenge was cut, and so were the scenes provided to dispose of the body of Polonius, to send Hamlet off to England, to acquaint us with Fortinbras and his army, and to arrange Laertes's scheme with Claudius. The fourth act was virtually given over to the crazed, heart-broken girl, and as her lover Hamlet in his tenderness and despair emerged as simple, elegant and 'wildly and strangely beautiful': the ambiguous Prince of the text became ineffably lovable, and William Winter reports that his character, 'long a favorite theme of the essayist, was discussed far and wide'.[16] Breath-taking beauty marked this and later productions, with the Ghost in one scene standing among huge rocks in moonlight and the dawn stealing across a great expanse of water; in another scene Ophelia's funeral cortège wound its way up a hill to the church-yard as the night slowly fell. Needless to say, in all this character work and tasteful 'harmony' of scenic illustration, audiences seemed not to mind that Irving's Hamlet was not Shakespeare's. Nor in 1884 was

Wilson Barrett's Hamlet — played as a teenage boy, consumed by love for his father; nor was Forbes Robertson's amazingly sane scholar-prince in 1897. There is no justice for Shakespeare when any part of the evidence is suppressed.

The young Poel presented himself as the iconoclast of the London stage at the age of 28, but he did so first armed to the teeth with the new scholarship of his time, gathered together in some haste. He made his position clear in a letter to *The Era*:

Managers must not repeat the mistakes of past actors and add to them more of their own. Stage conventionalities must be ignored, and tampering with the text and rearranging the order of scenes to meet the requirements of the modern stage, forbidden. Actors must endeavour, by a careful and searching study of the text, in its first published form, to originate a method of presentation that shall be just to the poet's dramatic intentions, and conformable to the conditions for which the plays were written.[17]

Opportunity to test theory with practice came with the controversy that surrounded the two *Hamlet* quartos, which had been published in cheap facsimile in 1880 by William Griggs, with a foreword by the great Furnivall, at that time President of the New Shakspere Society. Poel offered to read a paper on Shakespeare acting-editions to the Society, and wrote to Furnivall that actors would find the First Quarto of 1603 of special interest: its differences in scene arrangement, omissions and stage directions seemed to point to an acting-edition of Shakespeare's own time.[18] And he offered to mount an amateur performance to prove its effectiveness. He believed that the lost editor of Q1 had 'endeavoured to reproduce the play as *he* saw it represented', possibly as it was arranged for playing on tour at Court. Poel went even further and argued that Q1 'represents more truly Shakespeare's *dramatic conception* than either Q2 or our stage version'.[19] Incidentally, more than half *The Times*'s review of Poel's *Hamlet* was given over to a discussion of the inferiority of Q1, the reviewer rejecting Furnivall's (and Sidney Lee's) notion that it was the original draft for the play and that it 'supplies a far better and more compact acting play than the text commonly known and understood of the multitude'. Rather, Q1 consisted of imperfectly copied passages and 'some earlier and ruder work from which [Shakespeare] borrowed'.[20]

In addition to clinging to the text of the First Quarto, Poel had many settled ideas about the real Hamlet. He was not the sentimental figure of gloom whose very jokes were delivered with tragic solemnity, but he was to seem a smiling Elizabethan gallant in his thirties pursuing Gertrude as if she were an elderly Queen Elizabeth. Polonius was not the crafty old fox of a chief minister, but 'the essence of genteel foppishness, ceaselessly chattering'.[21] In the nunnery scene, Hamlet should see the King and Polonius concealing themselves behind the arras, thus avoiding the necessity for having the curtain shake and bulge, and he should not rail at Ophelia when she returned his gifts. In the play scene, it was essential to play the dumb show to start the tension in the King, and Hamlet should not anticipate the King's exit and drive him from the stage, which defeated his object, but Claudius should break up the performance himself. In the closet scene, Hamlet should not be tender with the Queen, but be as fiercely satirical as the lines demanded. Poel would also dress the Ghost in a white veil,[22] although he later followed the Q1 direction that the Ghost enter 'in his nightgown', since it explained Hamlet's cry, 'My father in his habit as he lived'. In the mad scene, Ophelia should carry a lute instead of wild flowers, since Poel believed that the Queen would not later have described them if we had already seen them; Ophelia 'should move from one person to another, unconscious of what she was saying, where she was going or to whom she was speaking'.[23] In the grave scene, 'such maimed rites' should not be represented by a full ceremonial procession of priests, with monks and nuns carrying Ophelia's coffin: a single priest would make the point (according to another pleasing direction in Q1), and he should not intone over the grave as if his lines were part of the very service to which the Church objected. For this scene, Hamlet should change into a sailor's costume to bear out the line, 'With my sea-gown scarf'd about me'. And of course the play must not end with the death of Hamlet, but with the appearance of Fortinbras who arrives in order to restore order to the distracted kingdom, flushed with his victories, 'a symbol of political virginity' as Poel saw it, 'life in the midst of death'.

As if these innovations were not alarming enough in the eyes of Poel's contemporaries, the absence of intervals in Q1 denied an actor the opportunity to make a point for applause at the end of a scene, and Poel seized his chance to recover the larger effect of Elizabethan performance in the pace, sweep and rhythm of continuous action possible on a bare platform.

The project took the stage with its team of amateurs on a Saturday afternoon, 16 April 1881.[24] The de Witt drawing of the Swan was, of course, not yet known, and Poel worked with curtains. *The Times* recognized, it thought, the work of Furnivall, who had introduced the performance with an introductory speech, and it failed to acknowledge Poel at all. Its correspondent therefore devoted his space to the novelty of the text and the staging, reporting that the play was presented 'without any of the adventitious adornments of scenery':

> The stage was enclosed with a pair of red curtains, through an aperture at the back of which, and through other openings at the right and left of the proscenium, the players came and went . . . . Two or three chairs and a small wooden platform, something like that provided by a painter for his model, formed the furniture, the latter being employed in the play scene . . . . The players were dressed, as the playbill informed us, in strict Elizabethan costume. . . .[25]

The writer found the performance 'a curious addition to the stock of public amusements', and his sarcasm was typical of those who came to scoff: 'Concerning the players themselves we are not disposed to be very critical. They were, as we have said, amateurs, playing, it is to be presumed, for their own gratification, and the gratification of their friends.' *The Era's* reviewer noted the titters in the audience at 'Saturday's pitiful exhibition',[26] and observed that the Ghost had a bad memory and that the King took 'a light comedy view of his duties'. Poel, playing Hamlet, was 'lachrymose' and 'ever in a hurry', running his lines together to produce results like, 'The rest shall remain as they are to a nunnery go' — a criticism which would be heard a generation later when Granville-Barker's mode of speaking Shakespeare replaced the former declamation.

The most violent attack was reserved for the text of Q1. Dutton Cook wrote of 'the muddled and mangled text . . . denied scenery and musical accompaniment'.[27] *The Era* spoke of it as 'the botcher's text, the barbarously mutilated and imperfect version of the piratical printer', and *The Saturday Review* reported that 'that degraded text was declaimed in a manner beneath criticism'.[28] The company's 'airy confidence of ineptitude' provoked from this reviewer the sarcastic suggestion that, to be accurate, the costumes should not be Elizabethan, but modern: 'Hamlet should have superintended the play in evening dress and killed Laertes in a fencing jacket.' He was not to know that his amusing notion was to be taken up soon enough by Barry Jackson as another step in the direction of finding Shakespeare's temporal range.

Poel's amateurs did not play well, let us concede. But the degree of indifference to the historical interest of the occasion shown by the gentlemen of the press points to the size of the task Poel had set himself: 'In my innocence', he wrote later, 'I fancied 'em all real Shakespeare students.'[29] And in the light of what we now know, Robert Speaight's verdict was right: that although the note of theatrical triumph was conspicuously absent, the performance announced the birth of a new idea. The experiment in St George's Hall 'was historic in the sense that it was seminal':

There is nothing new today in *Hamlet* being performed in curtains; there is nothing sensational in the appearance of Fortinbras. No one will raise an eyebrow if you suggest that *Hamlet* is a play drenched in Renaissance thought, or that while Hamlet should never behave like an actor, there is every reason why he should, on occasion, behave like a cad. The romantic Hamlet is now the reactionary Hamlet, and the sentimental Hamlet is obsolete. These changes might never have come about if William Poel had not had the startlingly original idea of reading the play as if he had just borrowed the prompter's copy from the Globe Theatre. He was on the side of logic against prejudice, of common sense against theatrical convention.[30]

Nearly twenty years later, on 21 February 1900, Poel and his brave amateurs again put on the First Quarto *Hamlet* (with additions from the Folio) for a single performance in the Carpenters' Hall, London (see Plate 6). This time the play was more Elizabethan than ever, with the female parts played by boys and men as they were originally, and Ophelia appearing as a comely maid in a ruff ('rather a blow to the imagination', complained *The Times*).[31] The jocular reviews indicate that Poel's experiment was taken no more seriously then than the first time.

But Poel was not discouraged from his search for Shakespearian immediacy, the 'special kind of realism' of the open stage and Elizabethan performance. After his *Hamlet*, he went on directing Elizabethan readings and productions in any hall he could rent, sometimes at the rate of four or five a year, for another fifty years. He preached and practised, unceasingly. He has the distinction of being the man who most clarified the critical issues for the twentieth century.

6 William Poel's First Quarto *Hamlet* in the Carpenters' Hall, 1900

In 1893 he studied the Fortune Theatre contract and attempted to build the old playhouse inside the Royalty Theatre for an Elizabethan *Measure for Measure* (see Plate 7). *The Times* of 7 September carried this announcement:

SHAKESPEARE READING SOCIETY

In order to test the dramatic effect of acting an Elizabethan play under the conditions it was written to fulfil, the Shakespeare Reading Society, of which Mr Irving is president, will on November 9, 10, and 11, at a West-end theatre, give a performance of *Measure for Measure* on a stage of the 16th Century style, with groups of spectators in appropriate costume.

If this sounds a little like a charade, so it was: but it was also the biggest step to date in seeking the non-illusory experience. There were four performances in all, on a curtained stage, 30 feet wide by 24 feet deep, without scenery, flanked by Elizabethan gentlemen who sat on the stage and in side boxes stripped of upholstery. These spectators ostentatiously puffed at clay pipes during the single interval.

What the members of the Shakespeare Reading Society have done is to erect a small proscenium within that of the Royalty, and in the background to raise the balcony or second stage above referred to, with two trans verse curtains, the drawing of one or other of which marks a change of scene.[32]

The Times printed a long notice, complaining that the effect was anachronistic: illumination was by gaslight, with a row of footlights (unknown before Garrick's return from France in 1765), women played the female parts instead of boys, and no placards were exhibited naming the place of the action. The correspondent indulged himself with a learned discussion on 'the rude playhouses of Shakespeare's time', describing the Swan drawing 'not long since brought to light in the University Library at Utrecht', and arguing that the adapted Royalty could not be said to bear 'even a distant resemblance' to an Elizabethan public playhouse. In three reports, Poel's name was not once mentioned, although he had played Angelo.

Yet attention was paid: Elizabethan dramatic experiment was actually invading the West End, and the issue of verisimilitude became a public controversy. The production was attacked by William Archer on technicalities — the curtain was too far forward and no doors provided the entrances.[33] In this and other productions C. E.

7 The Elizabethan revival: William Poel's *Measure for Measure* at the Royalty Theatre, 1893

Montague regretted that he did not get the Elizabethan sensation of 'having an actor come forward to the edge of a platform in the midst of ourselves',[34] missing what he called the 'fusion or interpenetration of stage and auditorium' which was 'the essence of the Elizabethan theatre' (Poel was, of course, still hampered by the proscenium arch). And *The Times*'s critic did not find what he expected:

Usually it is assumed that in such circumstances the imagination of the onlooker would be so stimulated as to conjure up streets and palaces surpassing the art of the modern *metteur-en-scène*. The present writer must confess that he had no such experience. In fact, though following the action closely, he had no picture of the scene before his mind at all. He found himself interested in the persons of the play, without considering whether they were English or foreign, ancient or modern. They were merely so many abstractions, like the characters of a fairy tale.[35]

Nevertheless, in this criticism paradoxically lies the success of the experiment. The critic expected that a bare stage would require him to exercise his visual imagination and build his own scenery, according to the textbooks; instead, it was the unlocalized and timeless action which became prominent. And Poel won a supporter in George Bernard Shaw, the apostle of the new drama, and in any case a man always ready for a fight against the establishment. Two years later, Shaw was to write:

'The more I see of these performances by the Elizabethan Stage Society, the more I am convinced that their method of presenting an Elizabethan play is not only the right method for that particular sort of play but that any play performed on a platform amidst the audience gets closer home to its hearers than when it is presented as a picture framed by a proscenium. Also, that we are less conscious of the artificiality of the stage when a few well-understood conventions, adroitly handled, are substituted for attempts at an impossible scenic verisimilitude.[36]

Again a paradox: that convention, previously considered a positive distraction from the reality of the play, can make us *less* conscious of its theatricality.

In 1897, Poel produced a *Twelfth Night* before the Prince of Wales and a distinguished audience. He chose to play it in the Hall of the Middle Temple, the location of its first performance on 2 February 1601 before Queen Elizabeth.[37] The occasion was of more than antiquarian interest, however: it was important in the light of recent conclusions about the influence of the Tudor halls upon the Elizabethan stage and presentation.[38] At the upper end of the hall Poel set up a stage consisting of a raised platform with a balcony above it, and arranged with upstage entrances on either side in the manner of the de Witt drawing. He again used a traverse, before which he could play an 'exterior' scene, as when Malvolio overtakes Viola on her way from Olivia's house. The only furnishing was a table and a chair, and the costumes were those of the Elizabethan Court. Except that electric light was used instead of candles, and 'lady members of the society' played the women's parts, the performance struck the note of authenticity. The music was played on 'an Italian virginal of about 1550, a treble and a bass viol, and a Venice-made lute of about the same period'; the songs had their original settings, with others composed by Arnold Dolmetsch, who directed the musicians in an Elizabethan hat — 'the most charming piece of archaism of all'. Halberdiers stood formally on the stage and outside the hall. The play was performed within two hours.

The Times, again not naming Poel, was still his severe critic:

> That the action as represented under these primitive conditions was clear enough cannot be denied, but it is certain that the great majority of the public were far from seeing or hearing as well as they would in an ordinary modern theatre. Middle Temple Hall, with its elaborate oak carvings, is sadly deficient in acoustic properties, and, seated as they were for the most part on the flat, the spectators, with the exception of those in the front rows, could see nothing but the heads of the performers.[39]

For the most part, however, discussion of this remarkable occasion again turned chiefly on the effect of performance without scenery, and Poel's production of *The Tempest* in November of that year raised the same issues. The work of the Society was regarded widely as an 'educational' exercise, but it took the percipience of Shaw to recognize that the nature of theatrical illusion itself was at issue. The force of Shakespeare's poetry was of such a kind that it would take 'an extraordinary degree of [scenic] art' to complement and not destroy the illusion of poetic drama.[40] He began to ask the fundamental question: what kind of play is to be performed on a bare stage?

Soon after the turn of the century, rival critical positions were taken more firmly. Max Beerbohm, who never liked Poel's work, found that the search for the authentic was 'somewhat too owlish', and he explained, 'I use the word "owlish" as implying a certain rather morbid and inhuman solemnity and a detachment from the light of day'[41] – he preferred the realistic and spectacular stage. In Poel's production of *Samson Agonistes* at Burlington House in December 1908, he dared to have his chorus enter through the auditorium, another step toward non-illusion, and Beerbohm's revealing comment was that 'it must obviously destroy all aesthetic illusion, and send us all into paroxysms of internal laughter'.[42] *The Times* continued to complain with heavy irony of the Society's 'self-denying frugality', yet began to admit 'some inexplicable, but genuine attraction' in the archaism, and confessed that the 'delightful simplicities' had their 'aesthetic effect'.[43] C. E. Montague, as we saw, was disappointed that Poel's actor did not truly move from a proscenium-arch relationship with the audience and speak as 'from a front bench in Parliament'. The Elizabethan actor performed, he believed,

with only the narrowest scope for theatrical illusion, with no incentive to naturalism, and with every motive for putting his strength into sheer energy and beauty of declamation, giving his performance the special qualities of fine recitation as distinct from those of realistic acting.[44]

However, in reviewing Poel's *Doctor Faustus* in 1904, Montague was pleased to find that 'the actors stood out "in the round" like statues' on the platform stage, in contrast with the modern picture stage 'where the actor is seen in the flat, framed in a recess, and planted on a background'.

The issue of Shakespearian illusion, and whether the audience's conviction of realism in a play was a help or a hindrance to its meaning, was at least alive. As usual, Shaw grasped the nettle first, and in a notable review of *The Tempest* performed in the Mansion House in 1897, he recognized that communication in the theatre always required a special assessment of the nature of a play in relation to the role of its audience:

Mr Poel says frankly, 'See that singers' gallery up there! Well, let's pretend that it's the ship'. We agree; and the thing is done.... The singing gallery makes no attempt to impose on us: it disarms criticism by unaffected submission to the facts of the case, and throws itself honestly on our fancy, with instant success.[45]

'The facts of the case' were to become the matter for debate, both on the stage and in the study. Thus, because of its essential unreality, Poel's *Two Gentlemen of Verona* in 1910 provoked a pertinent discussion of appropriate illusion, even in *The Times*. 'Of course, what they cannot reproduce is the Elizabethan audience with the Elizabethan frame of mind', the correspondent observed, but 'the puerile complications and improbabilities of the intrigue, which a "realistic" modern setting would only have made more glaring, became of little account' and the peculiarly romantic atmosphere of the comedy, its character as a 'brilliant fantasia on what Pascal called "les passions de l'amour"',[46] was thrust into prominence by Poel's presentation.

Thus, well before the new orientation of Shakespeare created by Granville-Barker, it had become commonplace to recognize that Poel's Elizabethanism was no mere archaeological affectation, but of historical importance and answering a public demand. Martin Harvey's *The Taming of the Shrew* at no less a theatre than the Prince of Wales in 1913 adopted Poel's staging methods (Poel was 'coadjutor' in the production), and excited almost Brechtian approval:

> The conventions of this method of production are at least no harder to swallow than the conventions of the 'realistic' method; and since it makes no pretence that anything but a play is toward, we are auditors not merely unhindered but positively helped by obvious indications that a play it is.[47]

In view of this conversion of *The Times*, Poel's experiments can hardly be accounted a failure.

In a notable article in 1927 in *The Saturday Review*[48] entitled 'Salute to William Poel', Ivor Brown brilliantly summarized Poel's extraordinary achievement. He acknowledged that Poel had worked against a tide of mockery as well as physical and financial difficulties. But 'he went quietly about his job, giving more of the poet and less of the upholsterer'. His influence had been pervasive, and 'the better type of Shakespearean presentation to-day is simply Poel popularized without acknowledgments'. Brown recognized clearly that stage practice had much to demonstrate about the meaning of the plays – the size of Poel's platform itself explained numerous things which otherwise seemed silly or unintelligible. Brown distinguished between the full platform and the compromise 'apron', perceiving in particular that the original staging stressed the formal experience intended:

The apron assists the delivery of soliloquies and asides which, on a full platform, are spoken naturally to the surrounding audience. The apron also assists in a small way the general scheme of rhetoric and grandiose movement. Here again the full platform does more than assist; it entirely alters and recreates. . . . The apron-stage opened the door of that cage in which the Elizabethan drama had been pent up; the platform-stage removes all the four walls of the prison.

In his observations Brown also anticipated our recent sense of Shakespeare's stage, and thus of his drama, as 'multiple', promoting 'the plasticity and variety' of Elizabethan dramatic communication, and he also perceived the 'to-and-fro technique' (the swift cut from scene to scene) which Shakespeare's stage and the new art of the 'kinema' had in common.

Poel always believed that Shakespeare demanded a close relationship between stage and auditorium. G. B. Harrison once asked him whether he liked the productions at the Old Vic, and he replied that the Old Vic was too big for a Shakespeare play, which was designed for a small and intimate playhouse. As soon as the actor has to 'project' over considerable space, he inevitably loses the flexibility of an intimate performance.[49] In a later contribution to *The Saturday Review*,[50] Brown pulled together the notion of the 'drastic intimacy between actor and audience' belonging to Shakespeare's theatre and the peculiar rhythm and movement of his poetic drama:

The Elizabethan platform was not only far larger than the average modern stage, but its triple division gave scope for swift alternations from one plane to another, both in structure and in temper. As soon as Mr Poel recreates his platform-stage he recreates the flow, the rhythm, and the energy of Elizabethan drama.

All this, of course, anticipated the course of modern criticism, which is more formalist, historically accurate and open to the actual trial of performance. And this, too, Brown seemed to anticipate in his 'Salute' when he asserted that Poel always achieved 'a performance, never an essay in pedantry': 'His reward is to have saved Shakespeare from stupidity. He could do that because he is the scholar—actor who knows the internal craft of the stage as well as the external lore of Elizabethanism.' He reclaimed Shakespeare the poet, prompting Robert Speaight and Bridges-Adams to characterize him as 'a rationalist whose mysticism is too much for him'.[51]

4

The advent of stage-centred criticism

'We all learn, borrow, steal, if you like, from one another', wrote Tyrone Guthrie,[1] and the chain of influences linking director to director is as strong as that between critics. In 1899, at the age of 22, Granville Barker played Richard II for William Poel. After 1902, Ben Greet had been co-producer with Poel for *Everyman*, and his simplified stage smacked of the master (although William Winter decided that Greet's Elizabethan *Twelfth Night* of 1904 smacked of humbug[2]). In the same year Barker directed a swift *Two Gentlemen* at the Court, working with Lewis Casson, who had appeared in Poel's *Alchemist* of 1899 and later played the Provost in Poel's *Measure for Measure* in 1908. Iden Payne at Manchester and Barry Jackson at Birmingham were both impressed by the simple strength of this production,[3] and Nugent Monck and Bridges-Adams were stage manager and ASM respectively for Poel's *Two Gentlemen* at His Majesty's in 1910. Robert Atkins was Poel's stage manager for *All's Well* in 1920, and Atkins borrowed Poel's ideas for his tenure at the Old Vic, 1920–5.

Entering the age of Granville-Barker, we find that Nigel Playfair was the Steward in his *Winter's Tale* of 1912, and Bottom in his *Dream* of 1914. In that year Tyrone Guthrie saw Monck's *Love's Labour's Lost* and has confessed a debt to him.[4] Poel also approved the efficiency of Bridges-Adams's scene design for *Henry V* in 1920. Harcourt Williams, a keen student of Poel and Granville-Barker, reigned at the Old Vic from 1929 to 1934, with John Gielgud as his young lead. Gielgud's *Hamlet* at the Lyceum in 1939 had enjoyed a special rehearsal under Granville-Barker and used his style of simple setting, and Gielgud's *Lear* at the Old Vic in 1940, with Lewis Casson as co-producer, acknowledged its debt to Granville-Barker's *Preface*.[5] When Gielgud revived *Lear* at Stratford in 1950, he thanked 'the spirit of Harley Granville-Barker who taught me all I know about this play'.[6] In 1946, Barry Jackson was running the Stratford Festival, to which he introduced a new and very young director for *Love's Labour's Lost*, one Peter Brook, aged 21.

So the catalogue proceeds, link upon link, until audiences lose sight of the beginning of the chain. But this is to rush ahead and pass over events of major importance affecting the life of Shakespeare in the early years of this century.

In England, an extraordinary growth of dramatic societies, amateur and professional, initiated by playgoers and by actors, bent upon exploring Shakespeare and neglected Elizabethan plays, coincided with the revival of interest in their appropriate staging. Among the oldest was the Stage Society of 1899, from which emerged the Phoenix in 1919, dedicated to the revival of old English drama and using simplified settings by Granville-Barker's designer Norman Wilkinson to achieve continuity of action. The British Empire Shakespeare Society, the London Shakespeare League and the English Dramatic Society (founded by Nugent Monck) were all begun in 1904—5. All devoted in some degree to playing Shakespeare, the Renaissance Society, the Fellowship of Players, the Pioneers (started in 1905 and becoming the Pioneer Players in 1911), the Play Actors' Society (started in 1907) and a dozen others[7] sprouted in the 1900s and withered by the end of the 1920s. This initiative was matched by organized groups of serious theatre-goers, the Playgoers' Club, the Gallery First Nighters' Club, the O.P. Club, the Dramatic Debaters, and others, who found their common ground in the British Drama League in 1919. It is perhaps a British social impulse to gather together in the name of play-acting, and the new simplified Shakespeare provided the perfect occasion. After the Second World War, societies variously associated with Elizabethanism were still blooming briefly overnight, forswearing the elaborate staging of the Victorians, austerely doubling the parts, keeping monotonous lighting in imitation of the daylight at the Globe, trusting that their earnest attempts to recapture the spirit of the original would compensate for their deficiencies in acting.

These societies came and went unheralded, but for the first time they brought together amateur and professional, scholar and player, in the name of Shakespeare and his contemporaries: they were symptomatic of a new consciousness of the Elizabethan heritage of great drama and theatre. Mention should be made of the little-known Mermaid Club, one of whose rules was that no member might report its proceedings in the press. The Club was founded by Martin Holmes of the London Museum, George Skillan, one of W. Bridges-Adams's actors at the Memorial Theatre, and G. B. Harrison, then Reader in English Literature at the University of London. It was a very modest London club with a subscription of 2s. 6d. a head. It had about 25 members, a mixture of actors, directors, critics, scholars, playwrights and antiquarians including W. W. Greg, John Dover Wilson, Ben Iden Payne, Ivor Brown, John Drinkwater, Donald Wolfit and John Laurie, some of the best of that generation. Members met once a month in the winter, when someone would introduce a topic for discussion in a 15-minute talk. The Club then sat down to a dinner and continued the exchange until each went about his own affairs. This society ran from 1933 to 1939, when the War brought it to an end. In reminiscence, Harrison writes that the members taught each other much.[8]

Meanwhile in the world of education there were parallel developments. At one extreme the summer of 1912 was given over to a 'Shakespeare's England' Exhibition at Earl's Court, with *tableaux vivants* and folk dances set in a mock Fortune Theatre, a replica of the Globe housing extracts from the plays, a Mermaid Tavern Club, a Tudor banqueting hall displaying Queen Elizabeth and her Court, and 'Plymouth Harbour' sporting the battleship *Revenge*. The festival was capped by a tournament in the Empress Hall, which included tilting before Queen Alexandra, the Empress of Russia and a brilliant social gathering. Circuses, joy wheels and water chutes completed Britain's homage to the Bard.

At another extreme Shakespeare became a new subject for the schools. In the 1870s Oxford's Clarendon Press had issued its first school Shakespeare, smothered in philological notes and word pedigrees by William George Clark and William Aldis Wright after the models of Greek and Latin texts. A. W. Verity's 13 volumes of The Pitt Press Shakespeare came from Cambridge between 1890 and 1905, rich with material on Elizabethan English and Shakespeare's use of metre, and in 1907 this was supplemented by notes from E. A. Abbott's *Shakespearian Grammar* (1869). The indigestion resulting from such excessive annotation and tortuous apparatus made Verity's name a grim household word for generations of schoolchildren in Britain.

There were other perils for young students of Shakespeare in the

The advent of stage-centred criticism

late nineteenth century, and in America in 1881 the Rev. Henry N. Hudson followed his 20-volume Harvard Shakespeare with an edition from Ginn and Company explicitly 'for use in schools and families': it offered a carefully bowdlerized text. Dr Hudson's moral justification of a school edition of a play like *Antony and Cleopatra* with its adulterous theme makes priceless reading today:

> The Poet makes us sympathize so far with their magnificent infatuation, that we cheerfully accord to them a sort of special privilege and exemption. Thus their action leaves our moral feelings altogether behind, and indeed soars, or, which comes to the same thing, sinks, quite beyond their ken. Nay, more; our thoughts and imaginations take with them, so to speak, a glad holiday in a strange country where the laws of duty undergo a willing suspension, and conscience temporarily abdicates her throne. Nor are we anywise damaged by this process. Rather say, the laws of duty are all the sweeter to us after such a brief escape from them; mark, I say escape from them, not transgression of them; which is a very different thing. So that the drama is perfectly free from anything approaching to moral taint or infection. The very extravagance of the leading characters causes their action to be felt by us as strictly exceptional.[9]

Hudson's sober editions were widely used on both sides of the Atlantic well into the twentieth century.

A slowly increasing sense that Shakespeare was not a dead author, however, changed the editorial approach: editions appeared with a short life of the author, the story of the play and more 'literary' notes. These would triumphantly list such considerations as Shakespeare's anachronisms, until any student could feel superior to a writer whose Romans could talk of plucking ope a doublet and whose Cleopatra could ask to have her lace cut. But the progress was increasingly towards a plain text, until the Clarendon Press issued *The Oxford Plain Text Shakespeare* actually without one word of introduction or annotation.

By 1920 the London County Council was paying for children to attend professional performances of Shakespeare in the West End, and in this period Blackie and Son came out with *The Warwick Shakespeare* edited by C. H. Herford, who declared forthrightly in his General Preface: 'In the Warwick Shakespeare an attempt is made to present the greater plays of the dramatist in their literary aspect, and not merely as material for the study of philology and grammar.' Herford went so far as to append four pages on 'Shakespeare's Stage in Its Bearing upon His Drama'. Thomas Nelson and Sons produced a school text in 1926 which carried the motto, 'The reader acts the play himself in the theatre of his own mind', and went so far as to include as its only introduction the list of *dramatis personae*, followed by a suggestion of their dress and appearance. Finally, the University of London Press issued a series of the plays in the 1930s under the general editorship of Allardyce Nicoll, who wrote a bold prefatory note to the student as follows:

1. Note the following remarks by Dr Johnson: 'Let him that is yet unacquainted with the powers of Shakespeare, and who desires to feel the greatest pleasure that the drama can give, read every play, from the first scene to the last, with utter negligence of all his commentators'.
2. As you read, try always to imagine exactly what is happening. Remember that this is, after all, a *play*.[10]

Quite a turn-about in 50 years.

In 1926 the Board of Education produced a momentous document, *The Drama in Adult Education*.[11] No greater official sanction of the propriety of the wayward muse could have been desired. The Adult Education Committee specifically encouraged the growth of amateur societies, to the surprising chagrin of William Poel, who believed that 'the country will be flooded with amateur entertainers, who will masquerade on our green and pleasant land under the impression that they are improving both themselves and their neighbours'.[12] The Report urged the teaching of drama because of its moral values — an extraordinary example of special pleading and loose thinking. It innocently advocated lectures such as one on 'the relationship between the comic spirit and laughter', which produced the scathing comment from Poel that no lecture on laughter could 'teach an amateur how to make a whole theatre full of others — that is, of those who are not professors — laugh at a line of Congreve's inimitable wit'.[13] He insisted that only one who had practised the art could teach it, and in his support he quoted Tree: 'It is better to send a sailor up a mast than a tailor'.

Nevertheless, a radical change in thinking about drama in education had taken place during the first quarter of the century. It was a change visible both in Britain and America, where increasing numbers of drama schools were being equipped with everything except staff. The change in Britain can be attributed to the work of many people: to Poel, to the leaders of the amateur movement, to Frank Benson who toured Shakespeare in repertory for thirty-three years from 1883 to 1914 and persuaded the schools that Shakespeare was not a dead author. But behind all this stand a great number of early adventures into stage-centred criticism, research into the early playhouses, attempts to recreate Shakespeare in his 'workshop' and historical studies of Elizabethan theatrical life and conventions of the stage.

While A. W. Pollard and W. W. Greg were attempting to establish as nearly as possible the original texts as they might have been printed directly from the playhouse manuscripts,[14] the character and methods of the Elizabethan playhouses became the life work of such men as Joseph Quincy Adams, Edmund Chambers, and W. J. Lawrence. In 1917, Adams edited *The Dramatic Records of Sir Henry Herbert, Master of the Revels, 1623–1673*, a work replete with insights into the life of the stage, and *Shakespearean Playhouses: A History of English Theatres from the Beginnings to the Restoration*, a model for all subsequent studies. His *Life of William Shakespeare* was the first to set Shakespeare in his true milieu as a busy manager, a ready actor and a practical playwright. The indispensable source-book was Chambers's four-volume *The Elizabethan Stage* published by Oxford in 1923, and he followed this in 1930 with the two-volume *William Shakespeare: A Study of Facts and Problems*. Together these volumes made a comprehensive collection of contemporary Elizabethan material so accessible that it could not be ignored.[15] Chambers brought to the forefront of discussion the importance of how an acting company was run and how the playhouse was built; he reviewed the relationship of the actors with the Court, the playhouse manuscripts, the chronology of the plays, shared authorship and many other essential considerations. Yet Chambers's terse objectivity precluded the possibility that he might be the scholar to speculate upon the plays on the stage and to attempt performance analysis. The excitement of this kind of study was left to men like the Irishman W. J. Lawrence.

Now neglected and in many details superseded, Lawrence was nevertheless in his time an extraordinary stimulus to new thinking about Shakespeare. With William Archer and W. H. Godfrey in 1907, he attempted the reconstruction of the Fortune Theatre plans. He began putting together his thoughts on the business of Elizabethan stagecraft in several collections of essays, beginning with two volumes of *The Elizabethan Playhouse and Other Studies* in 1912 and 1913,[16] and in 1927 he produced his central book, *The Physical Conditions of the Elizabethan Playhouse*. His interest started properly from the details of the playhouse structure: he speculated upon the size of the house, the shape of the platform and its height, the position of the doors and the trap, the location of an inner stage with the curtains presumed to conceal it, and the use of a 'chamber', two window-stages and the heavens.[17] It was a short step to speculation about the audience and the practice of the stage: its music, its off-stage effects of thunder, lightning and bell-ringing, the positioning of thrones, the use of the trap to suggest hell, and why rushes were strewn on the platform (answer: to protect the expensive costumes). He argued for the 'alternation theory', whereby one scene was supposed to have followed another without loss of 'illusion' by playing alternately before and behind the line of a curtain believed to have been strung between the stage posts. All this was necessary pioneer work.

Lawrence's most pertinent discussions were to follow. How was Antony raised aloft to Cleopatra's monument? In what ways did doubling affect the play-structure? Were *As You Like It* and *A Midsummer Night's Dream* written for private performance? What was the purpose of the dumb-show in *Hamlet*? Were stage ghosts visible, and why did Gertrude not see the ghost of Hamlet's father? He discussed the use of horns in *A Midsummer Night's Dream*, and how trumpets intensify the martial atmosphere in *Coriolanus*. He considered the antimasque and its effect in *Macbeth*, and raised the first teasing questions about the casting of boys in women's parts. He noted the tag couplets which announced an exit from the stage and speculated upon the so-called law of re-entry whereby an actor who closed one scene could not open the next. This bent of Lawrence's mind appealed to William Poel, and encouraged their friendship and correspondence over many years.[18] In this, director tempered scholar: both desired to prove that the life of the Elizabethan stage was different from that of the proscenium stage, but it was Poel, the practical man of the theatre, who urged restraint:

There was no finality in the form of the Elizabethan Stage which dramatists like Shakespeare would or could accept, because they knew that the play must be acted one day in their own theatre, another day in the palace, and, when they were travelling, in town halls.[19]

The advent of stage-centred criticism

However, it is interesting to note that Granville-Barker did not find himself much in accord with Lawrence, whom he thought too literal. In a review of *The Physical Conditions of the Elizabethan Public Playhouses* and *Pre-Restoration Stage Studies*, Granville-Barker observed that it was 'a rare type of scholar who is capable of appreciating Elizabethan drama as literature and of visualizing it in action under the original conditions', but went on to say that a prompt-book was a shaky foundation for fact. Of Lawrence's learned discussion of the stage direction for 'the noise of a sea-fight' in *Antony and Cleopatra*, III.x, he wrote dryly, 'I suspect it differed mainly from the noise of a land-fight by the addition of "Avasts" and "Belays".' Lawrence devoted a whole chapter to stage traps, so that it seemed there was little about traps that remained to be said. Granville-Barker, however, brought his stage sense to bear on the issues:

Does [Lawrence] really wish us to think that Juliet in her tomb was below stage and out of sight, that Romeo lowered the dead Paris on the top of her, and addressed his farewell speech − to a hole? And all because, by one stage direction, 'Juliet rises'!

Lawrence also believed that *Hamlet*'s Ghost 'took a step forward and flung itself down the suddenly yawning grave trap', to which Granville-Barker responded with the mild protest, 'I do beg him to free us from a vision of the immortal William flinging himself down that trap − six foot at the shallowest.'[20]

'Workshop' criticism[21] had properly begun with Richard Green Moulton of Cambridge and Chicago in his *Shakespeare as a Dramatic Artist: A Popular Illustration of Scientific Criticism* (Oxford, 1885). Hazlitt had felt that Shakespeare's characters were 'present in the poet's imagination, as at a kind of rehearsal' and he was fond of repeating how well the playwright had embodied them, animating their slightest impulses. Moulton's close scrutiny of chosen plays attempted to calculate Shakespeare's techniques and analyze his plot construction, even to the point of recasting *Macbeth* into the shape of a Greek tragedy, chorus and all. George Pierce Baker's *The Development of Shakespeare as a Dramatist* (1907) applied to Shakespeare the kind of structural enquiry he developed in his playwriting workshops at Harvard. Arthur Quiller-Couch published his Cambridge lectures on ten of the plays in a breezy, popular volume, *Shakespeare's Workmanship* (1918).

In his preface, Q wrote that he sought to discover 'just what Shakespeare was trying to do as a playwright', which had always seemed to him 'a sensible way of approaching him':

It is no disparagement to the erudition and scholarship that have so piously been heaped about Shakespeare to say that we shall sometimes find it salutary to disengage our minds from it all, and recollect that the poet was a playwright.

Shakespeare's plays were 'acting plays', those which succeeded on the boards and entertained an audience which had paid to be entertained: this differentiated them at once from 'a literary composition meant to be read by the fireside, where the kettle does all the hissing'. And he made the first assumption necessary to achieve perceptual criticism: 'To understand what Shakespeare as a workman was driving at, we must in imagination seat ourselves amid the audience he had in mind as he worked.'[22] Thus he began his discussion of *Macbeth* by first describing the Elizabethan playhouse, complete with inner stage, according to the received opinion of the day. Q's lectures ranged over a hundred and one engaging problems — boy actors, witches and fairies, the suggestion of atmosphere, comic relief, disguises in the comedies, blank verse as a vehicle for drama, scenic resources in the last plays, the nature of tragicomedy, and many more. The book is still as stimulating as it was when first published.

Stage-centred criticism is that which characteristically checks text against performance, and does not admit critical opinion as fully valid without reference to the physical circumstances of the medium. As a spectator judges by what he perceives in the theatre, so perceptual criticism assesses the intention, the conception, behind a play from a reconstruction of performance before a particular audience, and arrives at its meaning by recognizing its code of communication. When a new production of a play, perhaps in a different playhouse and before a different audience, reveals more of its qualities, then perceptual criticism must make an adjustment. As the play lives, so criticism is modified and refined to greater accuracy, until at some unseen vanishing point the focus is felt to be exact and the play defined.

It is ironic that Poel, with all his Victorian limitations, should be the one to initiate modern stage-centred criticism. He liberated Shakespeare criticism, because as a scholar—actor he learned to verify his ideas by scores of recitals and productions, an achievement equal to his

The advent of stage-centred criticism

rebellion against Victorian realism in performance which made possible Granville-Barker's much finer and visionary productions. Poel asked that scholars should have a sense of the theatre, which he defined broadly as 'the ability to forecast what degree of emotion or sympathy certain incidents can arouse in an audience when they are seen represented on the stage'.[23] In particular, audience response was to be estimated by an examination of the details of dramatic construction:

It is doubtful if any serious attention has been given yet to the way Shakespeare conducts his story and brings his characters on and off the stage, a matter of the highest moment, since the very life of the play depends upon the skill with which this is done. And how many realize that the art of Shakespeare's dramatic construction differs fundamentally from that of the modern dramatist?[24]

Poel's close criticism was done with the eye of a director, as any sample of his work will show.

His major paper on *Romeo and Juliet*[25] involve a scholarly comparison with the source poem of Arthur Brooke, mixed with an actor's frontal attack on the Irving acting version. The following extracts will indicate Poel's approach and the essay's distinction:

i.i In less than thirty lines we are introduced to seven persons, all of whom indicate their character by the attitude they assume towards the quarrel. . . . The quarrel is abruptly terminated by the entrance of the Prince, who speaks with a precision and decision which throws every other character on the stage into insignificance. . . . Shakespeare having wisely kept [Romeo] out of the quarrel, that the audience may see him indifferent to every other passion but the one of love.

i.v [In] Capulet's house, where Romeo and Juliet see each other for the first time, the audience now [are] fully aware of the conditions under which the two meet.

ii.ii It is incomprehensible to me why our stage Juliets, in the 'Balcony Scene', go through their billing-and-cooing as deliberately as they do their toilets, never for a moment thinking that the 'place is death' to Romeo.

ii.iv The advance of the love episode must move side by side with the quarrel episode, so in the next scene we hear of Romeo receiving a challenge from Tybalt.

iii.i Not to show, in action on the stage, the rage of the Capulets at the death of Tybalt, and the grief of the Montagues at the banishment of Romeo, is to weaken the tragic significance of the scenes which follow. Without it the audience cannot vividly realize that the hatred of the two houses has reached its acutest stage.

III.iv The scene that follows shows us Capulet fixing a day for the marriage of Juliet with Paris, [rendering] the parting of the lovers in the next scene highly dramatic. . . . The news is sprung upon her with terrible abruptness, though the audience have been in the secret from the first.

IV.ii Then follows what is perhaps the most dramatic episode in the whole play. We are shown Capulet's household busy with the preparations for the marriage-feast, and the father now bent on having a 'great ado'.

IV.iii The vision of Tybalt's ghost pursuing Romeo for vengeance, an incident not to be found in the originals, shows the touch of the master dramatist. We feel the need of some immediate incentive to nerve Juliet to raise the vial to her lips.

IV.iv While the poor child lies prostrate upon her bed in the likeness of death, we are shown the dawn of the morning, the rousing and bustle of the household; we hear the bridal march in the distance . . . the changing of the sound of instruments to that of melancholy bells, of solemn hymns to sullen dirges, of bridal flowers to funeral wreaths.

V.iii The Irving-version omits all but the entrance of the citizens with Montague, Capulet, and the Prince, who at once ends the play with the couplet —

> For never was a story of more woe
> Than this of Juliet and her Romeo.

Why open your play with the quarrel of the two houses if you do not intend to show them reconciled. . . ? No stage-version of 'Romeo and Juliet' is consistent with Shakespeare's intentions which does not give prominence to the hatred of the two houses and retain intact the three 'crowd scenes' — the one at the opening of the play, the second in the middle, and the third at the end.

In all this, Poel was not only alive to the details of the play's structure, but he was also judging its strength from the weight imposed upon it by an audience.

Poel looked for the simple relation of each scene to the whole play, its unity of design. In the opening of *King Lear*, Cordelia should enter affectionately with her father, in order to balance her last entrance when she is carried in his devoted arms.[26] The blinding of Gloucester in the same play is not mere sensationalism: that Regan and Goneril could be so inhuman makes Lear's plight more desperate. In *Macbeth*, the murder of Macduff's children is necessary to bring about the death of Macbeth himself. Poel's writings over many years are a mine of such observations, but his name could also be associated with a new historical criticism which was determined to remove the accretions of theatrical tradition. In *Twelfth Night*, Sir Toby should not appear in leather jerkin and stuffed breeches like an inn-keeper; Maria must seem by birth a lady attendant upon a countess, not wearing the aprons of a kitchen-maid.[27] In *The Merchant of Venice*, Poel always defied Irving and played Shylock for comedy, assuming a falsetto voice and scurrying back and forth in the trial scene to create a reductive image of the Jew.

Poel continued speaking and writing like this for half a century without bending too many academic ears. More respect was paid, however, to the historical criticism of two men unattached to the theatre, one German and one American, both writing independently. Levin Ludwig Schücking published *Character Problems in Shakespeare's Plays* in 1919.[28] He set out to stem the 'subjective current' fashionable in the discussion of Shakespeare's characters. Since Shakespeare was answerable to his public, the first question to ask was, 'What was the probable attitude of Shakespeare's contemporaries?':

To read and interpret the Shakespearean drama in the light of the same standards as we do that of Ibsen would be as wrong as tacitly to identify the mental qualities of Shakespeare's audience with that of Ibsen's.[29]

For the first time here was the promise of historical objectivity and a method of exegesis which would lead more surely to the Bard's intentions. Schücking's plan was to take Shakespeare more literally than was usual. Unhappily, he argued his case from a position which vitiated its force: he assumed that the Victorian theatre and audience were superior to the Elizabethan. Shakespeare's art was 'more naive', his methods frequently 'far more primitive'; the stage clowns were a concession to 'an ignorant mob'.

Time and again Schücking's findings were brilliantly original for the period. In discussing the soliloquy as 'direct self-explanation'[30] (which is not always its first *raison d'être*), he was aware of physical pressures, and recognized 'the close connexion which existed between the stage and the audience'. During a soliloquy, 'the actor may be said to stand in the midst of the audience', and his speech was a 'monologue in which the speaker, so to say, fraternizes with the audience'. He thus observed the difference between the modern and the Elizabethan theatres when he asserted, 'Our drama is enacted under the tacit agreement that there are no spectators present.' Indeed, he seemed always on the edge of making a profound statement, but arrived only at the conclusion, 'Our illusion in the theatre is entirely different from that of the Elizabethans.' On every occasion when he seemed about to take the momentous step towards an understanding of another mode of drama, his own limited notion of what was apt for realism and illusion stultified his thinking. Once again, rather than see the critic mastering the drama, we witness the drama defeating the critic.

Schücking was concerned to emphasize too literally what the characters said about themselves, as if they were themselves the makers of the play, and in vain he tried to schematize their comments. He heard Hamlet explain himself at length in soliloquy, and observed fallaciously that this made him introspective; he failed to ask himself why it was that a villain announcing his villainy, like Iago, or a comic character in his patter to the house, like Falstaff, did not also acquire a similar quality of introspection – an ignorant groundling would have known why he preferred Hamlet and Falstaff to Iago, in spite of their common technique. Schücking recognized that Shakespeare's characters often broke into uncharacteristic speech, as when Mercutio discourses on Queen Mab, but argued from this that they 'lack unity' because the words and ideas 'proceed immediately from the poet's own personality',[31] instead of finding Mercutio's ironic lyricism proper to its dramatic context in style and content. He believed that shifting modes of characterization, like Cleopatra's sea-change from strumpet to queen, arose from the episodic structure of primitive playwriting, and failed to see that the developing concept of human love as it became immortal remained consistent with the meaning of the play as a whole, without Shakespeare's giving a fig for psychological unity of character. He was on the mark in asserting that Hal's provocative first soliloquy was 'an explanatory remark, meant to be true to fact and belonging to the exposition, a statement which might have been put into the mouth of someone speaking as Chorus',[32] but went on fatuously to chide Shakespeare for seeking an immediate effect at the expense of the unity of his play, by which he implied the consistency of Hal's character.

When Schücking finally argued that Shakespeare's mixing of comedy and tragedy destroyed 'illusion', the reader of today may suspect that the critic was a prisoner of his own sense of an ideal dramatic form.[33]

The advent of stage-centred criticism

In attacking impressionistic criticism he indulged some of his own, and it took a clearer head than Schücking's to untangle the web of convention and illusion.

Elmer Edgar Stoll of the University of Minnesota was simultaneously attacking the impressionistic criticism of the old character studies of Shakespeare. The major incursions were made in 1915 with a study of *Othello* and in 1919 with a study of *Hamlet*.[34] He was immediately on surer ground than Schücking when he re-asserted the Aristotelian position that the 'core' of drama was situation: 'a situation is a character in contrast, and perhaps also in conflict, with other characters or with circumstances'.[35] The dramatist sought the sharpest and most striking contrast, 'the probability or psychological reasonableness of it being a secondary consideration'. The drama necessarily aimed at compression and condensation to produce the bigger effect, and Stoll triumphantly quoted Aristotle's teleological dictum that 'impossibilities are justifiable if they serve the end of poetry . . . if they make the effect of some portion of the work more striking'[36] [ἐκπληκτικός: variously translated 'astounding' (Bywater) and 'emotionally shattering' (Else)]. The end was everything for Aristotelians and for drama, the accumulative art. Longinus, too, was invoked for his contention that poets do not persuade their audiences, but enthral them, take them out of themselves. And Stoll summarized his priorities thus: 'The whole is more important than any part, the dramatic and poetic structure than the characters, and emotional illusion than verisimilitude. And they are, I think, to Shakespeare.' The sequence was: situation over character, and dramatic effect over situation – a design for improbability by any standard of psychological realism.

The psychological improbabilities in *Othello* were now to be explained dramatically. The Moor's uncharacteristic jealousy was an emotional development for the shape of the play – 'an eclipse, then an earthquake, then an avalanche' – traced by five meetings with Desdemona 'at each of which Othello is continually more brutal and outrageous',[37] the effect calculated dramatically for the audience. Desdemona 'like a child, continually says or does the wrong thing for herself, the right thing for the dramatist'.[38] Emilia's failure to speak up about the handkerchief increased tension, since the audience expected her every moment to save the situation, and her want of perception

77

was not stupidity, but carefully planned to enforce 'the fiction of the impenetrableness of Iago's mask'.[39] Stoll characterized these instances as 'musical manipulation':

The various repetition, whereby the contrasts are enforced and impressed upon us, is a sort of artistic manipulation, which, overriding the ordinary restrictions of psychology and realism, verges upon the confines of another art, that of music.[40]

His musical sense led him to associate the nature of dramatic illusion itself with the evocation of atmosphere and the ebb and flow in the intensity of the action.

With this, stage-centred criticism, if not perceptual criticism, took a giant stride forward. The delay in *Hamlet* was customary in Elizabethan revenge tragedies as a dramatic device,[41] and was not to be held to the Prince's discredit: it was a manoeuvre to make the best of an irrational old plot, a mechanical matter of postponing the catastrophe. Thus Hamlet's madness was really feigned, not partly involuntary, and 'this is in keeping with his perfect sanity when alone or with his friend':[42] this was less an invitation to see the play as a psychological case-study, of course, but much more dramatic. In the graveyard scene 'Shakespeare simply overreaches himself' when Hamlet and Laertes rant and leap into the grave, contriving for emotional effect the Clowns' jokes about Ophelia's tragedy and Hamlet's brooding, and capping all with a 'vast volume of utterance', as was Shakespeare's musical habit. Stoll followed this with a discussion on the grave scene, the best piece of perceptual criticism[43] in this period other than Granville-Barker's early *Prefaces*.

There was much more in Stoll which would guide criticism and performance in the years to come. He wrote chiefly of the tragedies, but his suggestion that the comedies dealt even more in fantasy, exaggeration and distortion was left for his readers to ponder. Shakespeare manipulated illusion at the expense of probability in order to manipulate his audience, and did so with an audacity designed to move and overwhelm the imagination. Art was not life, and Lear divided his kingdom, or Macbeth reacted to the Witches, by the laws of art. To attain his realities, Shakespeare ignored consistency of character, neglecting our familiar realism. He used the Elizabethan conventions, as a man of the theatre must, to quicken and expand the mind. Stoll had his touch of poetry, but in arguing thus historically, he left the closet far behind.

Closet Shakespeare was soon to receive a shattering blow, and the force for that blow was building up in other quarters. Edward Gordon Craig was the visionary spokesman for a new concept of theatre wholly opposed to the vogue of realism. He was also an outstanding innovator in scene design, and his ideas in that field afford an approach to his idea of a poetic drama, one which was neither Poel's nor Irving's: 'the middle path between ugly pedantry on the one hand, and superfluous detail on the other'.[44]

Craig's designs for his first production, Purcell's *Dido and Aeneas* in 1900, were simple and broad in effect – a throne, four walls of trellis and lights playing delicately upon a grey gauze hung before back-cloths of bright ultramarine blue and medium grey. It was a mere frame for the action. For Ibsen's *The Vikings*, designed for his mother Ellen Terry at the Imperial in 1903, fussy flies, borders, wings and foot-lights had gone, and shafts of light suggested, not reality, but impressions of reality, his effects towering beyond the limit of the proscenium itself, dwarfing the players.

Max Beerbohm at first argued that Craig's method of design lent itself to fantasy, but could not be well applied to an ordinary Shake-spearian comedy.[45] Poel went further and asserted that the central interest in drama is human, and 'there is no room for man in Mr Craig's world'.[46] But in the same year Craig designed *Much Ado About Nothing* at the Imperial, and Beerbohm came to think otherwise:

The men and women on the stage no longer symbolize the insignificance of the human race that crawls on our globe's surface. They have regained that fallacious magnitude that is so real to us. For the scenery itself is a sort of inner proscenium. True, in the church scene, the characters are dwarfed in Mr Craig's first manner. But it is realistically right that they should be.[47]

The church scene in act III was the sensation of the production. It was inspired by Sebastiano Serlio's *Five Books of Architecture* and the paint-ings of Taddeo Gaddi, and Craig's son described it thus:

Against a backing of grey curtains decorated with a varnished pattern that sparkled in the dim light, he built a long platform, reached by four wide steps. On the platform was a great altar, crowded with enormous candlesticks. High over the altar hung a giant crucifix, part of it disappearing into the shadows above (this was like the Cimabue crucifix in Florence). In the foreground he suggested two great columns by gathering together two clusters of enormous grey curtains. The only illumination in this dimly lit 'church' came from an imaginary stained-glass window above the proscenium arch that cast a great pool of light upon the floor below, while the distant candles twinkled mysteriously on the altar in the background. The characters were only lit when they entered the acting area which was the pool of coloured light; outside it, they too became silhouettes like the columns.[48]

This impressionism might today seem more Victorian than modern in its extravagance, but for Beerbohm it was 'not only the most decorative, but also the most dramatic, method of illustrating a play': 'By the elimination of details which in a real scene would be unnoticed, but which become salient on the stage, he gives to the persons of the play a salience never given to them before.'[49]

Craig believed that 'Realism is only Exposure, whereas Art is Revelation', and he endeavoured to reveal the spirit of a scene in his design. The shifting screens of his Moscow Art Theatre *Hamlet* of 1910 were the abstract background to a speaking costume design: the King in the first court scene 'in a golden cloak under which the whole Court sheltered', and the Players in gay coloured silks after the manner of Chinese jugglers, 'like so many birds flying in to bring joy to the young prince'.[50] Peter Brook recently summarized Craig's purpose simply: 'Craig wanted a token shadow to take the place of a complete painted forest and he only did so because he recognized that useless information absorbed our attention *at the expense of something more important*'.[51]

That 'something' was 'the drama', as Craig in his writings made clear. He dictated the two visionary dialogues of *The Art of the Theatre* between 22 April and 4 May 1905, adding additional material in 1910. The new book, *On the Art of the Theatre*, was soon being read all over Europe, and seen as the natural extension of Adolphe Appia's bible for the reform of play presentation, *Die Musik und die Inscenierung*. At the centre of Craig's conception was 'the art of the theatre', not the actor, not the playwright, nor any of the parts of the play. Just as Shakespeare rarely identifies the location of a scene, perhaps writing simply *'actus primus, scaena prima'*, so the stage-manager should aim 'not to *reproduce* nature, but to *suggest* some of her most beautiful and most living ways'[52] — not to compete with 'the strenuous photographer'. The actor in turn should be ready to subordinate himself to the drama, become a kind of *Übermarionette* which 'will not compete with life — rather will it go beyond it'.[53] Craig's was a conclusive assault on realism as the province of the theatre, and his provocative ideas tallied exactly with the new thinking about Shakespeare.

Another powerful force at work in pre-war London came from an unexpected quarter, Russia. Serge Diaghilev brought the Ballets Russes to Paris and London, and from 1909 to 1912 they conquered Europe. Their visit 'marked a turning point in the history of the Western theatre'.[54] Meyerhold at the Kommissarzhevskaya Theatre had been practising anti-realism, working to match moods and symbolic colours, characters and fixed gestures, and applying it even to Ibsen. But only Diaghilev and his ballet achieved the perfect blend of music, picture, dance and drama, acclaimed by all as a pure joy to the eye and ear. Rebecca West saw the Russian Ballet as of 'enormous aesthetic importance':

In this country people have forgotten how to use their eyes for anything except reading. It is a tendency encouraged in our schools, in which literature is absurdly overtaught and the art of painting undertaught. . . . The result is that an educated audience goes to the theatre intent on the dialogue, and is consequently blind to half the effect that can be got out of a stage performance.[55]

It may seem that the understanding of Shakespeare and the agreeable reception accorded to the Russian Ballet could have had little in common, but there is no more conventional art form than the dance, and for those who had a mind to see, the amalgam of its visual and aural elements was a revelation. In 1912 the most devoted student of Shakespeare and the stage was Harley Granville Barker, and he found in the successful fusing of dramatic elements by the Russian Ballet the example *par excellence* for the conventions of poetic drama.

5

Barker at the Savoy

In 1904, at the age of 27, Harley Granville Barker had produced the little-known *Two Gentlemen of Verona* (himself playing Speed) at the Court Theatre under J. H. Leigh. It was the prelude to the provocative seasons of non-commercial drama, enlivened with Shavian thunder-bolts, at the Court between 1904 and 1907. In all those 946 per-formances[1] under Barker and J. E. Vedrenne, there was not one of Shakespeare, but when Barker returned to Shakespearian comedy at the Savoy in 1912, he again shook the London theatre. Poel's anti-quarianism had vanished, the importance of an oral and paced pro-duction with speed and continuity was grasped by a more brilliant talent, and Shakespeare on the stage and in the study was meteorically impelled towards the later metaphorical interpretation of Wilson Knight and Peter Brook.

Like Poel, Barker believed that the actor must be a student of the drama, and be given opportunities 'especially for the co-operative study . . . involved in the rehearsing of a play'.[2] The search was for homogeneity between actor and dramatist,[3] for a true authenticity, but not merely one of historical fastidiousness and bleak archaeology.

We shall not save our souls by being Elizabethan. It is an easy way out, and strictly followed, an honourable one. But there's the difference. To be Eliza-bethan one must be strictly, logically, or quite ineffectively so. And even then, it is asking much of an audience to come to the theatre so historically sensed as that.[4]

The object was to reproduce 'those conditions of the Elizabethan theatre which had a spiritual significance in the shaping of the plays them-selves'.[5] The superficial placing of tapestries or pillars or audience on the stage, the mechanical retracing of the original stagecraft, the most elaborate of Elizabethan costumes, would not do it; the task was to recreate the spirit and intention of the original to the best effect. Nor was this a return to the realistic spectacle of the Victorian managers;

Barker at the Savoy

Beerbohm Tree's magnificent garden for *Twelfth Night* and rabbits for *The Dream* had gone forever. Barker worked undogmatically towards a few simple principles, governed by an even simpler rule: 'Gain Shakespeare's effects by Shakespeare's means when you can; for, obviously, this will be the better way. But gain Shakespeare's effects; and it is your business to discern them.'[6] Shakespeare was to re-appear centre-stage.

Barker rejected all realistically painted canvas and scenery, the great Victorian standby, because they were violently at odds with the non-illusory nature of the plays themselves. He substituted a simple, abstract setting, capable of quick adjustment, which would do duty for several different scenes. Time and place were to be found in the lines or in the acting, and although he would provide for entrances and upper levels, his settings were essentially conventional 'decorations', not scenery, designed to 'reflect light and suggest space'.[7] Muriel St Clare Byrne found this a derivation from 'the bare, stripped style' of pre-war German productions,[8] but it clearly stemmed from a desire to retain the principle of continuity which Poel had established. Guthrie faulted the over-use of curtains as a way of achieving the conventional effect:

Nothing can be simpler and more abstract than curtains; but . . . they make a very emphatic and often very unacceptable pictorial statement. . . . It is illogical and annoying if a stage which has been designed for a peep show . . . is then denied its whole function.[9]

But Barker's harmonious curtains were also designed to project his actors towards a swift, intimate performance.

His acquaintance with Poel's productions had taught him the virtues of Elizabethan intimacy between actor and audience. 'A producer of Shakespeare', he asserted, 'will find no more important and no more difficult task than the restoring of this intimacy of contact, without which the soliloquy must fail of its full emotional effect.'[10] He believed that the Elizabethan actor was meant to speak his lines with an audience around him, and forward of any setting; nor was the actor long embarrassed by a cage of light and the unnatural shadows cast by footlights. With intimacy between actor and audience a governing condition of performance, Barker built an arc of forestage over the orchestra pit at the Savoy, and lit it by spotlights attached to the front rail of the dress circle, an expedient imitated in the majority of old proscenium theatres afterwards.[11] W. Bridges-Adams bore witness to the effect created:

> He swept shadows from the stage as if they harboured germs. It was a hygienic light, the sort of light a surgeon likes to have above his operating table. It was a strictly democratic light, falling equally on principals and supers. And the stage it lit was as neat and mathematical as a chessboard.[12]

But this new lighting and its suggestion of an apron-stage met at first with general disapproval:

> The projection of the characters on the apron stage is radically bad in more ways than one. It is artistically unsound. It is bad for the stage illusion, because the proscenium line is thrown out and figures come into the auditorium, breaking down their fabled existence by intimacy of contact, and also showing details of make-up and the like that it is the province of art to hide.[13]

Enthusiasts for Brecht's way of stage presentation should find this amusing. Barker was, of course, urging a different kind of illusion upon his startled audience, an illusion which insisted that acting a play was a very real activity of consent and imagination between player and spectator.

More than this, the abstract setting and the movement outside the proscenium were designed to return Shakespeare to the oral tradition. Barker borrowed again from Poel in his insistence upon the primacy of the verse-speaking, and throughout his *Prefaces* he discussed the appropriate voices and pace. He thought of the plays as musically controlled: 'orchestrated' was his perfect word. He wrote of *A Midsummer Night's Dream* as if it were 'a musical symphony':

> The characterization will not repay very prolonged analysis. It can best be vivified and elaborated by the contrasting to eye and ear of individual with individual and group with group. Then the passing and repassing from the lyric to the dramatic mood has to be carefully judged and provided for. To hold an audience to the end entranced with the play's beauty one depends much upon the right changing of tune and time, and the shifting of key from scene to scene and from speech to speech. . . . All the time it must be delightful to listen to, musical, with each change in a definite and purposeful relation to what went before, to what will come after.[14]

Intimacy permitted speech that was swift, melodic and natural, and this kind of speaking was in turn the key to the rhythmic structure of Shakespeare's verse drama, the contrast of mood with mood, character with character and scene with scene in a continuous flow. Barker told the *New York Times*'s reporter, 'Some day I am going to ask a modern audience to sit through a play without an interval. I wonder if they will'. The intention was to assert the values of the play as paramount.

Barker directed three 'milestone' productions of Shakespeare at the Savoy: *The Winter's Tale* opening 21 September 1912; *Twelfth Night*, 15 November 1912; and *A Midsummer Night's Dream*, 6 February 1914. Happily, the prompt-books of the last two survive,[15] although that for *The Winter's Tale* is lost. The records are unusally full, but the purpose here is only to point to those elements of performance and presentation which moved Shakespeare boldly into the twentieth century.

Barker picked *The Winter's Tale* for his first broadside because it was not too well known on the stage – 'throwing one to the wolves', according to *The New York Times*.[16] Charles Kean's production of 1856 had established its pictorial possibilities, opening with a royal banquet in Greek Syracuse resplendent with musicians, slaves and dancing-girls. The Queen's trial before an imposing assembly of courtiers and councillors had Hermione carried on a litter in procession with her ladies. The speech of the Chorus was illustrated by a magnificent allegorical pageant of time, 'the greatest triumph of art ever exhibited on the stage' in the words of J. W. Cole, Kean's biographer. But above all, the scene of the pastoral festival became a Bacchic revel of three hundred frantic dancers, and that of the statue was one of surpassing beauty. All this encouraged Mary Anderson (doubling Hermione and Perdita for the first time) to mount the play again in 1887–8, and Beerbohm Tree to beat all in 1906 with a sensational storm scene and a rare display of priests and vestal virgins. Barker took up the challenge and sought to provide a fresh perspective on the play. In the unity of Barker's productions the art critic P. G. Konody thought he recognized 'the birth of the art of the theatre'.[17]

The attempt to break away from proscenium illusion succeeded as much through the staging as the setting.[18] Performance seemed to be thrust forward, moving fluently over three acting areas, each of which could be divided off by curtains: from an inset stage leading down four steps to the proscenium stage proper, which led down again to a forestage 12 feet in depth. Barker brought the actors forward whenever possible,[19] and sometimes they 'stood out like speakers on a platform'[20] untroubled by any footlights. *The Times* (A. B. Walkley) reported that set speeches were delivered 'at the very edge of the stage' and addressed directly to the audience, 'the proper method, of course, of the old "platform"',[21] and the act-drop occasionally descended upon the actors while they were speaking, so that they began a speech in mid-stage and finished it before the curtain.

While *The Tatler* found the Savoy unsuitable for this treatment, arguing that the spectator does not need to be on top of the action in order to feel that he is taking part in the play ('Nothing breaks the picture more than seeing people rushing about the stalls; all the time one has that uncomfortable feeling of watching a canary that has escaped its cage'[22]), John Palmer recognized the importance of what was happening:

The value of Mr Barker's revival . . . rests almost wholly upon his projection of the stage into the auditorium; for thereby hangs all that distinguished Elizabethan plays and playing from Restoration comedy. Mr Barker's innovation . . . is not a merely topographical trick of stage management. There were precious moments in the Savoy Theatre on Saturday when it was possible to be thrillingly conscious of precisely the appeal Burbage made as he issued from the tiring-house to the vacant platform before Elsinore. Personally, I was the more conscious of this, as I was sitting in the front of the stalls, almost in the position from which the good man of Beaumont and Fletcher interfered so successfully with the progress of 'The Knight of the Burning Pestle'. Like the Elizabethan critic, who was mercifully not required to print his opinion, I was in direct, almost personal, contact with the players. Gone was the centuries-old, needless and silly illusion of a picture stage, with scene and atmosphere ready-made, and mutoscopically viewed. I had no illusion, and could wait receptively for Shakespeare to build it. Never before had his splendid rhetoric, his glamour of resistless verse, the true and vivid illusion upon which he alone and so successfully relied, reached me in a London theatre.[23]

In an interview for *The Observer*, Bernard Shaw concurred:

The subject is really a highly technical one. Nobody but a practised stage craftsman can understand the importance of the revolution that Barker has effected in the lighting and general aspect of the stage. He has got rid of the footlights, and apparently trebled the spaciousness of the stage, though the actual addition consists only of a strip formerly occupied by the orchestra and the front row of the stalls. To the imagination it looks as if he had invented a new heaven and a new earth. Instead of the theatre being a huge auditorium, with a picture frame at one end of it, the theatre is now a stage with some unnoticed spectators round it. The crushing importance of the front of the house has gone.

Barker at the Savoy

You see, to Barker the play's the thing; and consequently in his theatre the stage is the thing. People used to talk of the tyranny of the actor–manager; but the real tyranny was that of the *acting*-manager, gloating over his rows of well-dressed deadheads, and oblivious and contemptuous of the Punch and Judy show in the corner called the stage. In Barker's house the stage is triumphant.[24]

The simplicity of this staging made possible a frank acceptance of Shakespeare's conventions.

Norman Wilkinson was responsible for the décor. The dead-white set with its white Graeco-Roman pillars on a white stage under white lighting made its contribution to non-illusion as the white set did at Stratford in 1969 for the same play.[25] Barker called it his stage 'decoration', and it was received with an expectedly mixed enthusiasm. Period flavour was lost, all sense of mystery was gone, nothing touched reality; and in their place Barker offered 'a suggestion, an impression, instead of realization'.[26] For 'G.M.' of the *Mail*, the staring white walls of 'Barkerized Shakespeare' reminded him of 'the palace a not very ingenious child will make out of the insides of cardboard boxes'.[27]

Albert Rothenstein (later Rutherston) created the costumes, and against this plain setting, they were extravagant to a degree (see Plate 8). Headgear flaunted preposterous plumes, legs were bare with gold and silver boots, dress was boldly embroidered and bespangled. The costumes were of no recognizable period or place, and the critics groped for points of reference: Layard's Nineveh, the Nice Carnival, Aubrey Beardsley, Leon Bakst and the Russian Ballet, the Chelsea Arts Ball, the Ideal Home Exhibition, Art Nouveau, Thomas Hardy, *Sûmûrun*, Beaumarchais, Tahiti, Ariosto and Boccaccio. There were Botticellian damsels, Roman warriors and Bohemian peasants. It was all attributed to Max Reinhardt out of Giulio Romano of the late Renaissance, who is mentioned in v.ii. Was this décor an irresponsible distraction? Or a Post-Impressionist Shakespeare, as *The Times* thought?[28] The extravagance and eccentricity, of course, was planned for the release of the imagination into the world of artifice.

The text used was all but complete, with only three cuts of eleven lines, and it was widely assumed that the speed of Barker's speech was to enable the whole text to be played with only one interval of fifteen minutes. The *Daily Mail* compared it with the Margate express,[29] and J. T. Grein in *The Sunday Times* felt its furious pace would 'beat a

8 Harley Granville Barker's *The Winter's Tale* at the Savoy Theatre, 1912

hundred horse-power scorching on the Portsmouth road. Not a soul, unfamiliar with the play, could follow its drift and pace'.[30] On the other hand, Konody asserted that he 'missed never a word of the play through the substitution of natural human speech for the slow and tedious droning of blank verse'. Barker was seeking that rhythmic continuity by which the play would 'spring to life', as he argued, and release its 'magic spell'.[31]

The cumulative effect of these elements was to return *The Winter's Tale* to its proper mode and style. The supers seemed to move like automata, lending an air of burlesque to the indictment of the trial scene. The frank asides of Leontes's first scene permitted that awkward and unnatural assertion of his jealous thoughts to work as good theatre: by its telescopic convention, the stage presented directly its two conflicting worlds of appearances and reality. Of this 'Elizabethan or rhetorical style of playing', Palmer wrote:

How gloriously effective ... upon an Elizabethan stage is the aside, vehemently declaimed full at the spectator, or secretly breathed in his ear. A very convincing book might be written, showing that the health of our national drama (as opposed to the naturalized French importation) was inextricably bound up with the stage aside and the soliloquy. No wonder Shakespeare so affected them.[32]

When Polixenes in disguise spied on Florizel, he 'merely marks the fact of being disguised by holding a grotesque mask in front of his face. It is, in a way, a crude convention, but it answers its purpose admirably; the impossible will be immediately and unquestioningly accepted'.[33] The complaint that the audience could not feel at home with the set was ironically well justified, and it was in line with the criticism in *The Referee* that Barker occasionally forced an effect when the stage struck 'a tapestry or tableau pose, which gives a suggestion more of artifice than art to the scene'.[34] *The Times* acknowledged an air of improvisation about the performance: 'you feel that [Barker] might vary his effects from night to night'.[35] John Palmer, in praise of the manner, wished that the production had discarded 'the whole sack of naturalistic artifices', even to playing Perdita with a boy rather than 'an obviously pretty young woman'; and he made the paradoxical and challenging point that 'in that case the illusion would have been stronger still'.[36]

The play was taken off after six weeks, except for matinées, but only after Palmer and others had acknowledged the importance of the innovations: it was 'probably the first performance in England of a play by Shakespeare that the author would have recognized for his own since Burbage'. Emerging through Barker's assembled conventions and devices was some sense of the true illusion at which Shakespeare aimed, the vision behind the external action of story and character seen on the stage. In the correspondence in *The Times* which followed the production, John Masefield insisted that, for the first time in any English theatre, he was given 'a sense of Shakespeare's power and art, of his mind at work shaping and directing, and of his dramatic intention'. And he added a statement of momentous implication for the future of Shakespeare studies: 'The performance seemed to me to be a riper and juster piece of Shakespearian criticism, a clearer perception and grasping of the Shakespearian idea, than I have seen hitherto in print.'[37]

Macbeth had been rehearsed through the summer of 1912 with *The Winter's Tale*, but it was dropped in favour of *Twelfth Night* because of the need for a financial success.[38] *Twelfth Night* stood high among the most popular Shakespeare revivals of the nineteenth century,[39] and it had been among the most readily abused. Its scenes were juggled to enable the carpenters and painters to erect magnificent palaces for Orsino and glorious gardens for Olivia. It was larded with songs stolen from other plays: a peasant chorus singing 'Come unto these yellow sands' from *The Tempest* welcomed Viola to shore, and 'Fair Olivia, what is she?' from *The Two Gentlemen of Verona* seemed a natural extension to the Duke's rhapsodies of love. By the time of Beerbohm Tree's 1901 production, the play had become so musical that he turned Feste's last wistful solo 'When that I was and a little tiny boy' into a song-and-dance finale for the whole company, a destructive act which has been perpetrated since. The over-elaboration of comic business in the Toby scenes had, however, been the greatest temptation, and still is, and regularly upset the structure and balance of the play: any prop introduced into the drinking (or so-called 'kitchen') scene, II.iii, whether a candle for Malvolio or a punchbowl for Sir Toby, could turn it into a riot.

Approval of Barker's method was this time almost universal. *The Times* found it to be 'the most enjoyable performance of *Twelfth Night* that we have had the fortune to see'[40] and John Masefield wrote that it was 'much the most beautiful thing I have ever seen done on the stage'.[41] This time there was almost no comment on the modified 'apron' stage, as if its directness of appeal and swift continuity of playing had been already assimilated. But every critic had something to say about the décor. The scenery remained sparse by Victorian standards, but the white set of *The Winter's Tale* had changed to pink — 'a nightmare' for 'G.M.' of the *Daily Mail* and 'hideous' for J. T. Grein in *The Sunday Times*. The cover of *Play Pictorial*[42] fortunately reproduced a picture of the main set of Olivia's garden in colour. Against a background of white walls, the columns of Olivia's summerhouse were in a deep pink with a baldachino over a golden throne like a sugar ornament. Pale green yew trees with box hedges in a topiarian arrangement reminded spectators of a child's Noah's Ark toy-box — again a foreshadowing of productions half-a-century to come (see Plate 9). Symmetrically arranged seats were covered in gold like the throne, and gilded garden gates appeared in v.i. The Duke's cloth of pink and black triangles exhibited 'pure Cubism', as did drops for the seacoast and part of the town. Black in the costumes was also set off by the pinkness, and particularly pleased the critic in *The Observer*:

[Norman Wilkinson's] costumes, from Orsino's pinks to the blacks of Olivia's court; from the strange, foreign seamen to the Elizabethan fashion-plate of Aguecheek . . . his beautiful work seems to hang together and to bring out the effect of the play. But this impression of artistic unity can hardly fail to strike any spectator of the production.[43]

Act v became a riot of colour, matching the confusions of the play's ending.

The *Mail* continued to argue obstinately that 'when "decoration" of this sort comes in at the stage door, poetry goes out of the window',[44] but *The Daily Telegraph* confessed that after the initial shock 'it became the inevitably right setting for the laughing romance of Olivia's love and the mad fantastics of Malvolio'.[45] Wilkinson's delicate sense of colour contributed wonder and surprise, even seemed to govern the scheme of the play, without dwarfing the players who stood out distinctly and rivetted the attention. Barker was in fact trying to invent 'a new hieroglyphic language of scenery':

A new formula has to be found. Realistic scenery won't do, if only because it

9   Harley Granville Barker's *Twelfth Night* at the Savoy Theatre, 1912

swears against everything in the plays. ... We want something that will reflect light and suggest space; if it's to be a background permanent for a play (this, for many reasons, it should be), something that will not tie us too rigidly indoors or out. Sky-blue then will be too like the sky; patterns suggest walls....[46]

Nor were the critics now troubled by the pace of speaking. Indeed, its quality of spontaneity received general approval, and J. T. Grein even found the pace at times 'rather too slow'. The *Telegraph* critic who had complained of the speed of *The Winter's Tale* could now exclaim, 'The long multiplex cadences, the sweet melody, the bewitching variety of the Shakespearean rhythm, find expression, if not quite perfect, as nearly perfect as mortal ear can enjoy.'[47] No doubt they thought Barker had taken their words to heart. According to the prompt-book, Barker had very little movement on the stage during the central speeches of lyrical feeling, and subtlety in the playing was encouraged by the gentlest of directorial touches. Upon Viola's first meeting with Olivia (I.v), her line, 'Good madam, let me see your face', had her merely 'turn slightly' to Olivia, suggesting a feminine reticence and apprehension, and Viola simply dropped to her knees for the 25 lines leading to and through the willow-cabin speech. Orsino held Viola's hand throughout the 'patience on a monument' poetry (II.iv), suggesting their proximity and her quiet tone, until she 'backs a little' upon his question, 'But died thy sister of her love, my boy?' When Olivia became the aggressor in III.i, she was most gently so, making a 'slight move' towards Viola, speaking of her 'tyrannous heart' with her eyes lowered. All was delicacy: Viola 'turns away a shade' in her embarrassment, and Olivia followed this with a touch of pathos in 'a movement'. A new intelligence was at work on the text.

Comic business was managed with the same sense of careful proportion. Toby and Andrew were gentlemen, not clowns, and Toby, whom the audience was accustomed to see played as the traditional drunken sot, had his weakness conveyed chiefly by a red face, a more careful step and an occasional stumble.

Before now we have seen Sir Toby Belch and Sir Andrew Aguecheek and the rest so lengthily consumed with laughter at their own fun that we have been too exhausted to enjoy the joke. At the Savoy all the singing of the catches and the gulling of Malvolio and the arranging of the duel between Cesario and Aguecheek goes pat, leaving us sorry that it is over so soon.[48]

Andrew, of course, properly cut his caper in ɪ.iii. The business in the drinking scene, ɪɪ.iii, was restricted to having Toby and Andrew enter with their shoes in their hands.

Approach, Sir Andrew: not to be a-bed after midnight is to be up betimes; and 'diluculo surgere', thou know'st.

Upon which Andrew stubbed his toe in the dark. For the catch, 'Hold thy peace', Barker introduced a comic moment when they tried to take the correct key from the virginal. Malvolio did not enter in the traditional nightgown and nightcap, but Andrew and Feste tried to hide from him, and gave the game away when a note was accidentally struck on the virginal. And on Feste's line, 'Sir Toby, there you lie', he tipped Toby out of his chair. The business in the letter scene, ɪɪ.v, would seem modest to a fault against the balletic freezing and high jinks familiar today: the comic trio hid behind the seats, hedges and trees on the lower level while Malvolio strutted above them. In ɪɪɪ.iv, the business in the duel was that of restrained ceremonial nonsense: much was made of preliminaries (prolonging the suspense which Shakespeare had already created), with Andrew facing the audience and throwing out his chest, coming *en garde* and saluting; all this Viola imitated exactly, until, step by step, they came together and their swords touched accidentally, he 'mightily pleased with himself', she 'horribly nervous'.[49] Following this, Antonio interrupted the fight after only three passes.

Malvolio (Henry Ainley) was played far more tactfully than usual: omitting nothing from the text, Barker aimed at consistency of character through the play. In the love scene with Olivia, ɪɪɪ.iv, he skittishly knelt before the lady, threw kisses, sat beside her on the seat, reclined, took her hand. When Toby and his crew teased Malvolio by 'exorcising' the devil, the business was fairly traditional: Maria screamed when Malvolio spoke to her, Toby chucked him under the chin and slapped him on the back, and Fabian tickled his legs with a stick. In the last scene, v.i, Malvolio tore the mischievous letter into pieces and threw them at the Clown on exit. Masefield wrote to Barker that it was a 'sudden and inspiring bit of vision' when he made 'Feste blaze out at Malvolio and Malvolio flame up in reply'.[50]

After this beautiful production J. M. Barrie wrote to Barker, 'I don't doubt that *The Winter's Tale* and *Twelfth Night* will make all Shakespearian productions a little better for all time to come.'[31] What had succeeded in *Twelfth Night* was that Barker had caught an appropriate style and tone for the play. It ended with the closing of Olivia's golden gates, Feste singing in the foreground. John Palmer was lyrical: 'We had wandered in Elia's fairyland, but the time had come for magic to be locked away',[52] and H. W. Massingham wrote of 'the Ariel mood of the play' and of the lovers as 'porcelain-lovers'.[53] But Norman Wilkinson in *The Stage Year Book* for 1914 hinted more accurately at what happened when there was no attempt at illusion:

> What one calls a 'natural effect' on the stage is got by cheating people, for the moment, into the idea that they are where they are not, and at the Savoy there was no attempt to convince the eye against the judgement of the mind that one was out-of-doors looking at clipped yew hedges and marble canopies.[54]

A production unimpeded by detail allowed the creative artifice of its conception to do its work, and the audience to enjoy its quality of playful ease.

Every student of stage history knows that Pepys found *A Midsummer Night's Dream* 'the most insipid ridiculous play' he ever saw in his life, and, for want of understanding, the 250 years that followed his unhappy experience seemed bent upon adopting any device of theatre that was vaguely admissible as reparation. As one of Shakespeare's most fantastic vehicles, the play lay open to every abuse. Until 1840 it had been treated as an operetta; Madame Vestris and Charles Kean brought back Shakespeare's lines, but dressed it for an archaeologist's Athenian holiday; Phelps advanced its popularity with the beauties of dreamy green gauze curtains which melted the actors into moonlight. By the twentieth century it had become a play of magic transformation scenes: Tree created his own scenic marvels and in 1905 and 1911 went so far as to grace his carpets of wild flowers and bosky thickets with live rabbits. The Victorian *Dream* was a thing traditionally embellished with Mendelssohn's music (which also involved the suppression of the lyrics), female Oberons, child Pucks and charming little girls for fairies. Barker departed utterly from all of this.

At the Savoy, the sense of an apron-stage structure was as before, lit from the front without footlights or side-strips against a white rectangular proscenium: the prompt-book indicates bold address to the

10   Harley Granville Barker's *A Midsummer Night's Dream* at the Savoy Theatre, 1914

audience from time to time, and for the court entertainment of the last act, Theseus and Hippolyta reclined on couches at the very front of the apron ('sprawled on couches ranged across the front of the stage, with their backs to the audience', according to William Winter,[55] who found them inaudible in this position). Winter complained that the front of the apron projected about 12 feet from the regular stage line and was only three feet high: it was so close to the front row that spectators could touch it with their feet. Two steps, the width of the opening, took the actor on to the original stage level, and stage boxes were replaced by entrances right and left. 'Pyramus and Thisbe' was played on a third level, an elevated platform in front of a line of 'short, ugly pillars painted black and silver'. 'The whole surface of this structure', reported Winter, 'was sheathed with canvas of a slate-gray hue, — the cold, flat colour usually seen on the decks of our harbour ferry boats when newly painted.'

Norman Wilkinson again designed the production, strongly contrasting the palace and woodland scenes. There were no gorgeous sets: rather, the design was thought to bear the hall-mark of 'Futurism' and Barker afterwards acknowledged a debt to the thinking of Gordon Craig in trying to achieve a unity of atmosphere appropriate to the whole play.[56] A grey painted drop was used for the first palace scene, another in pink with a painted door for Quince's house, another with shadowy green and indigo-blue trees for the first wood scene, and a starry night sky-cloth backed the pillars of the final scene. The central wood scenes were played upon a grassy knoll over which hung a wreath of flowers spangled with lights and surrounded with 'trees' of flimsy strips of green and purple sheer silk; a grey gauze served for Titania's bower. The effect was mystical and right, 'a strange and beautiful place', according to *The Observer*:

a wood in which the English hobgoblin, Puck, is quite at home, a wood where the lovers and other human beings can pass in and out of sight among the trees; and yet a wood which is august and dream-like, and none too exact and earthy.[57]

Realism, for both play and audience, was dispelled, and all was done by painting a curtain and hanging a few strips of gauze (see Plate 10).

It was Barker who first seems to have recognized that one's understanding of *A Midsummer Night's Dream* is to be measured by one's per-

11 Harley Granville Barker's golden fairies: the final dance

ception of the fairies. Beerbohm Tree's little sugar-cake girls with pretty wings and tutus, or Max Reinhardt's diaphanous young ladies, indicate the limitations of the director's imagination and the subsequent inhibition of the spectator's vision. Barker strove to create immortals who surpassed anyone's conception and were completely liberating. He dressed and painted them in shimmering gold from top to toe.[58] Faces were gilt and eyebrows picked out in crimson. They wore masks, and quaint Indian head-dresses, with moustachios and wigs of ravelled rope and metallic curls. They came in all sizes, all but four fully grown.[59] They did not skip and cavort, but stood in Oriental poses and moved with a dignified, shuffling gait, making weird mechanical gestures (see Plate 11). They were shocking, but unforgettable. According to William Winter, 'The effect was much as though a considerable number of steam-heat radiators, cast in human form, had become mechanically animated'.[60] They were 'peroxidized pixies' or 'an odd lot of brass ornaments' or 'bronzed or brazen-faced Indians' or 'strange Cambodian deities' for some, 'magic', 'quaint and comical' for others. Harold Child in *The Times* drew a little desperately upon comparisons from Bakst, Cambodian idols, Nijinsky in *Le Dieu Bleu*, *Sûmûrun* for its baggy trousers, *Petrouchka* and the Russian Ballet, Minos's palace in Crete, a Byzantine fresco from Ravenna and Grecian robes:

The golden fairies chase one another through the wood in single file or lie prone on a low green mound, grouped round Titania, under great shafts of green mounting to the sky, against a purple background. This colour-effect, the heavy mass of old gold against the purple and green, is wonderfully beautiful. . . . An inspiration, something to strike us all with wonder and delight.[61]

Other reviews reflected the uncertainty of the audience:

Titania was most unhappy in her make-up, which not only took away all chance of facial play but whenever one of Mr. Barker's searchlights focussed her from the front of the circle tier she looked like a quaint little golden idol from an Indian temple. . . . As for the fairy attendants, being such big and burly persons, of course they could not convey the accepted notion of the 'Little People'. Moreover, being made for the most part, certainly till nearly the end, to stand rigid and motionless through Oberon's and Puck's speeches and business — all the elfin poetry evaporated. . . . It may be that [Mr. Barker] was influenced by Titania's statement that Oberon has 'come from the farthest steppe of India'.[62]

While some found the effect a 'Shakespearian nightmare' and not *The Dream* at all, others waxed lyrical as they sensed what Barker was doing:

'Gilded fairies' gives indeed a poor notion of these elegant creatures, not children but tall and graceful, clad in the soft metallic shimmer of their web of gold over gold armour, all of the daintiest fancy of design. We knew how right the fancy of these fairies was when we found them not clashing with the mortals − Oberon standing like an ikon unperceived in the midst of the quarrelling lovers.[63]

The Nation recognized 'A New Fairy Convention' in its headline and perceived the fairies as symbolic agents:

It made a rich pageant when they marched across the stage in a glittering procession. It softened to the likeness of a shimmering cob-web when they danced around their knoll. It gave them an elusive unreality when they mingled, invisible, among the parti-coloured mortals. It was an original and wholly successful attempt to achieve romance without convention.[64]

The prompt-book offers further insights into Barker's conception of the fairies. At their general entrance in ii.i ('Ill met by moonlight'), they were designated by individual characteristics: one was a soldierly leader named as 'Major', who frightened small fairies on his entrance and twisted the 'Twins' round until they spun into their places. Three were intentionally grave, being named 'Professor', 'Doctor' and 'Ecclesiastic', and there was also an 'Old man fairy'. They were a complete fairy community. Oberon's train-bearers lined up in pairs behind him. Two male and female pairs of singers entered in step, and Oberon's and Titania's trains nodded and bowed their heads in unison. To become invisible to the lovers ('I will overhear their conference'), Oberon simply stepped back; when Helena and Demetrius exited, he stepped forward; the convention was repeated in iii.ii. Desmond MacCarthy described how the fairies seemed to make themselves invisible, believing that 'the very characteristics which made them at first so outlandishly arresting' contributed to making them inconspicuous:

They group themselves motionless about the stage, and the lovers move past and between them as casually as though they were stocks or stones. It is without effort we believe these quaintly gorgeous metallic creatures are invisible to human eyes.[65]

The dancers and singers of Titania's party were all in pairs for her sleep of iii.ii, and they wove and wound a symmetrical path around her bower. Cecil Sharp arranged his English folk music and dance for the impressive and poetic last scene of the play, the golden fairies blessing the house by weaving through the pillars and slowly fading away until there was but one girl left: according to Harold Child, 'the last patch of gold to fade from sight'.

Against the gold was a patch of scarlet. This was Puck, played by a man for the first time. He was dressed in a red cloak, a bright, shock-headed wig covered with berries, and baggy breeches, 'somewhat in the style of Struwwelpeter', an immensely attractive elf who 'seemed to be more nearly allied to Hans Andersen's fairies than those of Shake-speare'.[66] The critic for *The Nation* again recognized the importance of the innovation:

The really significant departure from the prettiness of Mid-Victorian convention . . . was the Puck of Mr. Donald Calthrop. Shakespeare's Puck is no romantic invention like Ariel. He is a genuine rustic hobgoblin, an authentic fragment of Warwickshire folk-lore, a crude deliberate patch of ugliness in a fairy play, and in this spirit he was acted. With his yellow wig, scarlet dress, and antic motions he seemed something sinister and alien among the golden elves of Oberon's court, and Mr. Calthrop carried out this conception in his elaborately harsh elocution. . . . The play absorbed him as music absorbs discords.[67]

With Theseus looking like a god, Hermia like a Tartar maiden, Helena like a Grecian Gretchen with flaxen hair, and Lysander and Demetrius with a touch of Japanese in their costume, the total visual image was unimaginable and other-worldly — which, as J. C. Trewin has recently observed,[68] was the whole idea.

'As soon as you see the thing, you know that Mendelssohn would never do. For our part, we should welcome Stravinsky'. This was Harold Child in *The Times*, and the consensus was that the visual surprises prompted a new awareness of every word in the play and the musical pattern of the whole. In his preface to the acting-edition, Barker showed his close concern with the word-music, acknowledging Poel, who had taught that the merit of Elizabethan verse lay in 'its consonantal swiftness, its gradations sudden or slow into vowelled liquidity, its comic rushes and stops, with, above all, the peculiar beauty of its rhymes'.[69] During the speaking of the major speeches, the prompt-book indicates, Barker again required his stage to be still: Lysander and Hermia were made to sit for their first amorous exchange, Titania and Oberon addressed each other in their quarrel over the changeling boy with hardly a motion, Puck squatted at Oberon's feet to receive his instructions to find the 'little western flower'. During the lovers' quarrel Barker struck a burlesque style, as suggested by the symmetrical kneeling of the young men, an 'exact' changing of places, kissing of hands and turns to the audience. The programme carried the unusual legend, 'With the indulgence of the Audience, no calls will be taken by the Actors until the end of the Play'.

The mechanicals were not clowns but countrymen of Warwickshire, and they did not play with the customary slapstick stupidity. Their business was simple, in spite of the host of invitations to improvise nonsense that this play offers: Flute found he had Starveling's part in I.ii; Bottom was granted some business with his sword and had a roaring match with Snug, Flute read his part to himself gesticulating wildly and Puck chased them away with general tripping and tumbling in III.i; in III.ii, Bottom sneezed upon introduction to Mustardseed and introduced business with his missing ears and tail when he woke in IV.i ('Methought I was, —and methought I had, —'). Altogether a modest allowance of comedy with which to extend these scenes. According to *The Referee*, the play-scene, 'with Theseus, Hippolyta, and all the guests reclining while the amateurs acted on the grand staircase, was a triumph of novel stage-management'.[70] Yet even in this scene the nonsense was restrained. One critic found Moonshine to be 'the funniest Moon of mortal memory', struggling with his superfluity of props, giggling and drying up, troubling Bottom with his dangling lantern on 'Sweet Moon, I thank thee for thy sunny beams', and upon his exit forgetting his stool and dog so that he had to stretch out an arm from behind a pillar to retrieve them. The death of Pyramus was also notable for his contest with Thisbe: the lady wanted the corpse on its back and accordingly rolled it over, but Bottom had other ideas and persisted in repeatedly rolling on his side to face the audience. *The Observer* thought that the play scene was 'never for a moment forced', and had 'never seemed so funny'.[71]

The prompt-book contains one striking direction which reveals the director's implicit attitude towards the play. When Oberon gave Puck his final orders to put right the mistakes of the night, Puck ended the scene by seeming to stage-manage the production himself. Two fairies opened the curtain, Puck came down centre and motioned for the lights to be dimmed, and then bent down as if raising the drop cloth as it ascended to bring in Demetrius and Lysander (III.ii). For Puck to be physically aware of the mechanics of the Savoy stage was an extra-dramatic device by which Barker's audience could be compelled to accept the mode of the play as one of conscious non-illusion. The spectator had in part become an immortal himself, granted the power to control and observe the antics of the earthly lovers. By this simple device, the theatre of Bertolt Brecht, Peter Brook and perhaps the real Shakespeare came a step closer. After the war, Barker would write, 'Upon the platform stage of the Elizabethan drama every detail of workmanship tells . . . you may turn all the lights full on if you want to, and not be ashamed to let the audience see everything just as it is. Not that the aim is to destroy illusion, but only to transfer it to the subliminal region of the actors' interpretation of the play.'[72]

Not all were content to have their own notion of the play's illusion damaged. John Palmer, a previous supporter, thought that Barker was 'suffering from brains' and that 'Shakespeare from the beginning never had a chance'.[73] And in New York, William Winter asserted baldly that 'illusion was destroyed. Dramatic effect was nullified'.

The absurd scenery was destructive of all right effect. It is impossible for the mind to abandon itself to the enchantment of the acted drama and allow itself to drift with the representation, self-forgetful and delighted, when it is continually compelled to consider that trees are indicated by long festoons of gray cloth, wooded banks by wooden benches, and flitting sylphs by prancing gnomes that no more suggest fairies than so many coal-scuttles would![74]

But among Barker's champions, the critic for *The Observer* claimed that the production was 'revolutionary in its attempt to get back to what the poet planned'. The play was not drama, farce, a musical or spectacle, nor all these combined, but 'the dream of a poet': 'That is what Mr Barker has tried to express, his first step being to go direct to the poet, and find out what sort of idea the poet had about the relative proportions of the elements of his play.'[75] Barker sought, in a phrase, 'the poetic whole'. J. T. Grein, founder of the Independent Theatre in London and sponsor of the Stage Society, joined those who recognized that another Shakespeare had been revealed, and is to be quoted at length:

As there was war in the critics' camp through the advent of Ibsen, so there will be war through the progress of Barker. . . . Is it wrong to infuse the new spirit of freedom into the interpretation of the master . . . ? Barker and his henchmen read Shakespeare as wholly human — they scorn the corset of the cathedral library, of academic solemnity, of ceremonial discomfort. As usual they overshot the mark — pioneers always do — and *The Winter's Tale* was grotesque. Then came *Twelfth Night* and people said: 'How much more fascinating this play is than I thought, what freshness pervades it in its unforced diction; of course there are eccentricities in the adornment, but on the whole I prefer Shakespeare in this modern, vital spirit.' And now comes *The Dream*, inspired by imagination, in plasticism and in colour, the eccentricities have mellowed into a new and definite manifestation of Art. . . . When the dovetailing begins, when the fairies and some mortals laze in the forest with its mound of green, its dome of flowers and leaves twined to a wreath, its wafting trees and mysterious horizon . . . then it becomes paramount enough that one thought guided a firm hand in the production. It is an effort to bring poetry, fancy and the living into line.[76]

With this beacon of a production came new understanding of what Shakespeare had achieved, of how he had engaged all the flexibility and licence of his medium to speak to his audience. Granville Barker's *Dream* granted the twentieth century an insight into his mode of vision as perhaps only Peter Brook's has done since.[77]

6

Granville-Barker's early criticism

Soon after the First World War Granville-Barker[1] stopped regular work as a director, and after *A Midsummer Night's Dream* in 1914, he touched only one other Shakespeare play: he shared the direction of *King Lear*[2] at the Old Vic in 1940 with Lewis Casson, and he died in 1946. He spent only ten days in rehearsal with the actors, giving most of his attention to the speaking of the verse and the balance of voices. John Gielgud reported that he encouraged 'grand entrances and exits centre-stage, a declamatory style, imposing gestures', and added, 'Only under his subtle hand these theatrical devices became classic, tragic, noble, not merely histrionic or melodramatic, because of the unerring taste and simplicity with which he ordered them.'[3] The notes which Gielgud scribbled into his copy bear out Granville-Barker's extreme care for nuance, as the following sample line readings suggest:

Kent on thy life no more (I.i)	Dead quiet. Turn. Stare at him.
Does any here know me? (I.iv)	Danger — end of careless exterior. Gasps. Feeling. Speech nothing.
O let me not be mad. (I.v)	Now afraid *inside*. Simple.
No Regan thou shalt never have my curse (II.iv)	Exhausted by the rage. Tender silly.
I gave you all. (II.iv)	Very big. To the front. Bewildered. Not as fast as their speeches.
O reason not the need. (II.iv)	Drop it right down. Ironic feeling. Dignity.
Come let's away to prison. (v.iii)	Delighted. Really happy. Dance the whole speech like a polka. Music up and down. Variety.

This is the work of a close reader with a sharp stage ear; there is no extravagant stagecraft, no revolutionary vistas. By this time the revolution had marched on.

Barker's aesthetic revolution had been carried on by a succession of distinguished men of the theatre, all of whom had been touched by his vision: Barry Jackson at the Birmingham Repertory Theatre, 1914 to 1918 and thereafter; W. Bridges-Adams directing the Stratford-upon-Avon Shakespeare Festival with the New Shakespeare Company, 1919 to 1934; Lewis Casson, with his wife Sybil Thorndike, between the wars; Robert Atkins, director at the Old Vic from 1920 to 1925; Harcourt Williams, also directing Shakespeare at the Old Vic from 1929 to 1934. Thus for *A Midsummer Night's Dream* in 1929, Williams threw out Mendelssohn and retained Cecil Sharp's folk music from Barker's production. His fairies were now green instead of gold, and dressed in costumes after the style of an Inigo Jones masque. The wood near Athens was of curtains hanging like tree trunks against a silvery sky-cloth. His *As You Like It* of 1932 again used curtains for trees, this time of blue net hanging in a circlet, and the forest scenes in both plays borrowed Barker's idea of a hillock centre-stage. All of Barker's disciples pursued an ideal of 'simple settings, speedy playing, continuity of action, reliance on team-work, and unabridged texts'.[4] Plain-text Shakespeare not only returned the emphasis to the words, reducing spectacle and recovering the shape of the plays, it also began to reveal their intention. In New York, innovations in design by Robert Edmond Jones and Norman Bel Geddes sought, like those of Gordon Craig, to capture the spirit and 'emotional idea' behind a play by scenic suggestion, as in Jones's *Macbeth* of 1921 whose toppling walls and arches reflected the insecurity of the King. The movement had also begun to shake off the particularity of historical association in the search for those faintly apprehended qualities, timelessness and universality.

If the Shakespeare experience was less dimly perceived in the theatre, 'workshop' criticism was simultaneously transforming our notion of how the experience could come about. The idolatrous concern with Shakespeare's life and personality was past, and what M. C. Bradbrook called the 'thinly disguised gossip about the private lives of the dramatis personae'[5] of second-rate Bradleyans grew fainter. The treatment of the plays as 'philosophers' playthings' was passing, and the impact of psychoanalysis and the 'new criticism' had yet to be felt. The man who continued to carry the torch for the new Shakespeare was Granville-Barker himself. In this period there is no more valuable application of theatrical wisdom to the understanding of Shakespeare than his series of long essays modestly entitled *Prefaces to Shakespeare*.[6]

Granville-Barker's early criticism

In his inaugural lecture at Edinburgh, John Dover Wilson claimed that these studies had begun 'a fresh epoch in Shakespearian criticism'[7] and Robert Speaight thought them to be Granville-Barker's 'monument', adding that 'any producer will always break his teeth against them in vain'.[8] If Granville-Barker did not direct Shakespeare on the stage, he recreated him on paper in some of the most vivid commentary we have.

Granville-Barker first proposed the theme of his work as a critic in a lecture read to the Royal Society of Literature on 7 June 1922.[9] There he asserted formally that the scholar and the actor depended upon each other: 'dramatic art has need of the services pure scholarship can render'. In the past the scholar's indifference to the theatre had been a serious limitation 'because he has often gone to great trouble to elucidate points which, if he could but have seen or even imagined the play in being – acted, that is, in a theatre, where a play belongs – would have elucidated themselves'. It had also been a limitation upon the actor 'because those of us who wish to inform ourselves thoroughly upon these matters, have to wade through a large amount of what is, frankly, very learned rubbish'.[10] He added that Shakespeare would respond to a performance by schoolboys while he might remain inert under the touch of the most learned professor. He praised Poel's experiments and argued that experiment, based upon research, could be the source of 'something very like a new school of Shakespearean criticism', and he concluded: 'We might project a Variorum edition of a new sort, one that would epitomise Shakespeare, the playwright.'[11] The editor's obligation would be always to exhibit the play in action by inferring Shakespeare's practice from the text and from classic and modern performances.

In this important paper, Granville-Barker also touched upon some of the ideas passing in his mind at the time. Elizabethan intimacy between actor and spectator must have influenced the method of the dialogue: it 'may have led Shakespeare to make certain demands on his actors of which their modern successors – not putting the plays to this same proof – remain unaware'.[12] And he offered an example from *Hamlet* of what might be tested:

A certain violence of attack which is indicated for the actor when it is necessary for the actor to capture the attention of the audience after a bustle of movement. Note the explosiveness of 'O that this too too solid flesh would melt' after the elaborate departure of the King and Queen and their attendants.

Note the same sort of opening 'O what a rogue and peasant slave am I' after the amusing medley of the players and Polonius is disposed of. On the other hand note the careful preparation by Polonius and the King for the necessarily quiet beginning of 'To be or not to be'.[13]

He discussed the awkward effect of those asides of Leontes in the opening scene of *The Winter's Tale* when the modern actor in the proscenium arch was trying to work from 'another plane of existence in respect of the audience'. The characters in *Hamlet* were contemporary Renaissance figures moving upon a stage, not as imagined in some historical Denmark 600 years earlier. Here were hints of good things to come.

Granville-Barker's first important project in publication was his *Players' Shakespeare* in expensive fine editions, designed to present the plays as for performance and with illustrations by distinguished artists. Seven plays appeared between 1923 and 1927, but an edition planned for students and actors at a minimum price of 4 guineas a volume was bound to fail. And although the introductions to the plays were stated as being 'the sort of addresses a producer might make to a company upon their first meeting to study the play',[14] they were strangely academic and illustrated by pictures which rarely suggested a stage performance. Nevertheless, the general introduction to the first book brilliantly summarized Granville-Barker's approach to Shakespeare at this time. His central statement about the plays was striking and straightforward:

We still remain so ignorant of their stagecraft, that our present task with them is, I think, to discover, even at the cost of some pedantry, what this stagecraft was. It may be that we can improve upon the original methods of their representation, but obviously we cannot until we know what these were. We must learn this, moreover, not in terms of archaeology, but by experimenting with the living body of the play. For this purpose precise knowledge of the structure and usages of Shakespeare's own theatre will be as useful as a philosophic study of Hamlet's character may be inspiring. Neither, however, can tell us so much about the play as a play as its performance can.... Amazing as the statement may appear — Shakespeare's case as a playwright has still to be fully proved, and the proving it must needs be a thorough process.[15]

Granville-Barker went on to point out several directions in which investigation might go, arguing that a practising playwright, then as now, would accept the conditions of his work and turn them to his advantage if he could. To have had spectators sitting on the stage might have been a nuisance to Shakespeare, 'but we shall be wrong if we think that he did not allow for and profit by the generally intimate relations between actors and audience that the platform stage permitted'.[16] Again, in the matter of the daylight convention:

It was doubtless most disturbing when the groundlings were rained on, and only a fanatic would say that an open theatre was necessary for the full enjoyment of the plays. But the fact that they were played in daylight is evident in a hundred turns of their writing.

Which led him to touch upon the verbal scene-painting in *A Midsummer Night's Dream* and *As You Like It*, with the warning that 'scenic illusion must not curtail Shakespeare's liberties with time and space'.[17] He struck straight to the heart of the convention of the soliloquy:

The physical proximity of the audience to the actor upon the apron stage, more importantly the absence of any barrier of light or of scenic illusion, bred a convention which fostered emotional intimacy. It was a case, as it often is with convention, of extremes meeting. As there was no illusion there was every illusion. Once grant that the man was Hamlet, the fact that you could touch him with your hand made him more actual to you, not less. And once admit that he thought aloud, you entered his thoughts the more easily if he moved in what was your own world still.[18]

Although he added that 'convention is habit', and that a lost device like the soliloquy could not be restored on demand, he was here reflecting what had emerged of the principles of non-illusory theatre from his time at the Savoy. Not least, these elusive notions of non-illusion were linked in his mind with the Elizabethan convention of boys playing the female parts. For Granville-Barker this was the most striking evidence of a mode of non-realistic drama: it matched other conventions of indefinite time and place, and was especially appropriate to the convention of verse.[19]

E. K. Chambers published his indispensable *The Elizabethan Stage* in 1923, and in 1925 Granville-Barker took up the cudgels with this redoubtable scholar in a note for the first issue of the *Review of English Studies*.[20] He applauded Chambers's mustering of the facts, but insisted that he lacked imagination: he was too wedded to the Swan drawing with its 'two foolish doors', rather than the inn-yards which better lent themselves to Shakespeare's true vitality. Chambers always made use of the stage structure with its withins and withouts, aboves and belows, writing as if there were a Victorian scene to be set (for battle, garden, street, hall, chamber) by an Elizabethan manager for whom no problem in fact existed. Rather, Juliet's room moved with her as she descended from balcony to platform. Romeo did not need an orchard wall to leap: 'nothing would worry an Elizabethan audience less than to see Romeo vanish through a door or behind a curtain'. And again Granville-Barker sounded his then familiar note: he wished that there existed 'something like a laboratory in which theories and deductions could be put to practical test'; if some of the theorists could act on a stage of their own devising, 'they would learn more in a week than they will persuade each other of in a generation'.[21]

In 1925 he was asked to deliver the British Academy Annual Shakespeare Lecture,[22] and he took that special occasion with its special audience to emphasize the mutual dependence of 'scholars of the printed page' and 'scholars of the spoken word', and to take up his usual theme:

At last it has seemed but common sense to return to Shakespeare as playwright, and even, for a fresh start, to Shakespeare as Elizabethan playwright. Upon which basis we have within these last five-and-twenty years largely relaid the foundations of our study of him. For this latter-day pioneering we have to thank scholars and men of the theatre both, men of diverse, not to say antagonistic, minds, methods, and standpoints. Mr William Poel, with a fine fanaticism, set himself to show us the Elizabethan stage as it was. Dr Pollard put us on the track of prompt-books. Dr Chambers, Sir Israel Gollancz (if in his presence I may name him), Mr Lawrence, Mr Dover Wilson – we are in debt to many. . . . We know well enough what the Elizabethan stage was like. We do not know fully all the effects that could be gained on it, for only experiment will show us. . . . His art has not yet, I think, been either very fruitfully studied or illustrated.

The paper sought out 'gleams of light', signs of dramatic vitality, in the early and mature plays, in the manner which was to be perfected in the *Prefaces*, but his next piece, 'Shakespeare and Modern Stagecraft',[23] seemed to focus more especially the principles by which he would give them their particular distinction.

'All art implies convention', he declared, and argued that the dramatist counted above all upon its tacit acceptance. Before we could understand Shakespeare, we must know the conditions and practices of his stage and thus 'prepare the ground for a due aesthetic appreciation'. He touched upon the notion that Shakespeare's theatre depended upon a totally different kind of illusion from that of more modern times. The drama of the twentieth century was one of visual illusion, whereas Shakespeare's appeal was primarily to the ear, and this was 'the mainspring of many differences'. Today, criticism is just beginning to take up the challenge he dropped by this remark, stimulated by the thinking of rare spirits like S. L. Bethell[24] and Anne Righter[25], with their sense of the multiple vision and 'multi-consciousness' of an Elizabethan audience in the act of watching a play. It is hard for us to recognize how purposefully Shakespeare exploited the spectator's awareness that he was indeed only in a theatre, while at the same time giving him sufficient rein for his illusory imagination. Actual time and place were made to interact with the timeless and the universal, the particular reality with the general application, in order to spur the spectator's perceptions in mysterious ways inaccessible to an audience watching the pictorial stage.

In this context, Granville-Barker pointed to the most elusive Elizabethan convention of all, that of the boy-actress:

Some up-to-date psychologist might well analyze the double paradox of the enjoyment derived by an audience of *Twelfth Night* who knew, as Olivia and the Duke did not know, that the boy Cesario—Viola was really a girl, but who also knew that the girl, Viola—Cesario was really a boy.[26]

Aesthetic distance and dramatic irony must have been greater still when the Elizabethan audience was aware that Olivia was also a boy, and Shakespeare repeatedly drew attention to the convention, not to undermine his art, but to bring sexual differences to a sharper focus. It was all done in a glorious game of appearances, played by both character and actor, with the playwright constantly extending his theatrical vehicle, its paradoxes of perception made more and more to reveal the ways of men and women. Granville-Barker's concern to identify what he called 'the Elizabethan illusion' was present in all his writing, and he continued to insist that the full enjoyment of Shakespeare depended upon 'a self-surrender as immediate and complete as possible'.[27]

Granville-Barker was enamoured of two great predecessors, William Poel and A. C. Bradley, the one urging him to think in terms of the Elizabethan stage and its non-illusory assumptions, and the other fascinating him with his modern revelation of realistic character and motivation. It may be said that Granville-Barker seemed to have devoted his writing to trying to absorb the one in the other to get the best of both worlds. Stage freedom seemed to have granted the dramatist freedom to explore character. Nevertheless, the attempt would have proved fruitless had not his superlative stage sense saved him from irretrievable blundering. For he believed that the Globe possessed an inner stage, and that in the development of the theatre it was this that became enlarged into a proscenium.[28] Happily, he also distinguished between the essentials of the Elizabethan stage and what he called its 'accidentals': Shakespeare's art did not depend upon any inner or outer stage, but upon

the things about it which gave him freedom in time and space, and the plays their swift mobility of action; the intimacy of the actors with their audience, which makes soliloquy effective and justifies the familiarity of the clowns; the neutral background which lets him, when he will, paint his scenery in poetry.[29]

But Granville-Barker also took Bradley at his word when he said that he felt like an actor of Shakespeare 'who had to study all the parts'.[30] From this Granville-Barker came to believe that Bradley's *Hamlet* and *Othello* commentaries were 'like a very great actor's conception of the parts' and that to Bradley 'the plays are plays and never cease to be plays'.[31] It was not so much important what a character did, as what he *was*, asserted Granville-Barker, echoing the master: '*Hamlet* is the triumph of dramatic idea over dramatic action and of character over plot'.[32]

Bradley's sense of Shakespeare's achievement as a profound investigation of the human psyche, treating characters as if they were all but alive as individuals, highly introspective and pitted one against another, was a limitation his criticism could never have overcome. In his *Prefaces*, Granville-Barker's saving grace was his instinct as an actor and director: he would always return to the play proper. It is true that, as his biographer C. B. Purdom says,[33] he devoted too much of his energy to scholarly issues of little account, like the discussion of the time-scheme in *Othello*, or act-division in *Hamlet*, or the separation of Shakespeare's hand from a collaborator's. He could not believe, for example, that *Macbeth*'s brilliant Witches were Shakespeare's own work, or that such a play could begin with such 'twaddle'. But Granville-Barker's very real triumph lay in his gift of recreating a performance on the page, and demonstrating Shakespeare's intention by showing vividly how a scene 'worked'. It was this that made these essays of outstanding importance for Shakespeare study and criticism between the wars.

The Introduction to the *First Series* reviewed much of what has already been said here: a plea for the study and the stage to merge, and for a primary understanding of Shakespeare's theatre. Behind this lay a lively notion of what charged a play with life and meaning:

> The dialogue of a play runs − and often intricately − upon lines of reason, but it is charged besides with an emotion which speech releases, yet only releases fully when the speaker is − as an actor is − identified with the character. There is further the incidental action, implicit in the dialogue, which springs to life only when a scene is in being. A play, in fact, as we find it written, is a magic spell; and even the magician cannot always foresee the full effect of it.[34]

Here were the ingredients: what an audience hears, what it sees, the elements of dramatic communication coming brilliantly together in performance to produce a *tertium aliquid* that is unpredictable.

Granville-Barker's emphasis was on the simplicity of Shakespeare's stage resources as the key to the development of the boldness and subtlety in his art. He commented brilliantly upon the unlocalized stage, by which 'no precious words need be wasted, nor ingenuity spent, in complying with the undramatic demands of space and time'.[35] He insisted again upon the importance of the verse-speaking as the actor's first and final source of control of his audience. He appreciated especially the strength of the soliloquy convention, whose intimacy 'allows the magnetism of personality full play'. Only in his uncertain attempt to show that the boy-actresses maintained their asexuality did he go seriously astray, yet even here he redeemed his argument by asserting that the relationships between men and women were 'made rarer and intenser by poetry'.

Love's Labour's Lost was the challenging subject of the first of the *Prefaces*. This elusive comedy he approached from the unexpected quarter of the director of the play, posing for literary criticism the unaccustomed question, Why produce it at all? 'Here is a fashionable play', he began, 'now, by three hundred years, out of fashion'.[36] His answer was to provide evidence to show that its comedy was nearly all 'instinct with dramatic life'. Of the characters, he believed that Berowne and the Princess, Costard and Sir Nathaniel the Curate come alive by unexpected 'outcroppings of pure dramatic gold'. Costard, for example, is merely the stage fool until at the end of the play (v.ii) he comes to act Pompey:

> COSTARD.   I Pompey am, Pompey surnam'd the big —
> DUMAIN.   The great.
> COSTARD.   It is great, sir; Pompey surnam'd the great;
> That oft in field, with targe and shield, did
> make my foe to sweat;
> And travelling along this coast, I here am
> come by chance,
> And lay my arms before the legs of this sweet
> lass of France.
> If your ladyship would say 'Thanks, Pompey'.
> I had done.
> PRINCESS.   Great thanks, great Pompey.
> COSTARD.   'Tis not so much worth; but I hope I was
> perfect: I made a little fault in 'great'.

Granville-Barker's comment was, 'These two last lines have, mysteriously and unexpectedly, given us the man beneath the jester.'[37] 'Drama, as Shakespeare will come to write it, is, first and last, the projection of character in action'[38] was Granville-Barker's somewhat tired maxim, after Bradley, but the refreshing excellence of his commentary springs from his actor's insights into what made stage sense. After a little gay repartee by Katharine and Longaville on cuckoldry, Granville-Barker's special ear hears the princess 'of a sudden' break out with

> Are these the breed of wits so wondered at?

just as the 'pretty speechifying' Mercutio would become

the stark man of
> A plague on both your houses!
> They have made worms' meat of me:
> I have it and soundly too . . .

and the word-spinning Romeo into that doomed taciturn figure of
> Is it ev'n so? Then I defy you, stars.

The dramatist was in the making who was to fashion a Falstaff out of the old pickpurse of Gadshill, who was to pitch on the preposterous tale of *The*

Merchant of Venice, and charge it (triumphantly, yet all but disastrously) with the passion of Shylock.[39]

Granville-Barker sought the kernel of success in the fantastic comedy of *Love's Labour's Lost*, and found it, simply, in its fantastic *style*:

> If the music is clear and fine, as Elizabethan music was, if the costumes strike their note of fantastic beauty, if, above all, the speech and movements of the actors are fine and rhythmical too, then this quaint medley of mask and play can still be made delightful. But it asks for style in the acting. The whole play, first and last, demands style. A vexingly indefinable thing, a hackneyed abracadabra of a word![40]

The magnificent assurance of the lines in *Love's Labour's Lost*, whether bombastic, parodistic or whatever, must be matched by an exquisite performance from the players. Never had a critic of Shakespeare pointed so resolutely to the essential ingredient of a play, and then proceeded to examine its implications for performance. The audience was to respond as Berowne did to Armado's letter: 'The style shall give us cause to climb in the merriness.' So Granville-Barker touched staging, costume and casting, capturing the contrasts of the last act between the lovers, 'glowingly apparelled', the village pageant loud against their delicate colouring, until all is clouded by the black Marcade. The blend and contrast of style, the shifts of key, governed the playing and the response. Granville-Barker, playing the words as he wrote, invited his readers to visualize the action behind the lines at every turn, until they could accept the proposition that 'the art of it is akin to the artifice of a ballet':

> The actor, in fine, must think of the dialogue in terms of music; of the tune and rhythm of it as at one with the sense – sometimes outbidding the sense – in telling him what to do and how to do it, in telling him, indeed, what to be.[41]

Love's Labour's Lost was a true test of the new approach in criticism, far more so than *Julius Caesar* and *King Lear*, the other *Prefaces* in the first volume. Granville-Barker passed the test by the most obvious of criteria: he sent his reader back to the play with every insight. The joy and energy of the comedy accumulate even now in the mind of the reader of this *Preface*, until he is undecided whether he has witnessed its performance or feels the urge to perform it himself. Nowhere did Granville-Barker attempt, or show any inclination, to say what the play 'meant'. His achievement was to track those experiential elements which would permit perception of meaning.

The *Julius Caesar Preface* was graced with a series of character studies in the best Bradleyan manner, and the Barker insights began only when he examined what he called the play's 'minor rhythms'. For one, he drew attention to the reiteration of the name Pompey before the Roman mob, until the name is dramatically supplanted by that of Caesar (i.ii): 'We hear the name sounded – sounded rather than spoken – seven times in twenty-four lines. The very name is to dominate.'[42] For another, in the same scene he caught the pace of Cassius's passionate speech into Brutus's ear, set off by the slower reactions of Brutus's less impulsive mind, divided in attention as it was by the implications of the off-stage shouting. Granville-Barker delicately traced the sequence of moods leading to the murder of Caesar, from Brutus's stoic calm and the details of the night's vigil, through the anti-climax of Portia's scene, to the tension of the storm and Calpurnia's fear; he was equally perceptive of the shifts of mood through the scene of the quarrel of Brutus and Cassius (iv.iii). But this play did not fully challenge the critic to probe the mystery of the poet dramatist.

The achievement of the *King Lear Preface* was of a different order. In this great essay, Granville-Barker dared to engage that curious tradition running from Lamb to Bradley which found the play 'too huge for the stage'. Writing after the great procession of Lears – Gielgud, Wolfit, Olivier, Redgrave – that took the stage following this *Preface*, T. C. Worsley paid special homage to Granville-Barker:

From being the least acted and least popular of the great tragedies, *King Lear* has recently been accepted into the repertoire as if it had never not had its place there. We owe this perhaps as much to Granville-Barker as to anyone. His authority as an actor and producer has weighed in the scales against those writers who for so long dominated Shakespearean criticism from the study.[43]

In an outstanding argument, Granville-Barker moved his reader towards the revolutionary position whereby the metaphysical experience could be understood in terms of the physical stage. Techniques of poetry and rhetoric must be dissociated from the limitations of visual illusion and realism, the plague of the nineteenth-century theatre. For his massive subject, Shakespeare rallied every resource of crafts-manship, trick of improvisation, every vital skill, to carry him through, so that at the core of the tragedy, the storm scenes, we should 'find this centre of the play a very epitome of Shakespeare's stagecraft — and we do'.[44] Granville-Barker then moved to the amazingly simple conclusion that the King, Kent and the rest must *act* the storm, and no effects of noise or music would finally serve in lieu: '[Shakespeare] solves his problem by making the actor impersonate Lear and the storm together, by identifying Lear's passion with the storm's'. Quoting 'Blow winds. . !' (III.ii), Granville-Barker commented,

This is the storm itself in its tragic purpose, as Shakespeare's imagination gives it voice. And any actor who should try to speak the lines realistically in the character of a feeble old man would be a fool. There is no realism about it. No real man could or would talk so. But the convention enables Shake-speare to isolate Lear for the time from all pettier circumstance, to symbolize the storm in him, and so to make him the great figure which the greater issues of the play demand.[45]

So the reader was led closer to the notion of a poetic drama winging swiftly through metaphor and symbol to ritual itself.

'Promethean Lear' was Granville-Barker's reverberating image to describe the actor in the storm scenes; but he did not seek the inspired idea of the play in a word or phrase any more than in his previous essays. He pointed instead to those rare qualities of feeling yoked unexpectedly together as they emerge in key scenes — the blinding, the fantasy of Gloucester's imaginary suicide, the meeting of mad Lear and blind Gloucester, the reconciliation of father and daughter. Of Lear's magnificent storm in the mind, Granville-Barker found that Shake-speare expended 'skill and imagination most recklessly till inspiration has had its will of him', and the scenes of madness 'pass beyond the needs of the plot, they belong to a far larger synthesis'.[46] There, Lear had his new vision of himself in Poor Tom, and the 'mad mummery of the trial comes near to being something we might call pure drama . . . in the sense that it cannot be rendered into other terms than its own . . . in that its effect can only be gained by due combination of sound, sight, and meaning, acting directly upon the sensibility of the audience'.[47]

In writing thus grandiloquently, Granville-Barker was motioning towards a finer statement of the way poetic vision is apprehended.

He juggled words as a critic must, but he was passing the performance before our eyes, pressing us to read the play again for its imaginative sweep. And in seeking to recreate the dramatic event by descriptive
evocation, he found himself, knowingly or not, selecting the ingredients
he felt to be essential for the particular chemistry of the play he was
discussing.

The second volume of his *Prefaces* was published in 1930: the
essays on *The Merchant of Venice* and *Cymbeline* derived from his *Players'
Shakespeare* introductions of 1923, and the *Romeo and Juliet* and *Antony
and Cleopatra* essays he had delivered as lectures at Aberystwyth. These
Prefaces are sufficient to show his method of chemical compounding
at work: the *Hamlet* volume, which did not appear after much labour
until 1937, already showed signs of academic atrophy and his divorce
from stage experience.

The *Romeo and Juliet* piece drove straight for the heart of its style.
The play 'is lyric tragedy', Granville-Barker began, 'and this must
be the key to its interpreting'.[48] By the two critical opposites of lyricism and tragedy he tried to characterize the play's uniquely mixed
elements: the simple power of its tragic story and the beauty of its
expression, the one thrusting it forward, the other suspending it in
inaction, the one of violence and death, the other touched by Queen
Mab. Granville-Barker wrote of 'something sacramental' in the
ceremony of the lovers' meeting, 'something shy and grave and
sweet'.[49] But he recognized as central the discord of Mercutio's ribaldry
set against the harmony of this meeting and that of the balcony scene.
He traced the vivid contrasts of tone created by the swift succession of
one scene in contradiction with another: Mercutio's death percipita-
ting Romeo's anger, while Juliet waits in the ecstasy of 'Gallop apace,
you fiery-footed steeds'. After the banishment of the young husband,
Shakespeare 'brings all his powers to bear upon the moulding of the
two figures to inevitable tragedy':

Over a succession of scenes – in all but one of which either Romeo or Juliet
is concerned – there is no relaxing of tension, vehemence or speed; for every
flagging moment in them there is some fresh spur, they reinforce each other
too, the common practice of contrast between scene and scene is more or
less foregone. And the play's declamatory method is heightened, now into
rhapsody, now into a veritable dervish-whirling of words.[50]

Thus was Granville-Barker keenly aware of pace and rhythm, lively action and rhetorical embroidery: he was searching for the assumed *convention* of a particular lyrical drama.

In tackling *The Merchant*, Granville-Barker again seized the play's characteristic manner, and tried to resolve the special contradictions of its mixture. 'The Merchant of Venice is a fairy tale', he began. 'There is no more reality in Shylock's bond and The Lord of Belmont's will than in Jack and the Beanstalk.' But if the stories of the play remain purely fabulous, the Jew is made real, and Portia and Bassanio become in great degree human:

Aesthetic logic may demand that a story and its characters should move consistently upon one plane or another, be it fantastic or real. But Shakespeare's practical business, once he had chosen these two stories for his play, was simply so to charge them with humanity that they did not betray belief in the human beings presenting them, yet not so uncompromisingly that the stories themselves became ridiculous.[51]

Here then was one problem to investigate: the presence of hard reality in the midst of that happy land of Faery. Another was the romance of the Portia story and how it was to be complemented by Shylock's sordid bond:

How to blend two such disparate themes into a dramatically organic whole; that was his real problem. The stories, linked in the first scene, will, of themselves, soon part company. Shakespeare has to run them neck and neck till he is ready to join them again in the scene of the trial. But the difficulty is less that they will not match each other by the clock than that their whole gait differs, their very nature. How is the flimsy theme of the caskets to be kept in countenance beside its grimly powerful rival?[52]

This was workshop criticism indeed, and posing the very questions which face every director of the play. Granville-Barker's answer was to find that the 'antiphony of high romance and rasping hate enhances the effect of both'. Shakespeare manoeuvred from mood to mood in masterly fashion, and the total effect must be valued 'very much in terms of music'. The action must sweep ahead, 'and no chance be given us to question its likelihood'.

Granville-Barker could not make head or tail of *Cymbeline* and its burlesque plot and style, any more than could his contemporaries. He fell back on Furness's theories of bad collaborators, or else found Shakespeare 'at odds with himself indeed', the master of stagecraft actually contriving 'structural clumsinesses'. He found the soliloquies too 'frankly informative', without recognizing that Shakespeare was having fun with the convention. And he descended to the confusion of a double conclusion, on the one hand that a fair amount of the play 'is pretty certainly not Shakespeare's'[53] and on the other that 'this art that displays art is a thing very likely to be to the taste of the mature and rather wearied artist'.[54] These lame observations were not characteristic of this volume, which also contained perhaps Granville-Barker's greatest achievement in dramatic criticism, the *Preface* to *Antony and Cleopatra*.

'The most spacious of the plays' was his immediate judgment: 'Shakespeare's eyes swept no wider horizon.'[55] Granville-Barker was thinking not of territorial excursions upon the Globe platform, but of the ease with which Shakespeare in this play ranges imaginatively in form and style. He cited with approval Coleridge's motto *'feliciter audax'* when he wrote of the wonder and vigour of the play's style and the flow of its multifarious life and activity. And Granville-Barker returned to his image of Shakespeare as a composer of music:

He was liker to a musician, master of an instrument, who takes a theme and, by generally recognized rules, improvises on it; or even to an orator, so accomplished that he can carry a complex subject through a two-hour speech, split it up, run it by divers channels, digress, but never for too long, and at last bring the streams abreast again to blend them in his peroration. Clarity of statement, a sense of proportion, of the value of contrast, justness of emphasis – in these lie the technique involved; and these, it will be found, are the dominant qualities of Shakespeare's stagecraft – of the craft merely, be it understood.[56]

Granville-Barker roamed through the play, touching here and there upon its artistry: the soldiers at their duty set against the rulers at their drinking bout; the quick shift from singing and dancing to the triumphant military entrance of Ventidius; the symbolic marching of the armies in the three days' battle, threaded by the 'hectic uncertainties through which Antony moves to his end'. He chastized Chambers for doubting that the Elizabethan stage could bear this load, and for thinking that 'Shakespeare is in some danger of outrunning the apprehensions of his auditory.' Granville-Barker conveyed a sense of the play which passed beyond mere stagecraft to what enthralled its audience when 'there is nothing left to stand between us and the essential drama', when we are 'at one with its realities'.[57] Where did these realities reside? At the centre of this *Preface* was a sustained commentary on 'the verse and its speaking', perhaps Granville-Barker's most subtle piece of writing, and in the poetry of *Antony and Cleopatra* he clearly located the fundamental spirit of the play. The tone and pitch and range of its language were at all times sufficiently ample and luminous in their power to sweep us into the special world of its heroism and its humanity.

In these remarkable *Prefaces* Granville-Barker was attempting a new descriptive dramatic criticism, fine in its particularity, and yet aiming at something more. He had left the closet far behind and moved his criticism on to the stage itself. Now he seemed to be straining to work out in each essay an ideal production, at once reaching backwards to Shakespeare's first intentions, and forwards to the realized essentials of each unique creation. He lacked, however, an element of some importance: a theatre.

7

Stylized Shakespeare and Nigel Playfair

'Stylization' — a term which first came into the language of art criticism at the turn of the century — was also a convenient notion by which a dramatic performance could be characterized when it conformed throughout to a general convention of speech and movement, costume and décor, set consistently at an appropriate distance from real life. Since the force of a play's content is inseparable from its style, in aesthetic theory at least a stylized performance would lead an audience to a fresh sense of a play's meaning.

A break-through to stylized Shakespeare followed hard upon Gordon Craig's theories of drama and the Granville Barker Savoy experiments. The new approach had begun visually. In 1910, John Martin Harvey had appeared in a *Hamlet* at Stratford which set and dressed the stage with a mere *suggestion* of an historical period and environment. The setting consisted of 'huge, prism-shaped triangular pillars, the Greek *periaktoi*. Placed at each end of the stage and decorated with simple designs, they suggested various localities as they were turned upon an axis'.[1] The revolve of the modern theatre has today made this quick change of illusion somewhat commonplace. In 1913, Martin Harvey directed *The Taming of the Shrew* at the Prince of Wales's with a single set consisting of 'a stylized picture of a gorgeous fifteenth-century summerhouse, the gardens of the Lord's mansion behind it'.[2]

In the same year, Lewis Casson had produced a *Julius Caesar* at Manchester using only a single piece of scenery, 'a large Roman arch which could be quickly and easily moved to different positions on the stage so as to give some slight indication of the changing locale'[3]: by this he achieved consistency of style as well as continuity of action. Casson was to go on to direct an outstanding production of *Cymbeline* in 1923 at the New Theatre: the stage was hung with 'futuristic' curtains of different colours which could be rearranged to change the mood of any scene.

Stylized Shakespeare and Nigel Playfair

In 1916, Martin Harvey tried another *Hamlet* at His Majesty's, a production in Max Reinhardt's style, in which he draped a variety of curtains against a great white canvas cyclorama:

> We looked at a dim and misty space, and beyond at the vast dim circle of the sky, and vague shapes like battlements showed black against it. . . . Everything was suggested, nothing was declared. The mind could not be distracted by detail, since no detail was visible. The stage picture was just the sufficient background and atmosphere for the great action which now began.[4]

In 1918, J. B. Fagan attempted a Granville-Barker style for *Twelfth Night* at the Court Theatre, a wholly emancipated production with a set of such simplicity that *The Times* found its scene changes 'almost as rapid as the kinematograph'.[5] However, the next Martin Harvey revival of *Hamlet*, that of December 1919 at Covent Garden, produced the first strong reaction to these new developments, and an outstanding contribution to *The Saturday Review*[6] pointed to the trap which stylization represented for the modern director of Shakespeare:

> For Shakespeare Mr. Craig's methods are fatal. . . . In Mr. Craig's theatre the actor is a necessary evil. In Shakespeare's theatre he is essentially the beginning and the end. Mr. Craig presents the actor in low relief against a background which is intended to include him. Shakespeare brings the actor out among the spectators, bidding him rely almost wholly on what he has to say. Mr. Craig aims at creating an impression by lines and colours, and to do this he reduces the bulk and stature of the actor, who is for him an incalculable and disconcerting element in the general scheme. Shakespeare aims at creating an impression by words delivered at close quarters, and to do this relies upon actors trained in every device whereby their speech and physical presence can be made most effectively to prevail. Mr. Craig desires us to contemplate his productions as one looks at a picture: it is something external to us and to be viewed as from a distance. Shakespeare desires us to be caught up into his production as an audience in personal touch with actors in a play: it is something in which we are directly implicated. Thus at Covent Garden . . . instead of hanging on every word that Hamlet says, we are almost surprised that he should speak at all.

So the critic found that the players were dwarfed by being presented as 'frail, drifting, remote figures moving against a lofty and spacious background'.

At the same time, some directors, following William Poel, were moved to recreate an impression of an Elizabethan playhouse structure. When Robert Atkins took over the direction of Shakespeare at the Old

Vic in 1920, he built the forestage out over the orchestra pit and set up a false proscenium in black velvet with flanking doors; inexpensive curtain sets proved to be immensely flexible. The actors played forward as much as possible, and in the 1930s Tyrone Guthrie built curved steps from the pit to the apron to accentuate the thrust still further. In 1947, Michel Saint-Denis remodelled the Old Vic forestage yet again, but, as Guthrie observed, 'so long as that picture frame remains, some kind of picture has to be put inside it'.[7] The Victorian theatre with its imposing and substantial arch, its brass-railed orchestra pit and its frontal rows of stalls has proved an obstinate agency by which to bring actor and audience into closer touch, but nothing could stop the growing tendency for the actor to speak directly to the house.

Meanwhile, in the country town of Norwich, Nugent Monck and his amateurs were setting an extraordinary example for the professional theatre by building their own Elizabethan-style playhouse. Monck was a producer of great enterprise:

He found, in the middle of one of those networks of back alleys so typical of Norwich, an old Georgian building with a gallery running round it. It had been built as a church, converted into a baking-powder factory, and afterwards acquired by the Salvation Army. At first sight it was hopeless to attempt to convert it into a theatre, as there was no space for offstage room. It was then that Monck had the inspiration of keeping the gallery as it was and building at one end an Elizabethan stage modelled on that of the old Fortune Theatre. It was christened 'The Maddermarket' because it was situated by the side of the medieval market where the madder roots were sold for dyeing turkey red the once famous Norwich wool.[8]

The Norwich Players opened the Maddermarket Theatre with *As You Like It* in 1921. It was a tiny theatre seating only 220 in a house 40 feet square. Poel called it 'this doll's house', since the greater part of it could have stood upon the original Globe stage itself. But the important point was that Monck had an instrument with which to rediscover the dramatic results of intimate acting. Norman Marshall reported that he achieved 'effects of great delicacy, using subtle touches of detail in expression and gesture which would be wasted in an ordinary theatre'.[9] His Shakespeare productions moved with great speed, one scene following another without pause: 'As a scene closes upon the balcony or the inner stage, the actors in the next scene are already walking on to the apron speaking the opening lines of their scene as they appear.'[10] In this way, *Twelfth Night*, for example, played for only an hour and three quarters. In his time (he died in 1958 at the age of 81), Monck produced every play in the canon, claiming only that he had spent his life 'trying to put Shakespeare simply on the stage'.[11] It is to be regretted that no analytical record remains of his findings, and his surviving prompt-books await attention.

These developments were straws in the wind. The first real aesthetic success for the new practice after Granville-Barker occurred at another small theatre also at some distance from the West End. The story of the Lyric Theatre, Hammersmith, is as romantic as that of the Maddermarket, but since it was professional, its manager, Nigel Playfair, took a far greater risk. In his introduction to Playfair's memoirs, Arnold Bennett wrote,

Nigel Playfair took what might fairly have been described as the unluckiest theatre in London. It is hidden in a slum; the slum lies off a street that the West End had never heard of, and the cab fare to which from the West End is about 4s. The trains of the Metropolitan Railway shriek, grind, and roar withing twenty yards of the building.[12]

The Lyric, Hammersmith, was known locally as 'The Blood-and-Flea-Pit', and in its time it had been everything from a mission hall to a boxing ring. Playfair wrote,

The theatre certainly took some finding, for it was almost lost in an old-clothes market. Whelk stalls, overcoats, and the establishments of fish-and-chip vendors jostled each other right round the very door; and on the steps an aged and incredibly miserable-looking man, hat in hand, was singing the sad story of his life to a tune of three notes, with intervals presumably corrupted from some Chinese composer, and in a voice which seemed to have been generated among all the internal diseases in the medical dictionary.[13]

The place was a shambles, in which half the destitutes of Hammersmith seemed to have found free lodging.

It was this theatre which originated one of the most refreshing and revealing Shakespeare productions of the 1920s, a landmark in stylization. At the invitation of Sir Frank Benson, Playfair's company was among those that opened the 1919 Birthday celebrations at Stratford, on St George's Day in Easter Week, the first after the war. They gave two performances of *As You Like It*, and then toured Manchester and Brighton, having to wait a year until their own theatre, the Lyric,

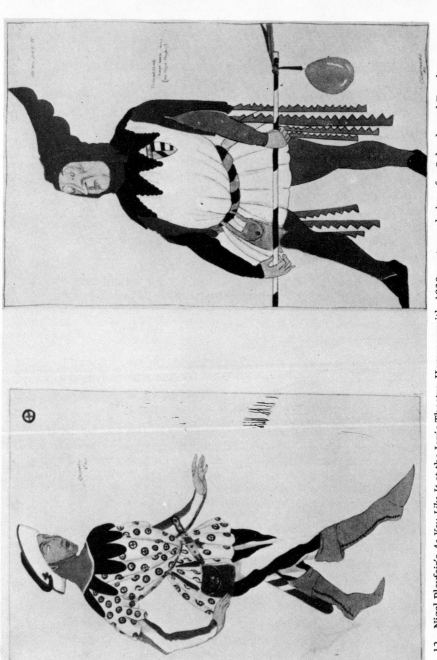

12 Nigel Playfair's *As You Like It* at the Lyric Theatre, Hammersmith, 1920: costume designs for Orlando and Touchstone

Hammersmith, was available. London saw the production on 21 April 1920.

It had raised both eyebrows and hackles at Stratford, and its reputation for being 'experimental' travelled before it. The outcry, as *The Observer* reported, was because it was thought 'that Shakespeare had been infused with or, rather, swamped by a mixture of futurism and Bolshevism — futurism, in that the costumes were of bright colour and unfamiliar design (see Plate 12); Bolshevism, in that stateliness of diction had been discarded in favour of something nearer the manner of playing modern comedy'.[14] *The Daily News* also spoke of 'this queer, affected, mixture of Shakespeare and futurism', and believed that Rosalind had 'failed in the main' because 'it is not easy to convince as Rosalind when you are dressed as a futurist pierrot at a Three Arts' Club Ball'.[15] Playfair confessed that when he went into his hotel, people turned their backs and even got up and walked out of the room. A woman went up to his designer and shook her fist in his face, saying impressively, 'Young man, how dare you meddle with Our Shakespeare!'[16] The production had denied the traditional idea of Shakespeare.

The designer was Claud Lovat Fraser, and most of the shock was caused by his settings and costumes, which radically altered the image of the play from that of a philosophical comedy to one of comic philosophy. In his preface to his book about the Lyric, Hammersmith, Playfair indicated that the public 'must learn to appreciate and find even better [than the sets of Irving and Tree] the simple decorative backgrounds which were certainly in the mind of Shakespeare when originally he wrote his plays'.[17] Lovat Fraser had gone for simplicity because his brilliant imagination was instinctively right; and also, it must be said, because his budget allowed for nothing more.[18] He represented the leaves of the forest by looped curves, which were not 'Futurist' or 'Cubist', not taken from Picasso or Derain, but copied exactly from a fourteenth-century missal. In a long letter to *The Observer*, Fraser explained his principle:

The period of the play is arbitrary, and in setting this production in the opening years of the fifteenth century, I have had recourse to the two best sources open to me, i.e., contemporary illuminated missals and tapestries. These two branches of art have preserved to us the gaiety, the freshness and fantasy of an age which otherwise in this country would have left but little trace of its form and character behind it.[19]

The first-act town background of bright pillars and medieval turrets came from a missal in the Bibliothèque de l'Arsénal in Paris, and the forest was taken from an illuminated English manuscript of 1426 showing Lydgate presenting his book to the Earl of Salisbury.

The Times was pleased to recognize the early source of the style, and added knowingly that it was 'perhaps not altogether unaffected by the Omega style in drawing. The forest, for instance, is ruthlessly simplified.'[20] *The Morning Post* saw the link with Granville-Barker: 'The scenery may best be described as Mr. Norman Wilkinson, only more so.'[21] Learned opinion was quite divided as a result. The *Stratford-upon-Avon Herald*, which sorely missed the *As You Like It* scenery it knew so well, including the moth-eaten stuffed deer from the Shakespeare Museum which was exhibited to remind visitors that young William was supposed to have been caught poaching in Sir Thomas Lucy's park, and which made a regular appearance in pastoral scenes, complained that 'all our appropriate scenery was discarded, and a lot of canvas, miserably painted and clumsily arranged, took its place', so that 'the environment of the play was altogether robbed of its picturesqueness'.[22] *The Observer* thought the whole thing 'a jumble of styles' and was particularly troubled that the Forest of Arden had become 'three sickly trees on the edge of an open field'.[23] But one letter-writer countered this by finding the scene of 'lyric freshness', and *The Birmingham Daily Post* saw a good reason for the break with tradition:

The old painted cloths in the manner of Alma Tadema . . . are now quite obsolete. . . . The scenes are, quite simply, no more than the penny plain outlines of the children's toy theatre of 40 years ago, carefully coloured by hand. And yet, with their simple green and purple washes, they were more effective and less obtrusive than the forests of the old convention.[24]

Realistic stage trees — no more than coloured cardboard stuck on strawberry netting — had in the past come between Shakespeare and his audience far more obtrusively.

No doubt it was the bizarre costuming, and especially the colouring, of the late French medieval style which most unsettled the audience. The colours were uncompromisingly vivid, of scarlet, lemon-yellow, saffron, emerald-green, Indian pink, crimson, ultramarine-blue, black and white: 'all the nicest colours known to Heal and the dyeing industry', wrote J. C. Squire.[25] The men wore particoloured tunics giving place to looser pleated clothes; the dagges on the sleeves and the edges of the tunics were fantastically slashed; the hose was also particoloured, with each leg a different colour – a device used for almost every male character in the play; the shoes were long and pointed, with stuffed toes designed to turn up. Monsieur le Beau, played by Miles Malleson, appeared in a flame-coloured suit and a great headdress of slightly Oriental design (the turbaned fashion of the period). The women wore high-waisted dresses, tight-fitting across the breast, with long and very full skirts. Celia wore the high, conical hennin draped with a muslin veil, and Rosalind's dress as Ganymede was so extravagant that it suggested to *The Morning Post* 'Arctic exploration, a Russian ballet, or anything rather than a simple old English forester'.[26]

The total effect was so arresting that audiences were hardly concerned with period authenticity. Instead, the issue became one of whether such designs were dramatically suitable or not. *The Morning Post* did not think so:

The dresses are so daring and colouring so extravagant in conception that they seem, to conservative minds at any rate, out of all key with Shakespeare. It surely does not, or should not, depend for its exposition on extraneous and factitious aids.

On the other hand, *The Times* found them 'very brilliant and exciting'[27] and *The Spectator* thought that they inspired 'a peculiarly gay and engaging sartorial "air with variations"'.[28] *The Observer* went so far as to assert that Lovat Fraser's riot of pure colour blended into 'striking and beautiful harmony'.[29] Clearly, these varying verdicts were quite subjective, and the final success of the production turned on something else: the director's consistency of vision, which depended upon his idea of the nature of *As You Like It*.

Playfair saw the play as a musical event, for which Arthur Bliss arranged Arne's Elizabethan settings for the songs, with 'some transcriptions from the Virginal Book made by Mr. Dent'. Bliss conducted the music himself, a string quartet of two violins, a viola and a violoncello. The musicians were dressed as pages, who sat in front of the curtain before the play began, and then took their places on the stage itself. They were regarded as a part of the play rather than as a musical addition or decoration, and their function returned the play to something like the spirit of good musical comedy, in which words and music, speech and song, remained in the same key throughout.

The play was given in its entirety without the customary cuts, and the dialogue was taken at a rattling pace, so much so that the former complaints were heard again, as they had been for Granville-Barker, that some of the actors were 'scarcely intelligible', and that most of them 'seemed quite unaware that they were speaking poetry'.[30] Athene Seyler gave a sparking performance as Rosalind, and judgments upon her confused the convention of the speech with the vitality of the character. *The Manchester Guardian* found her 'a chatterbox',[31] and *The Observer* at the London performance reported:

Miss Athene Seyler takes Rosalind at a pretty brisk pace — could a young woman with such an incredible fund of flippancy suddenly let loose in the vast freedom of a forest talk at anything less than a gallop?[32]

Tingling with life and humour, 'an almost electrical Rosalind . . . quick-witted, sportive, elfish, and charmingly defiant to an unusual degree',[33] she set the pace for the whole cast, which included Playfair himself as Touchstone. The theatre became a place of visual and also verbal magic.

Playfair, who had played Bottom in Granville-Barker's production of *A Midsummer Night's Dream*, had sought an appropriate convention for *As You Like It*, one which would characterize the comedy's exuberance and destroy all false tradition. Athene Seyler's exhilarating style of playing epitomized the exquisite fragility of Lovat Fraser's green and purple Arden, nicely set against the dignity and reserve of the sober Jaques, played by Herbert Marshall: 'Rosalind and Jaques, they made us feel, were the two clairvoyants of the "Golden World" — optimist and pessimist philosphers'.[34] *The Times* also remarked on Playfair's 'daring mixture of styles' which 'throws up the player against the scene'.[35] Playfair himself defended his production as an experiment in simplicity, formality and the unnaturalistic, designed to capture the spirit of the original conception.

At the first Stratford production, *The Birmingham Daily Post* had remarked that 'after five years' almost entire cessation of acting in Shakespeare, there must be an absolute reconsideration of methods and technique'.[36] This reconsideration Playfair had attempted in practice, not only in setting and décor, and in speech and movement, but also by exploring non-realistic conventions. The wrestling was performed on a bright sunlit patch of grass seen by the Duke, and the audience, through a cloister, so that it was half hidden, appearing and disappearing behind the spectators on the stage. *The Morning Post* was infuriated by this trick: 'All [Shakespeare] asked was that nothing should come between him and his audience', and that the wrestling should be 'played upstage in a corner, with Rosalind watching with her back to the audience' was unacceptable: at the Lyceum in 1890, the critic recalled nostalgically, 'all eyes were riveted on Miss Ada Rehan'.[37] Playfair seemed to be defying expectations wherever he could, and even J. C. Squire, full of praise for the production, protested at the scene in which 'the usurper, with a kneeling page at each side, posed facing the audience; I heard no words, I only saw a tableau vivant, as our fathers used to call it'.[38]

Playfair was aware that 'something of a revolution in the English Theatre' was being created, by embracing those earlier forms of drama built on many scenes and yet not neglecting the advantages of the modern pictorial stage. The scenic method at the Lyric, Hammersmith, was to find 'a background of scenery suitable in form for all revivals of classical plays'.[39] Fraser's trees and pillars were so simple and unreal that not only could they be quickly and easily handled, but they suited the mood and atmosphere of the whole play. The effect was so novel that the critics had difficulty in accounting for their new response, as Squire's account suggests:

The distraction was ephemeral; the scenes were not too frequently changed; and by the close of the evening one found the forest scene, for all the gulf between it and the scenery of Sir Herbert Tree, quite homely and natural, giving a sort of background of sensual pleasure to one's experience of the play, but not intruding itself in the least.[40]

This same 'background of sensual pleasure' could produce outrage, or, in the case of 'Tarn' of *The Spectator*, eulogy and something close to euphoria:

The lovers again stand fresh in immortal beauty. . . . In all truth and soberness, the entertainment at the Lyric is, taken all round – play, players, and the delight of the eye – nearer perfection than any stage production that I have ever seen. . . . It is difficult to know where to begin to particularize in praise. Was it the dress or the acting that pleased most, the music or the scene? Or was it a certain extraordinary impression of vitality and sensibility? In the first place, Mr. Nigel Playfair's methods succeed in leaving the audience with the impression that 'As You Like It' is very much the greatest of Shakespeare's plays.[41]

This kind of praise must seem nonsense at this distance, but it speaks exactly of what, at the moment of experience, every director asks of the playgoer at any play, an absorption in the play event, unique and complete unto itself.

Nigel Playfair did not direct another play by Shakespeare before he retired in 1932, but went on to revive the interest of London in Restoration and eighteenth-century comedy — perhaps his greatest achievement in stylization. The influence of his work, however, like that of Granville-Barker, was felt in a whole range of Shakespeare productions in the years which followed.

While the *As You Like It* of 1919 is the landmark production of the immediate post-war years, W. Bridges-Adams deserves a special place in the story. He had been associated with both Poel and Granville-Barker, and directed *The Merry Wives of Windsor* for Nigel Playfair in 1923. He also was attracted to the idea of simple, uncut Shakespeare, although he was not past cutting the Old Man and Ross in *Macbeth*, which he considered an imperfect and corrupt play. He was an Oxford graduate and for years a close friend of Professor Arthur Colby Sprague. Indeed, he was a considerable scholar in his own right, a man of discrimination, as his books on English drama testify. And he controlled the Shakespeare Memorial Theatre at Stratford in the crucial post-war years from 1919 to 1934, directing no less than 29 of the plays and designing his own settings on the backs of old envelopes. Bridges-Adams sought a less violent way of bringing 'true' Shakespeare back to the theatre, diplomatically and artistically eschewing both pictorial realism and alarming stylization. But he retained that essential speed and suggestiveness which marked the productions of Granville-Barker and Nigel Playfair, freeing the text — and Shakespeare — sufficiently to make the audience his collaborators. Unfortunately, Stratford's Memorial Theatre, a Victorian horseshoe, was unsuited to the new staging and in any case it was not yet the centre for Shakespeare it was to become later: at this time the London critics and playgoers rarely made the cross-country trip.

Bridges-Adams summarized his Stratford policy in a letter to J. C. Trewin:

It was briefly as follows (you will find most of it in Hamlet's advice to the Players): Tradition without traditionalism: fresh air and high spirits: grandeur of tone and gesture without ranting – 'using all gently': the virtues of the Elizabethan theatre without its vices, and its freedom without its fetters: scenic splendour where helpful, but the Play the Thing: all leading parts played by first-rate people: Hamlet one night and a servant the next: the smallest part well played, and balance and ensemble before everything: the play to be given as written: the text unmutilated whether in the interest of the stage carpenter or the leading man. Also (the ways of the human heart being inscrutable) that the Director should be forcibly spared all temptation to act himself, by a clause in his contract to that effect.[42]

Add to this catalogue that he could not abide recorded music: 'How can canned music follow the actor's eye?'[43] he demanded. Nor did he hesitate to criticize the master, Granville-Barker, whose challenge to tradition he felt to be 'too strident', and not quite authentic: 'People who would have blushed to speak of going to His Majesty's to see the scenery spoke without shame of going to the Savoy to see the *décor*.' But like Granville-Barker he wanted to be 'real without realism'.[44]

It was Bridges-Adams who dared to produce the first *A Midsummer Night's Dream* after Granville-Barker's golden vision. However, he fell back on Mendelssohn and had a woman play Puck in the traditional way. Moreover, if the interpretation of the immortals is the clue to the concept behind any production of this play, Bridges-Adams's fairies must be thought to have been a sorry retreat: they appeared as charming little children once more. H. C. Bailey admitted to finding them 'a trifle too substantial',[45] but he and nearly everyone else admired the 'tiny children playing in a Warwickshire copse'. For *The Stratford-upon-Avon Herald* it was 'typical fairyland', and not as bad as 'a host of children endeavouring to imitate an Alhambra ballet'.[46] Nevertheless, the notion of 'typical' fairyland disturbs, for it was this very need to upset typical expectations which had motivated Bridges-Adams's distinguished predecessor, and he had not approved of Granville-Barker's golden fairies:

The trouble with the stylistic treatment of Shakespeare is that it is not easy to be stylistic without being – what shall I say? – stylish, sophisticated, *towny*. Shakespeare was first and last a countryman; and his fairies, although they have a wealth of classical allusions on the tips of their tongues and can turn a pretty compliment to royalty, are first and last country fairies. They are scurrying, scudding, skimming creatures, not static little figurines on a London mantlepiece.[47]

The feature which induced a proper suggestiveness was what *The Yorkshire Telegraph* called his 'perpetual darkness',[48] or what *The Birmingham Post* thought 'his favourite device of obscurity'.[49] His scenes were characterized by soft colours and uncertain outlines, lending 'a drowsy and dreamlike appearance without that false theatricality which comes from the use of a veil of gauze'. They were beautiful stage pictures, suggesting an air of fantasy, and loose enough to allow Shakespeare to maintain control over his own play. Bridges-Adams had a true eye for delicate effects, and William Archer's verdict, that this was 'originality without eccentricity',[50] was probably right. The Stratford *Dream* was compromised Shakespeare, and stylized Shakespeare seemed to be evaporating before being perfected. *The Observer* summed up the 1920 season at Stratford more generously:

Mr. Bridges-Adams is not freakish, or futurist, or rebellious in any direction . . . but behind all his work lies the strong tradition of a drama that is feeling its way back to its origins. Breaking finally away from the outworn, 'representational', sham-realistic style of production which was reduced to its *absurdum* by the live rabbits in *A Midsummer Night's Dream*, he has returned to something which is precious near the Elizabethan system of an open stage with traverses and 'alternation' scenes; but, since modern stage art is capable of more definite suggestion than was Elizabethan stage art, he gives you, when needed, a landscape, a garden, or what not, which the scene painter shows as definitely a landscape or a garden, yet maintains as rather a suggestion than a statement, a setting for actors, not a 'landscape with figures'. And many of these scenes – simple, easily moved, lightly built though they are – have been deservedly welcomed at Stratford as very beautiful to eye and mind. As for the time saved by this method of dividing the play into scenes that follow one another rapidly, with only one interval for cigarettes and chatter, it enables them to give so much more of Shakespeare's text than is usually given. . . . Or, rather, it is the company which is the star. . . . They play for the play. They play it as a whole – swiftly, cleanly, faithfully.[51]

Elizabethan coherence seemed to have been achieved.

Meanwhile, in London, others like Lewis Casson were mixing the styles with unpredictable results. On the one hand, *Henry VIII* at the Empire in 1925 was dressed with splendid realism, as befitted a spectacular play. *Macbeth* at the Prince's Theatre the following year received the same treatment with disastrous effect:

134

This production reproduced some of the worst faults of the old tradition. The play was constantly tripped up by the scenery. The many changes of elaborate sets necessitated the curtain being lowered twenty-two times during the course of the performance, and although *Macbeth* is one of the shortest of Shakespeare's plays, it lasted for nearly three and a half hours.[52]

'A scenic progress by Charles Ricketts', according to J. C. Trewin, 'with a tragedy by Shakespeare interspersed'.[53] On the other hand, Casson's *Cymbeline* at the New Theatre in 1923 had jumbled the styles quite successfully, employing curtains on a semi-circular track, changing the colour with the mood, and dividing the stage with a traverse curtain. This was at once labelled Futurist, as usual, and seemed just right for a play in which Shakespeare was deliberately playing with style to produce what *The Times* described as 'a fascinating, repellent, quaint, confusing piece of romantic art ... throughout wonderfully strange'. The correspondent continued, 'It is strange to see stately Romans (out of Holinshed) and ratiocinative early Britons (who might be out of Shaw) cheek by jowl with Renaissance Italians (out of Boccaccio), all busy with an elaborate complication of plots (which rather suggest the libretto of an unusually conscientious musical comedy).'[54] Arbitrary stage methods somewhat arbitrarily carried an arbitrary sort of play.

Following the burning of the old Stratford Memorial Theatre in 1926, the new building with its modern mechanical devices opened for Shakespeare's birthday, 23 April 1932. A short study of Bridges-Adams's *A Midsummer Night's Dream* of that season may indicate the direction his talents had taken during his tenure at Stratford, and the distance travelled from Granville-Barker in a mere 18 years, especially since Bridges-Adams had the services of none other than Norman Wilkinson, the Savoy designer. It seems that stylization can take many forms, not all of them necessarily helpful to the playwright's intention.

Wilkinson's art had mellowed since the occasion of his gilded fairies; he now offered up a 'Nocturne in Blue and Silver'.[55] All remarked the beauty and enchantment of the stage image, but then Bridges-Adams had conceived the play in the happy spirit of an epithalamium. The court set was some great chamber in an Elizabethan palace, 'which threw out on either side broad corridors of glass hinting at yet greater chambers beyond'.[56] The wood was represented by a huge hollow oak riven by ancient lightning: this served as Oberon's chamber, and in it also Titania could later sleep. The immortals were 'the King and Queen of Shadows'.[57] *The Times* noted that 'the occasional shifting of this tree really conveyed the impression that we were exploring the wood'. Theseus and Hippolyta came from the hunt 'in clothes as white as marriage garments, with great sashes of scarlet-royal', and the lovers were 'Elizabethan figures in alabaster, slipping through some fold of Time across the centuries, from a golden age when love and all the world were young'.[58] We may judge from these lyrical sentiments whether the splendour of the new Shakespeare was not of the same romantic order as that of Beerbohm Tree a generation before, wedding march and all.

Bridges-Adams's fairy world was more saccharine than ever, and thoroughly approved. His creatures appeared and disappeared delightfully, small insubstantial shadows, so that the solid correspondent to *The Times* not only remarked how they danced, 'the darting moonbeams shining upon their faces and turning them to gold', but also drew attention to their size: 'How did Mr. Bridges-Adams discover performers so tiny and yet so amenable to discipline?' Puck, in a scarlet cloak, flashed amid the gloom, playing tricks on any fairy he caught, and the prompt-book[59] indicates what a conventional business this was:

Fairy enters left. Crosses right around tree. Crosses left followed by Puck. Crosses right, crosses left to centre, Puck following catches her as she falls on Bank (II.i).

Puck enters left, puts scarf over fairy's head. She screams. . . . Puck takes off fairies screaming (II.ii, just before Oberon squeezes the purple flower in Titania's eyes).

And so on. When Titania entered calling for 'a roundel, and a fairy song' (II.ii), the direction reads,

Fairies enter right running in single file. Circle around stage making a big semi-circle at foot of bank. On last note of entrance music all kneel. . . . Titania enters right, goes up bank and stands in bower. At the end of song, fairies bend forward with heads touching ground.

When Titania led Bottom to her bower, the fairies carried a garland and formed a chain to follow them off.

The prompt-book also shows that the business with the mechanicals was entirely conventional. When Puck entered upon their rehearsal in III.i, he touched them on the shoulder so that 'all sneeze'. When

Bottom appeared with the ass's head, the entry reads, 'Bottom chases Snug around right. Bottom goes to Starveling who screams and exits left. Flute and Snug run across from right to left and back.' In the play scene, a great deal was made of false cues and Quince's prompting. Moonshine and Pyramus both began their lines in error when they were first introduced, and were hastily suppressed by the others. Pyramus waited for applause on his first line, 'O grim-look'd night', and Quince had repeatedly to prompt him. Flute slipped from Thisbe's falsetto in a deep male voice on her exit line, '"Tide life, 'tide death, I come without delay'. Moonshine was so upset by Quince's prompting that he dissolved into tears on 'All that I have to say, is to tell you, that the lanthorn is the moon; I, the man i' the' moon; this thorn-bush, my thorn-bush; and this dog, my dog'. Lion himself held Thisbe's mantle for Quince to stain with blood. Unable to draw his sword from its scabbard, Bottom had to stab himself with scabbard and all. And on Thisbe's 'Come trusty sword', her suicide was graced with a wealth of burlesque business when Bottom realized that he was lying on it: 'Looks around and repeats. Bottom slowly raises sword. Thisbe draws it. Bottom sits up and is pushed back.' While Thisbe scurried frantically about the stage looking for the sword, Bottom hoisted himself up 'inconspicuously' and slid it out from under him with a 'pssst'. When Thisbe drew the sword, it came out instantly and Bottom sat up in amazement, whereupon Thisbe pushed him back with her foot.[60]

Bridges-Adams's stage became increasingly spectacular as Stratford prospered, and against mild complaints that his sets were 'a shade too representational', in his last season he mounted a *Tempest* with all the splendour of a masque. Since the play was supposedly written for the bridal of the Princess Elizabeth, *The Times* remarked a 'pageantry that would indeed have sufficed to adorn the nuptials of the royal paragon':

He gave us an actual ship, storm-tossed on a lee shore, which lost her masts and plunged beneath the spouting waves. It was no mere capful of stage wind, but a full gale fortifying the allusion of Prospero's mastery of the elements.[61]

Granville-Barker's requirement of a convention of indefinite place was no doubt in some danger of being ignored. But at least Bridges-Adams kept his stage fluid and swift, and he was never insensitive to the poetry of the plays. Robert Speaight quotes him as saying, 'I always felt nearer to the true music of Shakespeare at a rehearsal on a summer evening with a bare stage and a property chair, and the voices of a young actor and actress running quietly through the balcony scene from *Romeo and Juliet*',[62] and he never contemplated 'mechanical orgies as a substitute for Shakespeare's verse'.[63] In a little guidebook for playgoers which Bridges-Adams wrote during his retirement, he advised his reader always to cut through to the heart of a play:

The test of a good Shakespearean playgoer is his ability to see right through the trappings of the current mode to the heart of the performance. Whoever can do this soon discovers how far any novel treatment is a matter of externals merely.[64]

It was to his credit that he, like Shakespeare, worked through particulars and practised the art of making little things interesting: 'The dying Lear must have his button.'

In that both the critic and the director, and, indeed, all parties to the play, seek its heart and spirit, the primary decision about its style is their equal concern. However, the factors are elusive which decide an appropriate stylization for a non-realistic play. The style in which a play is performed represents that chosen level of decorum which will aesthetically reveal and release its power and dramatic properties. Its style authorizes a coherence of playing to match the content, and demands a consistency by which actor and audience alike can make and recognize the links of meaning. The style thus becomes part of the code most suitable for making understood and transmitting a play's dramatic idea and feeling. Granville-Barker, Nigel Playfair and Bridges-Adams were each in his own way seeking the right code, but the hunt had merely begun.

8

Barry Jackson and dizzy modernity

The pretty notion that Shakespeare was not of an age but for all time is to be traced throughout the history of Shakespeare criticism from Ben Jonson to Jan Kott. L. C. Knights has put the matter well:

The true Shakespeare critic will be concerned to make himself, as far as possible, a contemporary of Shakespeare's. . . . But, more important, he will also be concerned to make Shakespeare a contemporary, to see his particular relevance for our time.[1]

'Shakespeare our contemporary' was an idea that could be extended to embrace universal truth, too, and the cries, 'Shakespeare is Germany!', 'Poland is Hamlet!', have been raised in the past and will be again. 'Why', asked Logan Pearsall Smith, 'at the three-hundredth anniversary of [Shakespeare's] death, were tributes of passion and adoration, sent to celebrate it from all over Europe, — North and South America; why did Brahmin, Muslim, Egyptian, Burmese, Japanese and Chinese poets, the inhabitants of Iceland, the negroes of South Africa, "the scalded Indian, and the poor boy that shakes at the foot of the Riphean hills", why did they all burst into song, and raise the vast babel of their discordant voices to hymn his praise?'[2] It was a commonplace that the plays had a life of their own, and had continued over the years to grow in their significance. The abiding strain in modern Shakespeare criticism, felt in A. C. Bradley, pursued in Ernest Jones, has been strikingly anti-historical, and in 1930 Lascelles Abercrombie could make his famous 'Plea for the Liberty of Interpreting Shakespeare':[3] 'Anything which may be found [in Shakespeare's art], even if it is only the modern reader who can find it there, may legitimately be taken as its meaning.'

Perhaps the thought of timelessness and universality in Shakespeare is not quite unscientific. When in *Julius Caesar*, iii,i Cassius calls upon the conspirators to stoop and wash their hands in Caesar's blood, he adds,

The Shakespeare Revolution

How many ages hence
Shall this our lofty scene be acted over
In states unborn and accents yet unknown!

Unexpectedly the collapsing of time which follows when the audience's attention is drawn to the fact that these Romans are only actors and the blood a pretence makes the death of Caesar an event which is both Roman and Elizabethan, Elizabethan and modern. The device of the image of play-acting insists that the audience recognize its role of observer and see itself as one of many similar audiences in the past and in the future.[4] Just as on the Elizabethan stage there was rarely any need to represent space and time literally, so was there small interest in historical authenticity: indeed, the persistence of the anachronism of Elizabethan manners and attitudes seems deliberate in play after play. On a stage without illusion, all dramatic subjects, historical or fictional, offer analogues to contemporary life. In particular, costumes and properties, speech and behaviour, all in the contemporary vein, lent an enviable immediacy to Elizabethan performance, and it is no wonder that the actors in the years that followed should wish to share this privilege.

Burbage, Betterton, Garrick — they all played in the dress of their own period. For a Roman play, a length of cloth draped across a shoulder would sit quite comfortably over a seventeenth or eighteenth-century doublet, coat or waistcoat. Not until the nineteenth century did the vogue for historical accuracy arrive. Suddenly it became necessary to determine the place and time of the play — Imperial Rome, Renaissance Italy or ancient Britain — and Charles Kemble and Charles Kean set new standards of pedantry in costume and setting. Poel's return to an Elizabethan dress was in some ways the rebellion of one pedant against others, but at least he acknowledged that the plays were not history lessons. However, to watch a *Julius Caesar* or a *Timon of Athens* played in Elizabethan dress placed a double distance between the modern audience and Shakespeare, and was clearly not the final solution. Now, after the return to non-illusion with Granville-Barker and Nigel Playfair, the issue of contemporaneity again became acute. One solution might have been to find 'a setting and costumes which would be free of historical or decorative associations so that the timeless, universal, and mythical qualities of the story may be clear',[5] as the designer Isamu Noguchi declared for John Gielgud's 'Japanese'

Barry Jackson and dizzy modernity

King Lear in 1955. Barry Jackson's personal plan for timelessness was a Shakespeare in modern twentieth-century dress.

The Birmingham Repertory Theatre under Barry Jackson was unique among the provincial repertory theatres of Great Britain in that from the beginning it set its own artistic standards often far above those of London. It had begun in 1907 as a group of amateur drama enthusiasts calling themselves the Pilgrim Players. They performed in Barry Jackson's private house until they opened their own theatre in 1913 – according to Norman Marshall, this was the first theatre to be built in England for the purposes of repertory.[6] The name had become the Birmingham Repertory Company, but there never had been such a repertory: plays classical and modern from Shakespeare to Shaw, with shockers from Ibsen and Pirandello. And in all this Jackson was solely responsible for the solvency of the enterprise and its challenging policy of high standards in the selection of plays. The 'Birmingham Rep' was uniquely the creation of one man, exciting and unpredictable. Then in 1922 he dared to carry his uncommercial attitudes to London itself, disregarding all warnings about what made for success with the public, and always following his own taste. In twelve years he produced forty-two plays ranging from a medieval miracle play to the whole of Shaw's *Back to Methuselah*, done in five consecutive evenings. One of his most eccentric productions was of *Hamlet* in modern dress in 1925 at the Kingsway. It was a memorable success financially, but an even more important one critically and artistically.

Jackson's Shakespeare productions at Birmingham,[7] with John Drinkwater as his manager, had doggedly pursued Granville-Barker's principles of simplicity. On a well-raked stage with a suggestion of an apron he could give the spectator a strong sense of intimacy with the actor. Writing in 1919, an enthusiast offered this description:

The theatre was constructed especially to allow for performances of the Shakespearian drama. The proscenium is something after the manner of that of the old Georgian playhouse during the transition from the platform stage to the picture stage, at the point when footlights were first introduced. That is to say, it has proscenium doors and a dwindled forestage, both of which are used in performance with the new compromise between the Elizabethan method of presentation and the Victorian method of presentation. The plays are never, therefore, trimmed to fit the stage or the players, and the full text of Shakespeare is given unaltered.[8]

A permanent set made for an Elizabethan continuity of scenes, and this usually included an approximation to an 'inner stage' without its becoming the supposed Elizabethan 'study' — a Tudor arch for *The Merry Wives of Windsor* or thick pillars for Macbeth's castle at Inverness, approached by steps, would supply that necessary depth for an inner acting area. A cyclorama beyond, and lit by Mariano Fortuny's soft, reflected lighting, lent to the actors that dimension of dramatic and symbolic suggestion of light and shadow achieved by European designers like Adolphe Appia.

J. C. Trewin describes Jackson's imaginative sense of colour and style as worked upon this tidy stage for a memorable *Twelfth Night* in 1916:

Three concave steps stretched across the stage. Above them were eight slender columns, four on each side, that supported a slightly arched roof. The bases and capitals were black; there were black lines along the edges of the steps; and the remainder, including the stage itself, was a warm yellow. For certain of the interior scenes Jackson removed the background, showing a blue sky beyond the pillars. Curtains, dropped sometimes in front of the pillars and sometimes behind them, could vary the setting, and the passage for Viola and the sailors on the Illyrian shore was played upon the apron stage with the tableau curtains lowered.[9]

A striking *Much Ado About Nothing* was mounted in 1919, with Guy Kortright the designer achieving a medieval splendour of colour by using only reds and yellows in the costumes. The correspondent with *The Birmingham Post* wrote:

The background is a setting of white marble, and the spacious sky; the only other colour employed is black in the costumes of Don John and his followers.... Pictorially, [the production is] a thing of pure beauty, at once the most simple, the most sumptuous, and the most sustained of any production of Shakespeare in the new English manner. Compared with it, Mr. Lovat Fraser's painstaking decorations of *As You Like It* are only the efforts of a clever little boy with a paint box.[10]

Barry Jackson had pursued the impressionistic unreality of Granville-Barker's approach as far as this 'new English manner' would take him, and he was now ready for a further adventure into the unexplored experience of Shakespeare.

The grand idea for modern-dress Shakespeare came to Jackson after he had witnessed a group of poor children from Birmingham perform the mechanicals' scenes from *A Midsummer Night's Dream*. Without the aid of proper costumes, their 'Pyramus and Thisbe' had succeeded beyond belief: the essence of the comedy had been distilled by the children's demand for a simple attention to their performance and not its decoration. He resolved to test his idea in Birmingham on a romantic comedy whose burlesque mixture of styles and periods regularly defeated the principle of consistency of design. He wanted to see 'whether his audience, which had to face so many anachronisms in *Cymbeline*, would accept the major anachronism of modern dress'.[11] His director, H. K. Ayliff, arranged for the wager between Posthumus and Iachimo over the incorruptibility of Imogen to take place in evening dress at a dinner party. Cymbeline and his queen appeared in court dress, with Cloten in the uniform of a Guards' lieutenant. The sons who had been reared in a Welsh mountain cave suggested their outdoor life by wearing shorts and open-necked shirts, and Imogen in disguise did her mountaineering in knickerbockers and peaked cap. The audience was bewildered, but the production proved that its perception could be wonderfully controlled by this simple expedient of modernity.

At *Cymbeline* critics used for the first time the catch-phrase, 'Shakespeare in plus-fours'. Among local debate, for the news did not spread far, it was conceded that Jackson had pushed a door open; soon it would be opened wide.[12]

But no one could guess what would blow in.

Hamlet, that most sacrosanct of all plays, the one most encrusted with tradition, was to be the real test. Under Ayliff's direction, it opened in London at the Kingsway on 25 August 1925.[13] The first scene on the battlements was played in half darkness, thought to obviate the early danger of laughter in the wrong place. When the lights went up on the court scene, the actors seemed to be in the throne room of a small pre-war Balkan court: several critics named, not Denmark, but Ruritania. There, ambassadors and diplomats, and Polonius (A. Bromley-Davenport), dressed in white ties and tail-coats smothered in decorations, mingled with elegant women in *haute couture*. A tired dowager was 'conspicuous with her tiara'. And, lounging on a bench, was 'the Lord Hamlet (Colin Keith-Johnston), in a rather shabby dinner-jacket and a soft shirt'.[14]

13   Barry Jackson's *Hamlet* at the Kingsway Theatre, 1925

The focus of attention was at first naturally upon the clothes each character wore as he appeared (see Plate 13).[15] The King (Frank Vosper) had 'ordinary dress clothes, white tie and waistcoat, and a sort of pale blue Garter ribbon across his chest, while the courtiers, similarly arrayed, wore monocles and smoked cigarettes, with syncopated music "off"'.[16] Claudius appeared later in a dressing-gown over his evening dress and with another cigarette. Hamlet did not wear his famous plus-fours until the graveyard scene, and Laertes (Robert Holmes) and his second arrived for the duel in Oxford 'bags': 'the younger men from the 'Varsity, Laertes, Rosencrantz, Hamlet himself, [showed] a predilection for tweeds'.[17] The Ghost was in modern Danish uniform, although *The Spectator*, which considered the character to be 'undeniably romantic', was 'much relieved that he appeared only in the coinage of Hamlet's brain, later on'. On the battlements he was 'a faintly silvered Father Christmas'.[18] The First Grave-digger (Cedric Hardwicke) was on hand in the grave scene dressed in his Sunday best with a rusty bowler hat. Perhaps Ophelia (Muriel Hewitt) was the most disturbing: in bobbed hair and the short skirt of the twenties, she sang every line of her songs, and the notice in *The Times* observed that the scene of her madness was damaged by 'the inescapable shortness of [her] skirt' and her consequent 'loss of dignity'.[19] Yet the consensus was that the modern costumes were eminently successful:

They are easy, natural, appropriate. None of them gets a laugh, and none of them is meant to. They merely transport us to the modern world. But, as Wordsworth said, 'Oh, the difference to me!' The difference in the main is not to Hamlet himself, who at once becomes easier to play because his surroundings become ten times as interesting, but in the others, who surprise one by suddenly leaping to life.[20]

The simple effect of these powerful visual changes was, unexpectedly, to make *Hamlet* seem like a new play. I say 'unexpectedly', because Jackson had taken pains to promote the production as 'Hamlet in Modern Dress', and audiences went to the theatre hunting for anachronisms. In the event, awkwardnesses of period seemed hardly noticeable:

There are surprisingly few places where text and action clash. True, the Queen tells how Hamlet 'whipped out his rapier' to kill Polonius, whereas he had seized the sword from a convenient armoured figure against the wall, and

Ophelia's description of Hamlet with 'his doublet all unbraced' is hardly apt. But these do not seem matters of very great moment'.[21]

Rather, the overwhelming effect was to revitalize the characters, and Muriel St Clare Byrne later summed up the issue by saying that 'on to the scrap heap, with the incredible clothes and the wigs and the beards, went the whole accumulation of conventional characterization which had been stifling everybody'.[22] Modern dress tended to strip the parts to the bone, and the actors had to start again to clothe the characters in flesh. The Prince seemed more morose than melancholy in his new manner, unable as he was to strike the traditional attitudes. The cigarette-smoking Claudius, traditionally played as a second Player King, now appeared a polished, if foxy, ruler, with a clean-shaven face and well-groomed manners to match his clothing. Polonius, always played as a tedious old fool, became a dapper little minister of state. If Ophelia seemed too much the flapper, likely at any moment to break into a Charleston, her brother Laertes became 'an ordinary decent undergraduate, warped by a rancorous hatred in his heart for the young man who he thinks has seduced his sister'. So wrote Hubert Griffith in *The Observer*, declaring that he never wanted to see again 'the Laertes of the trunk-hose, or, alternatively, of the winged-helmeted Viking tradition'.

Of no less importance, speech and gesture also underwent a sea-change. Everyone was sharply aware of the contrast between verse-speaking and the modern idiom, always associated with prose dialogue until W. H. Auden's *The Dance of Death* (1933), Maxwell Anderson's *Winterset* (1935) and T. S. Eliot's *The Family Reunion* (1939). Some, like the correspondent with *The Daily News*, were unsure of the strong tendency towards rapid, naturalistic speech which resulted: 'The prosaic clothes make for prosaic speech', he argued, and for him Hamlet's exclamation, 'What a piece of work is man' might have been, 'What a fine sportsman is Hobbs'.[23] The critic in *The Spectator* described how Hamlet 'hammers out "To be" argumentatively as he strides up and down'.[24] The same writer believed that to discard romantic period costume was more remedial for the actors than for the audience, and *The Nation and Athenaeum* also made the point that 'the words lose none of their beauty through being spoken as though the actors understood them'.[25] Norman Marshall was an eloquent witness to this effect:

The clothes enforced a naturalism which admittedly entailed some sacrifices. Some of the declamatory passages had to be pruned, others had to be underplayed. Some of the music of the verse and much of its magnificence was lost. But never before had I heard Shakespeare's verse spoken with such directness and simplicity, or the sense of the lines made so clear.[26]

If modern dress restricted the actors to modern speaking and gesture, and if it was a little irritating to watch Laertes delivering his lecture to his sister while addressing a luggage-label to Paris, 'the play gained in point, in speed, in clarity'.[27]

'Gained in point': the blunted edges of the play's themes and meaning became sharp. The King and Queen acquired a new terror, and the audience felt itself nearer to Hamlet than ever before. He was no longer a romantic prince, but a man:

Only a man, naturally currish and then driven to despair by self-torturing philosophy, would have poured into his mother's ears all those relentless and filthy lines about the pinches and reechy kisses of the bloat king. When Hamlet is played as a modern youngster, all this beautification can be sloughed away. . . . Mr Keith-Johnston's performance, with its gabbling cynical worldhatred and its fiery mood of relentless raillery, was a perfect expression of a shell-shocked world.[28]

Several critics, indeed, noticed the similarity between the closet scene in *Hamlet* and the exchange between another mother and son, the effete Florence Lancaster and the degenerate dandy Nicky, in Noël Coward's *The Vortex*, which had been produced the year before. Nicky, like Hamlet, forces his mother to face the truth, with tragic results. Ophelia, too, played with a demure charm in the early scenes, became unusually poignant in her madness, as Barry Jackson explained in an interview:

Here you have a thoroughly charming girl, such as you would be glad to meet and know, suddenly saying things which no girl would say. When, on the other hand, traditional costume is worn, audiences say, 'Oh this all happened hundreds of years ago, and girls talked like this then'.[29]

Costume seems to speak for time, but time provides one of the illusions of the stage which the playwright, the actor and the director most desire to manipulate. When one critic called for the same company to complete the experiment and play *Hamlet* in costume, he was asking for the mystery of the theatre to be impossibly demonstrated to him:

147

the perception of a play's timelessness always remains imprisoned inside the spectator's head.

The newspapers made a fine joke of Jackson's *Hamlet*, heading their columns with tags like 'The knickerbocker Hamlet', 'Hamlet in plus-fours', 'Ophelia in a jumper', 'The gloomy Dane with a cigarette', and so on. A production of this kind was certainly a butt for easy witticism: 'The Court of Denmark was peopled by a throng of smartly dressed women in Paris models and men in well-cut evening clothes. They kept "wassail" to jazz music, and the older folk had a penchant for bridge.'[30] This writer also found the play 'almost denuded of beauty'. Nevertheless, there was surprisingly little condemnation with this type of criticism, and the majority of correspondents were overwhelmed by their experience. Ivor Brown believed that 'many of the first-night audience came to scoff and remained to hold its breath, to marvel and enjoy'.[31] Hubert Griffith found it 'the richest and deepest *Hamlet* I have ever seen', delighted that he was able to judge the play 'as though, by some inconceivable flight of burning genius, a modern playwright, say Tchekhov, had written it'.[32] The novelty of the décor soon wore off, the production ceased to seem a freak, and the 'new angle' on Shakespeare which Jackson had promised in his apologia in the programme was realized: a moving quality of humanity and the vitality of the original play were felt as never before. The notice in *The Times* attempted an explanation of this phenomenon:

How much is all aesthetic judgment weighed down by association that has no essential relevance . . . particularly when the play is *Hamlet* — history, tradition, custom, and so, inevitably, prejudice are in formidable alliance to obscure judgement. Recognition of this fact, and not any desire for extravagant innovation, is the basis of Sir Barry Jackson's experiment in putting *Hamlet* on the stage in the dress of today. It is clear from the treatment of the play that the motive of it is not a showman's but an artist's. There is from first to last no attempt to make any easy profit of eccentricity, or, in short, to turn tragedy to nonsense . . . there is, and must be until we are accustomed to the convention, a sensation of shock; for a moment the mind is turned away from what is important to the new non-essentials — to the fact, for instance, that the music of the dance is syncopated or that the courtiers drink cocktails and light cigarettes. And the question is — it is the question by which the whole experiment must stand or fall — how long will this diversion of mind last. . . ? The answer is that the diversion is short. . . . The initial strangeness vanishes, leaving a clear gain in freshness and life and vigour. . . . Here was not an addition of obscurity, but an opening out of fresh light upon the play.[33]

This writer added, however, that the experiment was not one which others should lightly repeat; nevertheless, after the revealing success of this *Hamlet* in modern dress, nothing could have stopped them.

Less by luck than judgment, Horace Brisbin Liveright's modern dress *Hamlet* opened in New York at the Booth Theater on the same night that Jackson took his production to Birmingham (9 November 1925). America was not to be outdone, and Aline Bernstein dressed Basil Sydney as a sensitive Prince in a sober lounge suit, Ernest Lawford as a fatuous Polonius in a monocle and Adrienne Morrison as the Queen in 'a frock more suggestive of Paris than Elsinore'. It was all bobbed hair and cocktails. This production was known more dryly, and perhaps with a touch of something more sinister, as 'the plain-clothes *Hamlet*': the Prince puffed a cigarette on a gilt divan as he meditated the life to come, and then shot Polonius through the arras with a pistol. But this production failed to repeat the success of its London counterpart.

It was a 'prose' production, a 'grand opera without music'. Joseph Wood Krutch in *The Nation*[34] found the production unexpectedly impressive, but he, like other New York reviewers, thought the rhythm of the lines at odds with the illusion of modern manners and twentieth-century chatter. Brooks Atkinson particularly complained of the actors' breaking up the verse into 'the snippets of casual conversation'. The game of anachronisms provided dubious fun for all: a telephone which stood on a table in one scene was never used, but it was hard to miss Claudius's agitated line following the murder of Polonius, 'Come, Gertrude, we'll call up our wisest friends' (IV.i.38). Otherwise, Gilbert Seldes seemed to sum the matter up with the terse conclusion that 'psychologically Mr John Barrymore was more modern'.[35]

Jackson himself followed *Hamlet* with a *Macbeth* in modern dress at the Court Theatre in 1928, again with Ayliff as director, but this time the magic did not always work. The play was set as if in World War I, with Macbeth (Eric Maturin) a khaki-clad general in riding-breeches and high polished boots. Battle scenes at start and finish of the play were brought up-to-date with exploding shells and rattling machine-guns. The Porter (Frank Pettingell) scored a success as a drunken Scottish butler: why? asked *The Times* — 'because intoxicated Scotsmen change not much with the years'.[36] Lady Macduff (Chris Castor) was murdered over a cup of afternoon tea by killers who entered through a casement window, with her son looking like a scrubbed and frightened schoolboy (see Plate 14). Macduff (Scott Sunderland) received the news of their deaths wearing a felt hat and a lounge suit in the fashion, and his realistic acting was fresh and moving. Such naturalistic scenes matched the modernity, but too much of this play is written in high style and too many of the speeches are rhetorical.

The modern Witches were a disaster from the beginning. Ivor Brown wrote:

If, as I believe, they are a severe handicap to a drama in which a Nordic Thane is plunging across blasted heaths wrapped in primeval mists, what an impossibility must they be when a modern major-general encounters them in the guise of distressed charwomen and discusses his career with them![37]

Lady Macbeth (Mary Merrall), in a short sleeveless evening dress with waistline around the hips, screwed her courage ridiculously to the sticking-place with a stiff drink on the line, 'That which hath made them drunk hath made me bold', although her nightdress for the sleep-walking scene was less embarrassing because it seemed less restricted in period. Macbeth emptied his revolver into the charmed Macduff at point-blank range, and then took to a sword with an uncomfortable effect of farce. It was all very troubling to the audience. The associations of khaki particularized the period of the play, and it was never clear why there was a war going on in contemporary Scotland: 'The director forgot that in modern Scotland there was no king to be killed, and that Duncan should have been modernized into George V'.[38] The mechanics of a production designed for timelessness in fact resulted in a raging anachronism, enough to prompt *The Times* to remind its readers that 'men who aspire to be kings in Scotland do not now forward their ambition by Macbeth's method, [and] great ladies who murder their guests do not wander about with daggers'.[39]

In the same season at the Court, Jackson produced *The Taming of the Shrew* in modern dress with more success: the farcical level of the original readily admitted the jokes and inventions of the director. J. C. Trewin reported that 'Petruchio addressed "Come on, i'God's name" to the starting-handle of a battered Ford. "And that his bags shall prove" was applied to trousers. Asked for a stove, Curtis brought on an electric fire',[40] and so on. Norman Marshall thought that the wedding scene was more successful than usual because modern audiences did not know how an Elizabethan bridegroom should look any-

14   Barry Jackson's *Macbeth* at the Court Theatre, 1928

way; it was far more ridiculous 'when Petruchio, dressed in a top hat,
a red handkerchief round his neck, morning coat, highly coloured pull-
over, a pair of khaki breeches, a riding boot on one foot and a patent
leather shoe on the other, was seen against a crowd dressed with the
formal correctitude of the guests at a fashionable wedding at St
George's, Hanover Square'.[41] The process of modernizing Shakespeare
took a new turn and became one of 'democratizing' the Bard when in
the next year (1929) Oscar Asche presented a modern version of *The
Merry Wives of Windsor* at the Apollo: Pistol recited 'The Charge of the
Light Brigade' while a small boy yelled 'Get your 'air cut!'; the Welsh
parson Sir Hugh Evans rode in on a bicycle and Shallow was pushed
in a wheelchair; and to cap all, Master Fenton carried off sweet Anne
Page on the pillion of his motor-cycle. All this was roundly condemned,
but thoroughly enjoyed.

151

It would be tedious to list all the productions of modern-dress Shakespeare which followed,[42] but the unusual work of Terence Gray at the Festival Theatre, Cambridge, between 1926 and 1933 thrust Shakespeare production in yet another direction in the frantic years of the twenties. The Festival Theatre was Gordon Craig's 'director's theatre' *par excellence*. Gray wrote in his *Festival Review* that his aim was

not to interpret any author's text but to create an independent work of theatre-art. The producer is an independent artist, using other artists and co-ordinating their arts into a whole which is the composite art-of-the-theatre. The author contributes a frame-work, ideas, dialogue, the designer contributes line and colour and architectural form, the actors contribute sound and movement by means of the human body in speech and action, and the whole is designed and built up by the producer into what should be a work of theatre-art.[43]

His attack was also upon what he referred to as 'the old game of illusion and glamour and all the rest of the nineteenth-century hocus pocus and bamboozle', and he, like Brecht, set out to wage war on the tradition of the theatre in which 'the audience creeps in, listens to a play, claps ritually, and creeps out'. Gray needed an open stage which would encourage the actors to play in the auditorium as well as on the stage, so that the audience was 'no longer asked to imagine that it is spying on reality'.

At Cambridge, he accordingly converted the old Regency theatre known as the Theatre Royal, Barnwell, so that naturalism must seem unnatural:

The Festival stage was so designed that conventional realistic production was almost impossible. The first essential to a photographically realistic production is a picture-frame proscenium isolating the actors from the audience. At the Festival it was difficult to find any definite point at which the stage ended and the auditorium began. There was no proscenium. The width of the stage was the width of the auditorium itself. The broad forestage merging into a great fan-shaped flight of steps extending to the feet of the audience sitting in the front row abolished any boundary line between actor and audience.[44]

Gray's stage was always, as the Globe platform was for Shakespeare, a focal place for the actors, who were never withdrawn from the audience behind a proscenium, but on occasion were even to be seen waiting to make their entrances. Gray believed that his stage was ideally suited to Shakespeare. He wrote in a programme note,

Barry Jackson and dizzy modernity

The withdrawal of the stage from the auditorium and its seclusion behind a proscenium, placing the audience in a different world from that in which the actors are living on the stage, was a bad blow for Shakespeare. Shakespeare's plays are essentially three-dimensional: the West End picture stage is essentially two-dimensional. Shakespeare's characters live and move among the audience, they speak to the spectators, who are often nearer to them than the fellow actors with whom they are in converse, whereas the picture stage actor is a specimen on a slide observed through a microscope. From behind a proscenium an 'aside' is an amazing absurdity which no realistic and no expressionist technique of production can justify.[45]

However, with none of the restrictions of illusion, Gray's productions in the late twenties seemed wildly eccentric. He permitted himself every liberty in his assertion of a director's theatre. His notorious production of *The Merchant of Venice* was presented with an outrageous cynicism: Shylock was to be seen fishing in a canal, and was last seen destitute and turning the handle of a barrel organ; Portia delivered her speech on the quality of mercy in a listless voice, while the Duke diverted himself with a yo-yo and his court yawned and assumed attitudes of boredom. In *Twelfth Night*, Toby Belch and Andrew Aguecheek entered on roller skates, and in *As You Like It*, Rosalind and Celia appeared in the Forest of Arden as boy scout and girl guide. *Romeo and Juliet* became 'Spanish', with the lovers dressed in flamenco costume; the stage was set with triangles of scarlet, black and emerald green, and cerise and mauve light was projected upon the cyclorama. *Henry VIII* was treated as an ironic masque: the actors were dressed as playing cards and entered down a high aluminium ramp on a revolve curving down to the auditorium; during the final scene of the christening of Princess Elizabeth, the stage revolved madly and the property baby was tossed with a shout out into the audience. On the first night of this production, 'the curtain fell to a pandemonium equally compounded of cries of rage and shouts of delight'.[46] Nevertheless, Terence Gray's use of a revolve set and his constant changes of lighting not only achieved Shakespeare's continuity of scenes, but managed to avoid particularity of time and place. More than this, his aggressive productions, disconcerting though they may have been, asserted the right of a director of Shakespeare to seek out all manner of means to adapt mood, tone and style to an audience's needs.

Theodore Komisarjevsky revelled in this tradition for his six productions as guest director at Stratford-upon-Avon between 1932 and 1939. After leaving Russia in 1919, Komisarjevsky had established his reputation as a most meticulous Chekhovian naturalist, so that his fantastic and apparently frivolous treatment of Shakespeare came as a surprise to everybody. In the summer of 1932, he handled *The Merchant of Venice* like a child with a new toy. J. C. Trewin describes the occasion:

Prefaced by a capering of *commedia dell'arte* masquers, it ended with a yawning Launcelot Gobbo. The Stratford stage was put through every trick. The Lion of St Mark slid one way and the Rialto another. Belmont rose shakily from the depths; Arragon and a nigger-minstrel Morocco were burlesqued; the Duke was senile and drowsy, his Clerk a dodderer; Portia in court wore bicycle-wheel spectacles; Antonio, who had a large ruff that made his face look like the head of John the Baptist on a charger, faced Shylock with a languid indifference.[47]

Komisarjevsky saw the production as an opportunity, without fear or favour, to improvize flamboyantly upon themes and notions in Shakespeare. Next year at Stratford came a *Macbeth* which in part echoed Barry Jackson's First World War version of a decade before: Macbeth was a neurotic soldier in a world of machine-guns and howitzers, rifles and steel helmets. His Witches were old women seen plundering the bodies of the battlefield, an idea which has since been borrowed by others, notably by Joseph Papp in New York, in order to eliminate the supernatural while retaining the play's sense of terror. In this way, Banquo's Ghost was seen to be Macbeth's own shadow and his visions the result of a nightmare.

Komisarjevsky's *The Merry Wives of Windsor* in 1935 struck out for innovation again by translating the play from the England of Elizabeth to a green, pink and ochre Vienna, with Falstaff looking like the Emperor Franz Joseph. *The Times* explained,

To show how independent [the play] may be made of English character and English humour he gives it a Viennese background and imposes on the actors the artificiality that would be appropriate to a Goldoni comedy.[48]

Just as the world was Shakespeare's oyster, so period and place could be ransacked to discover an apt medium by which to express the spirit of his drama. For our purposes we may pass over the Stratford *King Lear* of 1936 and 1937, although the production is notable for its attempt to eliminate the particularity of place, and instead focus upon tone and atmosphere by building on the stage a great flight of steps leading off in various directions, its acting areas lit by pools of changing light. But with his productions of two lighter comedies, *The Comedy of Errors* in 1938 and 1939 and *The Taming of the Shrew* in 1939, Komisarjevsky returned to his sportive attack upon place and time. *The Comedy of Errors* was as fantasticated as a ballet, 'the men wearing plumed pink bowler hats, the women in farthingales and carrying modern hand-bags'.[49] *The Taming of the Shrew* was lit with what J. C. Trewin called 'polychromatic artificiality' − carnation and blue and citron and apple-green − and its actors were dressed in a motley bewigged Resto-ration style mixed with traces of the *commedia dell'arte*.

Some playgoers concluded that Komisarjevsky was a charlatan, on the grounds that he did not know enough English to direct Shake-speare. It is hard to resist repeating the withering comments of Charles Morgan upon his production of *Antony and Cleopatra* at the New Theatre in 1936. Komisarjevsky cast a Russian comedienne, Eugenie Leon-tovich, as the Queen of the Nile, and Donald Wolfit, who played Antony, recalled that she was 'clad in the scantiest of draperies sur-mounted by a fireman's helmet, adorned with large white plumes'.[50] Unhappily, her English was rudimentary, and Morgan turned a sorry occasion into a prime joke:

The part of Cleopatra was written in English and in verse; Mme. Leontovich has neither. A phonetic script would be needed to describe what she makes of the great speeches, but plain lettering may serve to illustrate her difficulties.

  O weederdee degarlano devar
  Desolderspo lees falln: yong boisenguls
  Alefelnow wimen.

Whoever, reading that once in a perpetual *tremolo*, can interpret it as: −
  O, wither'd is the garland of the war.
  The soldier's pole is fall'n: young boys and girls
  Are level now with men.

may attend this performance in peace. . . . But who plays with this Cleopatra is lost, for she is so occupied by her own vain struggle with a text which, like her fantastic skirts, is forever getting in her way that she cannot listen to or understand anyone else, and Mr Donald Wolfit, who has the equipment of a good Antony, and proves it on occasions, finds himself, in passionate scenes with the Queen, one of two vocal islands apparently without communication.

Nor are these difficult circumstances Shakespeare's only rival. M. Komisarjevsky, doubtless in his pursuit of 'synthetic' theatre, has decided to treat *Antony and Cleopatra* as if it were a cross between a *ballet*, an operetta, and a *revue* at the Folies Bergères. . . .

Seldom has a play been so tormented and twisted and stifled or a work of genius so casually scorned.[51]

James Agate's headline for his own review was 'ANTON AND CLEOPATROVA: A TRAGEDY BY KOMISPEARE'.

The shadow of war descended on a stage crackling with Komisarjevsky's fireworks. As might be expected, all this was not, in the eyes of many, playing Shakespeare, but playing *with* him. These were the final steps in the process of democratizing Shakespeare, a delusion of vain outward shows for modern groundlings who were as susceptible to such temptations as 'any chuckle-headed pittite on Bankside'. W. Bridges-Adams complained bitterly that when a Lady Macbeth offered King Duncan, uninvited, her left hand palm upward, she had managed to drop three dreadful bricks in one. 'We no longer mutilated Shakespeare, but we gabbled his lines, and slapped him on the back and called him William.' Pranking him out in the new finery of modern dress was not necessarily going to disclose his mysteries:

Is there any real freshness, or is the actuality any greater, when we see the same old Hamlet and the same old King in gentleman's suitings? There are two arguments for modern-dress Shakespeare: that it attracts an audience who otherwise would not come, and that it compels the players and the public to think of the characters as real people; both are surely arguments of desperation. Of those against, the homeliest is as good as any. Modern tailoring does not allow for the great gestures that go with great lines, and if the play is to be re-dressed in this fashion it should be re-written also.[52]

While it was generally agreed that it was good that Shakespeare should occasionally be shaken out of the customary 'deadening ritual', and that 'a dash of the ridiculous may even have its uses', few saw much real significance in the use of modern dress for the development of our understanding of the plays. 'A joke's a joke. And, our medicine taken, it can go back to its cupboard till next time.' The author of this witticism was none other than Harley Granville-Barker.[53]

Yet we have to account for the response of a former professor of poetry at Oxford, J. W. Mackail, who believed that Jackson's *Hamlet* allowed him almost 'to see the drama itself in direct unclogged action for the first time',[54] and of John Dover Wilson, who saw Jackson's

Hamlet four times and 'learned more on each successive occasion'.[55] Critic and academic alike sensed that the undeniable new insights they had received called for reasons.

The historical explanation was reiterated: modern-dress Shakespeare was simply a reversion to older custom. Did not medieval religious pictures represent their characters in attire contemporary with the artist?[56] The Elizabethans themselves, after all, dressed Greece and Rome in doublet and hose, and in the eighteenth century Shakespeare's tragic heroes appeared in periwigs. It seemed logical to argue that when the Elizabethans saw, say, Roman characters in Elizabethan dress, they could more readily accept them as contemporaries; and that the same reasoning must apply to a modern audience seeing Elizabethan characters in modern dress; and that the same reasoning must also apply to a choice of dress from *any* period that would make the play more understandable. The evolution of Maurice Evans's 'G.I. *Hamlet*' during the Second World War illustrates this sequence of possible fallacies. Evans had played a traditional Hamlet in New York in 1938, but when he was sent to Hawaii to entertain the troops quartered there in readiness to invade Japan, he decided that Elizabethan dress would repel an audience of soldiers, most of whom had never seen a play before. However, the anachronisms of a modern-dress production, he believed, would also confuse them, and so he finally chose what he took to be the last romantic period which had any meaning for Americans of that generation. This period was that of the Civil War, when family daguerreotypes were fairly common. In this way Evans produced his Civil War *Hamlet*, revived it in New York in 1945 and toured it with great success for two years afterwards.

However, Ivor Brown believed that there was more to the matter than costume: '[Sir Barry Jackson] has proved that when you cut away the trappings and the suits of Wardour Street you can also cut away the frosty formalism of Wardour Street acting'.[57] Perhaps the elusive quality of 'style', coupled with good acting, was really responsible for any revelation, as Norman Marshall insisted:

Ayliff, by putting his actors into modern clothes, was simply using a drastic method of forcing them to act Shakespeare according to Granville-Barker – to speak the lines directly, simply, and swiftly, to reconsider the characters without reference to the traditional methods of playing them, to abandon silly, musty business, to pay scrupulous attention to the exact meaning of the lines, to make no thoughtless gestures, to realize above all that the plays of Shakespeare are not just about people who lived in the past, with strange ways of speech and dress, but are about human nature, which, during the passage of the centuries, has changed far less than the ways of speech and dress. If the actors are fully conscious of this, it really does not matter much whether they play Shakespeare in ruffs and doublets or in collars and coats.[58]

Other reasons were offered for the excitement of the experience: both the shock of incongruity stemming from the modern perspective given to ancient plays, and the surprise of congruity when so many of Shakespeare's themes and ideas seemed up-to-date. The programme note to Jackson's *Macbeth* discussed the sense of seeing a play with new eyes, and, writing of the *Hamlet*, he explained that 'after one had been in the theatre for five minutes, one was no longer concerned with what Hamlet wore or how Hamlet looked, but with what he said and did'. Muriel St Clare Byrne later suggested that people were surprised to discover what an extraordinarily good play *Hamlet* was, as if they were seeing it for the first time, and offered the reason that Jackson's production had 'earned the right to be regarded not as a stunt but as a serious excursion in search of authenticity. . . . He has forced his audience back to the text and the pursuit of the authentic Shakespeare.'[59] 'The authentic Shakespeare' is a challenging phrase indeed: a Shakespeare performance which wins acceptance because it affords what the sharpest imagination believes to be the genuine experience of the play is the end of all scholarship and every innovation in production. It is the subject of this book.

That a serious discovery had been made is scarcely in doubt, and nearly every critic of these developments in production was teased by the notion of timelessness in the plays. *The Observer* argued that the modern dress treatment was best suited to tragedies, because 'tragedy is unchanging'.[60] *The Spectator* was troubled that modern costume creates modern characters and manners, since clothes inevitably localize persons: 'Let Hamlet appear so that you cannot tell him from Adam. Or, if that might remind us – laden as we are with many memories – of an advanced ballet, vaguely symbolical dress might be better.'[61] And the writer waxed metaphysical: a modern-dress performance elicits 'what is of value in the play for our own time; for our own moment of this *time*'. If Pitoeff, who was directing Shakespeare in Paris at this time, believed that interpretation for one's own age was the sole object of any production, *The Spectator* evidently wanted more. Jackson's note to his *Macbeth* also touched this issue:

We take Hamlet out of his sable habit, not because we want to see him in the 'actuality' of plus fours, but because we wish to neutralize an oppressive convention and to see the man free of historical or theatrical limitations. The trouble is that the man must wear something, and our purpose is to discover the dress which will least cloak, with irrelevant suggestions of period, the essence of his tragedy. When the 'actuality of present-day happenings' makes itself felt the experiment is nearer failure than success.

Ivor Brown, with his usual astuteness, thought to return the question to Shakespeare himself:

If anything stands out conspicuously about Shakespeare, it is his disdain of dates: he thought in terms of mind and mood and threw the year-book out of the window. Naturally, then, the proper way to dress Shakespeare is to stop the audience considering period at all instead of forcing it on their attention.[62]

When was Shakespeare's stage ever concerned with the calendar? It was time to look again for what mattered to him.

When the correspondent of *The Daily Telegraph* asserted simplistically of Jackson's *Hamlet* that Shakespeare the dramatist gained effect at the expense of Shakespeare the poet,[63] he was in effect denying the unity of Shakespeare's art in a way that today would not be acceptable: twentieth-century criticism has led inevitably to the point where we now see that the poetry *is* the drama, and the drama the poetry, divisible only when taken off the stage. But unwittingly, perhaps, he was requiring the stage to synthesize our multifarious perceptions of Shakespeare. Whether Shakespeare is performed in modern dress or in the nude (at the time of writing, the latter is well within the bounds of possibility), the secret does not lie in so superficial an element of perception as costume, but in the mode of presentation which will embrace his infinite variety: his timelessness and his modernity, his symbolism and his actuality, his ritualism and his realism. When Barry Jackson and his successors were struggling with this puzzle, literary criticism was struggling too.

9

Criticism: retreat and advance

It does the world little good to see *The Tempest* as a mere modern spectacle, *A Midsummer Night's Dream* as an orgy of colour and dance, or *The Taming of the Shrew* as a vulgar farce. . . . It is a disservice to Shakespeare and to the modern world to misinterpret his plays.

The unease of the careful scholar on witnessing the licence of the stage is felt in Hardin Craig's words.[1] While the directors of the twenties and thirties expressed a riotous joy at their new-found Shakespeare, there was a perceptible withdrawal into propriety by his students and scholars. And yet every critical withdrawal was shown to be an instance of scholarly *reculer pour mieux sauter*.

After 1925, it seemed that Shakespeare criticism had two ways to go: towards the application of new psychoanalytical studies to the understanding of his characters, and perhaps of the author himself, and towards a more accurate knowledge of the Elizabethan stage and background. Both of these directions were taken, and both helped to guide the modern production of the plays. But it is true to say that in the thirties the strongest thrust of Shakespeare criticism, its major energies, went in neither of these ways. The rapid growth of the 'new criticism' in England and America, with its emphasis on the language of poetry, provided a technique of analysis which absorbed the interest of those literary critics less inclined to track Shakespeare back to the theatre. Why should the stage rob the study of its immortal poet? Yet even here, the flood of work done upon his word-choices, his imagery and his symbolism, and the values these implied, deposited a fertile alluvium for the stage. At the same time, every new researcher risked the limitations of his field and the excesses of his enthusiasm.

After John Barrymore's American *Hamlet* of 1925 — a very gentle and romantic, not to say dull and low-toned, prince, with Fay Compton as the sweetest of nineteenth-century maidens — 'R.J.' of *The Spectator* concluded that 'some day an up-to-date actor will give us the psychoanalyst's Hamlet'.[2] Ernest Jones's *The Oedipus-complex as an Explanation of Hamlet's Mystery* had been a response to a footnote by Freud in 1900 and published in *The American Journal of Psychology* in 1910. Thence it was translated into German, and thence it was revised and translated back to English as 'A Psycho-Analytic Study of Hamlet' in 1923, finally to be published as *Hamlet and Oedipus* in 1949. Freud joined forces with Shakespeare, therefore, late and circuitously. His studies in the infantile desires of Shakespeare's heroes embraced Lear's relationship with his daughter Cordelia, Lady Macbeth's with her father, and Richard III's with his hump.

Freud's thinking was a special force in the study of Hamlet, whose Elizabethan melancholia seemed quite insufficient to identify his traits of personality. The Prince's procrastination, his despair and his suicidal tendencies, his cynicism and his quick changes of mood, could be as readily explained by his Oedipal desire to kill his father and marry his mother — which, after all, Claudius had managed to do with far less conscience — as by Elizabethan treatises on the psychology of the humours, the pattern of an Elizabethan revenge tragedy or Hamlet's sense of personal and political corruption in Denmark. Of course, subconscious urges towards incest and parricide fail to explain Hamlet's Christian thinking, the 'divinity that shapes our ends'. Hamlet may be Oedipal, 'but there is more to his mystery than that', argues Arthur Eastman. 'Though the rest of us were to slay our fathers and marry our mothers, as Jones well knows, no such miracles of wit and passion would come from our lips as come from Hamlet's.'[3] However, a psychoanalytical study seemed to be the natural, and far more scientific, extension of the impressive work on character and motive done by A. C. Bradley. The troubling difference was that Bradley had assumed that Shakespeare knew what he was doing, whereas Freud's theories implied that he did not. The question of Hamlet's sanity might well become a question of Shakespeare's.

Writing in 1934, John Dover Wilson put his finger on the problem of examining Hamlet's psyche as an analyst would, at least as it seemed to actors and directors:

A fundamental misconception vitiates [psychoanalytical diagnosis] and most previous attempts of this kind: that of treating Hamlet as if he were a living man or a historical character, instead of being a single figure, if the central figure, in a dramatic composition. Prospero Shakespeare has put his spell upon the world; he has filled his plays with creatures so life-like that we imagine they must have an existence beyond the element they move in. Yet they are confined spirits; and though the illusion of their freedom is perhaps the highest of all tributes to the potency of the magician's wand, the fact that he has thus enchanted his greatest critics gives rise to grave errors concerning the nature of his art. . . . Apart from the play, apart from his actions, from what he tells us about himself and what other characters tell us about him, there is no Hamlet.[4]

In *What Happens in Hamlet*,[5] Wilson persisted in his belief that to abstract one figure from a dramatic composition and examine it as a clinical case made for wrong-headed criticism. Nevertheless, it was a fine testimony to the influence of Dr Jones that what had traditionally been referred to as the closet scene (*Hamlet*, III.iv) suddenly became 'the bedroom scene' in Wilson's seventh chapter.[6] Surprisingly, there never had been a bed on the London stage in the scene between Hamlet and his mother. Not surprisingly, playgoers had to wait only another year for the bed to make its appearance.

John Gielgud, an actor who used his voice as the subtlest of instruments, had played Hamlet at the Old Vic in 1930 as a romantically lonely youth in a hostile environment. He revived the play at the New Theatre four years later, and this became the most celebrated *Hamlet* of modern times, running for 155 performances. The voice was more thrilling than ever, a presence in itself, and it spoke of a poignant melancholy and the deepest pain of the soul. Or so it seemed. Was it in part the voice of Freudian sexuality and inner conflict? This production used centre curtains for the closet scene, suggesting a hidden bed. When Gielgud played Hamlet in New York in 1936, the 'couch for luxury and damned incest' had materialized as a real bed, upon which Hamlet leaped irreverently in order to stab Polonius through the arras. If Gielgud does not speak of an interest in Freud in his autobiographical *Early Stages*,[7] Rosamond Gilder, who kept a record of the New York performance, certainly recognized Freud's presence:

Modern psychology must be as much a part of [Gielgud's] thinking as the Darwinian theory was of our fathers'. The Freudian aspects of Hamlet's character are not startling for those to whom the revelations of the psychoanalytical technique are an accepted part of thought and experience. He can see and understand as perfectly sound and accurate portraiture Hamlet's split personality, his mother-fixation, his sense of guilt, his battles that will not stay won, his desperate efforts to reconcile the conflicting elements in his psychic make-up, his tendency to unpack his heart in words, his heroism and cowardice, his final integration.[8]

Gielgud's Hamlet was in part the success it was because he embodied the 'modern man' of psychological self-consciousness.

Tyrone Guthrie's production of *Hamlet* at the Old Vic in 1937, with Laurence Olivier as a more fiery prince, was also inspired by the director's interest in Ernest Jones's ideas, and doubtless others have followed him.[9] On this issue Ivor Brown made perhaps the shrewdest comment some years later in response to the tremulous Hamlet of Michael Redgrave at the Old Vic in 1950: 'Does hesitation to murder need all the argle-bargle that the professors have bestowed on the psychology of Hamlet?'[10] But if *Hamlet* was the focus for most Freudian speculation about Shakespeare, others of his plays did not escape. Before the production of *Othello* at the Old Vic in 1937, Guthrie and Olivier took the unusual step of consulting Jones in person about the playing of Iago. For Jones,

the clue to the play was not Iago's hatred for Othello, but his deep affection for him. His jealousy was not because he envied Othello's position, not because he was in love with Desdemona, but because he himself possessed a subconscious affection for the Moor, the homosexual foundation of which he did not understand.

In this way,

the great climax in Act III, when Iago and Othello kneel together planning the death of Cassio, became virtually a love scene with Othello's 'Now art thou my lieutenant', and Iago's reply, 'I am your own forever' taking on a new significance.[11]

The result was disastrous, since Olivier's jaunty Iago seemed more of a practical joker than a tragic villain. However, Guthrie's interest in psychology also extended to *Coriolanus*, and he introduced the homosexual element into the relationship between Coriolanus and Aufidius in his Nottingham Playhouse production of 1963. This time the structure of the play was not disturbed, perhaps because the two leaders come together only twice in the play.

Work on the Elizabethan stage and audience before the Second World War proceeded apace, and the next chapter will take up this pursuit again. 1932 was the year of publication of M. C. Bradbrook's challenging Harness Prize essay of 1931, *Elizabethan Stage Conditions: A Study of their Place in the Interpretation of Shakespeare's Plays.*[12] Bradbrook's study examined first where and why Shakespeare criticism had erred. In his *Shakespeare* of 1907, one of the best of the 'English Men of Letters' series, Walter Raleigh had asserted that '[Shakespeare's] poetry has been used like wedding-cake, not to eat but to dream upon. . . . Let us make an end of this, and do justice to Shakespeare the craftsman.' In the introduction to her *Shakespeare Criticism, 1919–1935*, a collection prepared for Oxford's 'The World's Classics', Anne Bradby could look back and say that 'Shakespeare's context as it is now seen is the theatre, and England under Elizabeth'.[13] Bradbrook's contribution was to tell the story of the development of stage and historical criticism, as we have seen.[14] And she insisted that a critic must know of the conditions and conventions of playing before offering an opinion of their content. Otherwise, wrong assumptions about meaning and style were sure to follow.

Bradbrook's scholarship over many years has been to discover essentially what those conditions and conventions were. In her first book, she asked the basic questions: How can a student of Shakespeare reconstruct conventions which the dramatist merely accepted automatically? What is the effect of writing for, of working on, of watching a non-representational stage? In what way should the modern theatre approximate to its Elizabethan forerunner? What is the 'vital tradition' in which Shakespeare should be understood and played in the future? She was, of course, thinking along lines traced by Stoll and Granville-Barker, but she brought a formidable new scholarship to bear upon the fundamental questions. Some of the answers began to emerge almost immediately in her next book, *Themes and Conventions in Elizabethan Tragedy*,[15] in which the chapter headings themselves outlined the breadth of her important new interests: 'Conventions of presentation and acting', 'Conventions of action', 'Elizabethan habits of reading, writing, and listening', 'Conventions of speech'. She was concerned with communication within the medium, and what she believed to be the 'general informing conditions' of Elizabethan drama. These were to provide an apparatus of approach to the study of the plays, and she confessed that 'an attempt to understand the conventions as a whole has revolutionized my personal outlook on the Elizabethan drama'.[16]

Bradbrook went on to examine the elements of Elizabethan comedy in 1955, and the role of the actor in Elizabethan society in 1962. But before this, her ideas were brilliantly picked up by S. L. Bethell in 1944 with *Shakespeare and the Popular Dramatic Tradition,* a book which surely deserves to be re-issued.[17] Bethell's study was of Elizabethan conventions as a sign of the 'multi-consciousness' of their audience, an audience which apparently had the facility of recognizing allegory and symbol in character and scene, adjusting imaginatively to elements of realism as well as those which were highly conventional, and losing itself in the play while remaining aware of its artifice. It is appropriate to recall Dr Johnson's apparent self-contradiction: 'It is false, that any representation is mistaken for reality; that any dramatic fable in its materiality was ever credible, or, for a single moment, was ever credited,' and 'Delusion, if delusion be admitted, has no certain limitation.'[18] Bethell set himself the task of resolving the problem by looking into the raw material of the plays themselves, which in scene after scene reveal the complex ironies of simultaneous action on the great Elizabethan platform (action with which the 'split screen' of the best experimental films can hardly compare).

To judge from the elaborate, if somewhat irresponsible, stage directions which John Dover Wilson scattered through the text of *The New Shakespeare* which began to appear in 1921 under the editorship he shared with Arthur Quiller-Couch, Wilson was something of a director *manqué.* Bradbrook had scolded him in her *Elizabethan Stage Conditions* because the detail and realism of these directions seemed to supersede the descriptive poetry of the scenes themselves. When in 1934 Wilson published a two-volume study of *Hamlet* and simultaneously his edition of the text with a lengthy introduction, he astonished his readers further by publishing the next year a full-length study of the play's problems of plotting and dramatic technique, *What Happens in Hamlet.*[19] In the second edition of this book in 1937, Wilson, greatly daring, stated a fresh critical position:

My book was written . . . to raise issues which will, I hope, after further discussion and experiment in the theatre, lead to the clearer understanding of Shakespeare's purposes and the better playing of *Hamlet.* If it does that, it will have fulfilled its aim, even if every notion within its covers proves to be unworkable on the stage. For it is with the stage that the final decision rests.

And he insisted that both the director and the critic of Shakespeare should possess a competent knowledge of Elizabethan stage conditions:

> Without such knowledge, the man of the theatre, however accomplished
> be his production of modern plays, is a blind guide so far as Shakespeare
> is concerned. Scarcely less dangerous, on questions of stage-technique, is
> the judgment of the man of the study who lacks direct theatrical experience,
> however learned a scholar he may be.[20]

What is perhaps even more remarkable is that the book provoked new
productions of this, the most overworked play in the canon, almost
immediately.

What Happens in Hamlet turned over hoary problems like the madness of the Prince and the credibility of the Ghost, whether Hamlet
knew that the King and Polonius were eavesdropping on his fiery
encounter with Ophelia, and why Claudius did not explode upon
seeing the dumb show. These discussions would excite little comment
here, were it not that Wilson refreshingly declared that he would seek
'a *dramatic* reason' in each case.[21] And he did so only after a year's
exchange of almost weekly letters with no less a theatre-man than
Granville-Barker, who happened to be writing his *Hamlet* preface at
the time. Hamlet's 'antic disposition' and its several manifestations
were argued as partly deliberate and partly involuntary: 'In a word,
Shakespeare wishes us to feel that Hamlet assumed madness because
he cannot help it'.[22] In the 'fishmonger' episode (ii.ii), Wilson believed
that Hamlet must have heard what Polonius said to the King about
loosing his daughter to him: the conspirators could be downstage when
Polonius spoke what seemed to be a stage direction for Hamlet's
entrance to an inner-stage, 'You know sometimes he walks four
hours together/Here in the lobby'. By this eavesdropping device,
Hamlet's discovery of the plot 'renders the nunnery scene playable
and intelligible as never before'.[23] Less plausibly, Wilson argued that
Shakespeare introduced the dumb show (iii.ii) in order that the
audience should have all the 'facts' it needs before the play proper
begins, but that Claudius, who 'must be lured gradually and unconsciously into the trap',[24] must not see it. Rather, he had been distracted by Hamlet's outrageous conduct with Ophelia, so that the
pantomime was performed 'entirely unnoticed' by the throne.

Dover Wilson's suggestions were put to the test the very next year,
1936, by the Cambridge Marlowe Society, but the success of the new

interpretations remained in dispute. That summer, *Hamlet* was also played at Stratford. Ben Iden Payne, another disciple of William Poel, and a director academically inclined, had succeeded Bridges-Adams in 1935. Like Poel, he aimed at a rattling Elizabethan pace, and on the Stratford stage set a penthouse roof on two pillars to form a curtained inner-stage. The resulting mock-Elizabethan above and below, inner and outer, acting areas gave him the speed and continuity he wanted. He scorned eccentric stagecraft, had a fondness for Elizabethan costume and tried for an authentic simplicity and flexibility. In the fishmonger scene, the Hamlet of Donald Wolfit was glimpsed upstage with his book on the implicit direction 'he walks four hours together', and then made a full entrance in the usual place. It was enough to suggest that he had overheard the plot. The Play Scene was confused by a stage composition flattened by the proscenium arch, but Payne invented the business of having Hamlet stop Claudius from seeing the dumb show by rushing from his place and pushing the script under his nose.

In 1937, Michael MacOwan directed the play at the Westminster Theatre. His was an avowed attempt to work out Wilson's ideas in practice, and the changes were publicly debated after the production. Harold Child reported that the actor playing Hamlet (Christopher Oldham) could express in performance both that Hamlet's antic disposition was put on for particular ends and that he was also, up to a point, mad: the best of both worlds. Child also found convincing MacOwan's arrangement for Hamlet's earlier entrance in the fishmonger scene in order to show that he had overheard Polonius's plot: 'It gave certainty and point to Hamlet's attack on Polonius, and prepared clearly for a dangerous mood that in the Nunnery Scene would not spare any slip that Ophelia might make.'[25] Again, the Play Scene at the Westminster proved very little, probably because the two-dimensional quality of the proscenium stage, even without scenery, disallowed those actor–audience lines of tension which come naturally to the three-dimensional platform for which the scene was written. Polonius (Cecil Trouncer) merely seemed to be purposely blocking Claudius's view of the dumb show. However, the fact that the whole scene was played, and that the director had a clear idea of what he wanted it to mean, 'seemed to make the poison–moustrap–murder–nephew dialogue blaze like lightning'.[26]

In the thirties the world of scholarship must have been gratified to feel that the stage was paying it so much attention. The historical study of the theatre and its Elizabethan context was pursued vigorously and productively by G. B. Harrison, and the several volumes of his *Elizabethan Journals* and *Jacobean Journals* began to appear from 1928, bringing to life in day-by-day accounts the events which were the background to the plays. When in 1934 Harrison joined with Granville-Barker, scholar with actor, to produce *A Companion to Shakespeare Studies*, a book which dealt with both academic and practical matters and received widespread acclaim, a new era seemed to have arrived. This impulse by stage and study to join forces culminated in an extraordinary gesture ten years later. In 1944, John Gielgud asked George Rylands of King's College, Cambridge, and director of the Cambridge Marlowe Society, to produce his *Hamlet* at the Haymarket; and in 1945, he asked Nevill Coghill of Exeter College, Oxford, and director of the Oxford University Drama Society, to produce *A Midsummer Night's Dream*, also at the Haymarket. After the war, university men were to flow into the directorial ranks of the Royal Shakespeare Company. Unhappily, the war was soon to divert energy from the pursuit of Shakespeare on the stage, but not before another powerful diversion had long since begun to distract the Shakespearian scholar.

When in 1941 the southern American poet and critic John Crowe Ransom published *The New Criticism*, he gave a name to a movement in literary criticism which had been gathering force since 1924, when I. A. Richards published *The Principles of Literary Criticism*. The movement had swept both Europe and America: in America it was associated with Allen Tate, R. P. Blackmur, Robert Penn Warren and Cleanth Brooks writing in *The Southern Review, The Sewanee Review* and *The Kenyon Review*; in France with the pre-1914 criticism of Rémy de Gourmont, leader of the *symboliste* critics writing in *Mercure de France*, and the development of *explication de texte* as a method; in England with the criticism of T. S. Eliot, followed by Richards's pupil William Empson, F. R. Leavis and L. C. Knights of the Cambridge *Scrutiny* group. A 'new critic', reacting against the undisciplined comments of *belles-lettrists*, believed that a work of literature should ideally be examined and judged as an object in itself, without reference to the personality of its author, the facts of its composition, its historical context, the audience its author intended or its effect upon them. He attempted to arrive at critical judgments by the close analysis of language, since he held that a work of literature communicates only in its own terms. The intense semantic scrutiny of the new critics undoubtedly worked wonders for our understanding of poetry – it produced the apotheosis of the lyric poem – and was surprisingly adaptable to prose fiction; it produced exciting insights into the nature of imagery and symbolism; but it stumbled badly when confronted with drama.

The first failure of the new critical attempt to analyze a play was its inability to recognize that a play is not made of words alone. The infinite variety of visual and aural signals in drama includes gesture and movement and visual relationships, acting style and the living character, voice and tone and pace, as well as the complexities of verbal meaning. Signals from the stage embrace colour and costume and music; they are chosen to shape dramatic form, establish dramatic genre, manipulate a plot; they reckon with a particular playhouse and a particular audience, often a particular acting company and a particular actor. While it is possible to read a poem as a linguistic or symbolic entity, our understanding of a play must take into account its physical and historical milieu, and the pressures upon it from wholly external sources – perhaps governmental, economic, religious, political, cultural or sociological forces both national and local. The intentions of the author of a play and the expectations of its audience are absolutely relevant to any value judgment passed upon it. If the new criticism insisted upon the autonomy of the text, drama as an art form demands attention to the primacy of context.

The importance of the poetry in Shakespeare goes without question, and the interest it generated in our own time and earlier is completely understandable. Yet in one sense it has been our greatest delusion. Shakespeare's poetry is first a stage tool, and the worth of the countless studies of his words is to be measured by their success in revealing this. The study of language can, like that of the physical sciences, be pure or applied. The texture of Shakespeare's verse indicates the delicacy of his mind, but in the theatre laboratory it reveals his character's mind, and the actor-in-the-character, since a work of *dramatic* literature communicates only in *its* own terms. Thus, in writing exquisitely of Shakespeare's 'incessant victory over language' in *The Problem of Style* (London, 1922), and of 'his unprecedented power of keeping this overcharged, exploded, tense, swollen language supple under his fingers',[27] John

Middleton Murry failed to ask what work it must perform. In writing of Shakespeare's use of metaphor in *Countries of the Mind, Second Series* (London, 1931), Murry produced a brilliant essay on his audacious images, vivid sense-perceptions and the unifying relationships between his verbal ideas. But Murry was still concerned only with the mystery of how Shakespeare reduced what Coleridge considered 'multitude to unity', and he wove his own nimble word patterns upon Shakespeare's.

However, when George Rylands examined the development of Shakespeare's style from the early to the mature plays in *Words and Poetry* (London, 1928), he was able to show that the earlier plays were in fact weak in dramatic movement: 'there are no *gestures*, as it were, and little variety of speed'. He observed how the graceful paradoxes of the early 'artificial' style gave way to Shakespeare's sense of character and dramatic realism:

Beside Berowne place Richard III, Hotspur, the Bastard. They all speak with the same accent; they are all realistic, commonsensical, prosaic, energetic figures. They take the verse into their own hands and break down the barriers of diction. . . . These voices demanded a new medium, verse which will allow colloquial emphases and prose order.[28]

In writing of the mature style, 'packed with matter, a style that could gallop at a touch, with freer rhythms and higher emotional pressure', Rylands was arguing for the quality which gave the plays their dramatic vitality. Shakespeare's true dexterity with words was demonstrated through character and actor and the sense-perceptions of an audience.

After this, the playgoer might rightly have felt a certain unease to have read I.A. Richards writing of *Hamlet* in an appendix on the poetry of T.S. Eliot:

The truth is that very much of the best poetry is necessarily ambiguous in its immediate effect. Even the most careful and responsive reader must reread and do hard work before the poem forms itself clearly and unambiguously in his mind.[29]

This was an invitation to approach a play as would an analytical critic a poem – and a seventeenth-century metaphysical poem at that. And if Richards related Shakespeare to Donne and Eliot, F.R. Leavis linked him with Gerard Manley Hopkins.[30] In his polemical *Education and the*

University, Leavis pursued his attack on the character studies of Brad-leyan criticism by making this alarming statement: 'At an early stage, then, the attempt should be made to apply seriously the axiom that poetry is made of words to the reading of Shakespeare.'[31] He then demonstrated his position by analyzing Banquo's 'temple-haunting martlet' speech to show that its effect was 'to a great extent independent of the speaker', and only in parentheses acknowledged that it was Shakespeare's choice of this particular speaker which makes the speech ironically ominous. William Empson found verbal ambiguity every-where in Shakespeare, who supplied him with text after text for his analytical studies in *Seven Types of Ambiguity* (1930); but he nowhere considered how ambiguities spoken from the stage might produce a desirable dramatic ambivalence in a playgoer, ambivalence of the kind that creates a participatory, not a passive, auditory.

Taking his cue from a note in A.C. Bradley's *Shakespearean Tragedy,* L.C. Knights chose the provocative title 'How Many Children had Lady Macbeth?' (1933) in order to launch the first frontal attack on the character-study approach of the nineteenth century. This essay in-cluded a fine verbal reconstruction of *Macbeth* as a poem of evil and disorder, but Knights gratuitously asserted that the only valid approach to poetic drama was through the poetry, as these selected statements show:

The only profitable approach to Shakespeare is a consideration of his plays as dramatic poems, of his use of language to obtain a total emotional response. The total response to a Shakespeare play can only be obtained by an exact and sensitive study of the quality of the verse, of the rhythm and imagery, of the controlled associations of the words and their emotional and intel-lectual force.

We start with so many lines of verse on a printed page which we read as we should read any other poem.

The apprehension of the whole can be obtained from a lively attention to the parts, whether they have an immediate bearing on the main action or 'il-lustrate character' or not.[32]

The validity of such criticism must depend upon what a play is taken to be. Knights has since withdrawn from this extreme position, and J. I. M. Stewart has also argued[33] for more balance in judgment, pointing out that this treatment would not only give *Hamlet* without the Prince, but the complete works without their *dramatis personae.*

In the same vein as the work of L.C. Knights, another 'Scrutineer', D.A. Traversi, published the first of several editions of *An Approach to Shakespeare* in 1938, praised by Leavis as 'by far the best introduction' to the critical study of Shakespeare.[34] Traversi also questioned the Victorian insistence on the centrality of character, believing it to have its foundation in Romanticism and a subjective reading of literature:

> *Hamlet* the tragedy — to take the stock example — became, when considered in the light of this tradition, a fruitful mirror for the dissatisfaction of the romantic self, and even the greatest students of the plays . . . found it difficult to avoid confusing Shakespeare's aims with their own often quite different concerns.[35]

Traversi also believed that the study of Shakespeare must begin with the words, 'the language through which [the total] impact makes itself most immediately felt in any given moment'.[36] He would then proceed to incorporate the word into the verse structure to which it belonged, examine how it conveyed character, and build this and other aspects into the complete concept of a dramatic action. He rightly insisted that 'no analysis of the first stage, *the word*, that does not illuminate some part of the last, the complete *dramatic action*, can be valid', and writing some thirty years after his first *Approach*, urged that this kind of reading should be done in the context of Shakespeare's own stage: 'The stress laid in the preceding argument on the dramatic action implies, as a necessary corollary, awareness that the plays were written for the stage, and for a given type of stage at that.'[37] He acknowledged that the neutral stage of the Elizabethans concentrated attention on the action, not on spectacle, and that its conventions were not limitations, but a source of life permitting the poetic impulse to flower with the greatest intensity. Alas, Traversi's insistence on the stage was merely paying lip service to Granville-Barker, and whatever theatrical test or effect is applied as a check against his understanding of the plays — an audience's realization that Poor Tom is really only Edgar in disguise, that Gloucester 'falls' on his face on a flat stage when he tries to jump from Dover Cliff, that Viola and Olivia are to be seen as two boys in their wooing scenes, that the level of the farce in *Twelfth Night* determines our judgment on Malvolio — Traversi seems blind to point after point which is transparent on the stage.

The thirties were a period rich in the study of Shakespeare on the page, and in the middle of the decade occurred an event which gave analytical new criticism its stamp of scientific authority. Caroline Spurgeon had lectured to the Shakespeare Association on the 'Leading Motives in the Imagery of Shakespeare's Tragedies' in 1930, and argued that recurrent images played a part in raising, developing, sustaining and repeating emotion in the tragedies, on analogy to recurrent motifs in music — images of light in *Romeo and Juliet* and of disease in *Hamlet*, for example, offer a suggestion about the 'texture' of each play and its atmosphere in performance, designed to control an audience's response. In 1935 Spurgeon presented the results of an exhaustive indexing of the images in *Shakespeare's Imagery and What It Tells Us*. Her book reported strange and alarming things about William: he did not like spaniels; he blushed easily; and so forth. Much of this improper psychoanalysis must now seem naive, but Spurgeon's initial work inspired others to follow more profitable ways: statistics were interpreted to show how images could inform and direct drama in action. The dramatic function of the imagery received more attention in Wolfgang Clemen's *Shakespeares Bilder: Ihre Entwicklung und Ihre Funktionen im dramatischen Werk*,[38] in which he traced Shakespeare's style from its early decorative figures to the more organic, functional imagery of the mature plays, and recognized how it contributed to character, plot and mood, and pulled a play together. At about the same time, Una Ellis-Fermor began writing about the imagery of the Jacobean playwrights, including Shakespeare, and her essay 'The Function of Imagery in Drama'[39] succinctly summarized what contributions imagery could make to a play on the stage: it could be dynamic like the action itself. She asked the question, 'Can we . . . describe what are or have been some of the functions by which imagery helps drama to overcome the limitations inherent in its brevity?' And she argued that verbal imagery increased dramatic concentration, indicated the underlying mood, anticipated the course of the action itself, revealed character rapidly and vividly, and could supply a process of argument or reflection without diluting the dramatic concentration.

In spite of this more constructive approach to Shakespeare's poetic method, H.B. Charlton had been previously led to make a stern protest:

The present trend to fashionable criticism appears to have little use even for drama. To our most modern coteries, drama is poetry or it is nothing; and by poetry they mean some sort of allegorical arabesque in which the images of Shakespeare's plays are far more important than their men and women. . . . To our simple sense the actors . . . look more or less like human beings; where-fore, to consider them as images of men and women seems the safest way of trying to understand them.[40]

Charlton was at the time writing about the comedies, which lend themselves less to the business of image-hunting, if for no other reason than they often contain a large proportion of prose. It is true that the new criticism risked its excesses more than most, but by this time there had been one other major critical development, one which seem-ed on the surface to bypass the theatre entirely, but which on closer inspection may well lead directly back to the stage. This was the 'symbolic' interpretation associated with the writing of G. Wilson Knight, himself an actor and director of Shakespeare.

Wilson Knight's work on Shakespeare frequently bordered on myst-icism, and yet in the end he may prove to be the one great critic of the century who pointed the way for post-war directors. This paradox remains to be explored. Certainly the effect of his criticism was all-pervasive during and after the thirties. After reading him, even a pragmatic Shakespearian like Dover Wilson could say in 1936 that 'the true meaning of dramatic poetry is only just beginning to be revealed to us' and spoke of the plays as 'dramatic symphonies': 'I call them sym-phonies, and think of them in terms of orchestration, counterpoint, *leitmotiv* and the rest, because the language appropriate to musical composition seems to me less misleading than any other.'[41] For all the obscurity of Knight's thinking, its fever was infectious, and few judges would now deny him his place as the most disturbing and sed-uctive critic of recent years. For those who searched for a pattern for the understanding of Shakespeare, he supplied one.

Bradley had spoken loosely of the 'worlds' of Lear and Macbeth, each coloured by an insistent mood and poetic ambience. *King Lear*'s world, for example, was one of pervasive gloom, and he wrote of

the vastness of the convulsion both of nature and of human passion; the vagueness of the scene where the action takes place, and of the movements of the figures which cross this scene; the strange atmosphere, cold and dark, which strikes on us as we enter this scene, enfolding these figures and magnify-ing their dim outlines like a winter mist; the half-realised suggestions of univ-ersal powers working in the world of individual fates and passions. . . .[42]

It was in this context that Bradley remarkably anticipated Spurgeon by drawing attention to the play's constant reference to animals and man's

Criticism: retreat and advance

likeness to them. And when Bradley found *Lear* 'overloaded', it was also as if he were anticipating T.S.Eliot's criticism in *The Sacred Wood* (1920) of the deficiency in *Hamlet* as a play 'dominated by an emotion which is inexpressible'. From this argument Eliot evolved the idea of a play's 'objective correlative', the formula of elements which would evoke the particular emotion its author desired. Knight's dramatic symphonies, informed by recurrent images and evoking a particular atmosphere at some remove from reality, were in the direct line of succession. His essays, abstract as they seem to be, were his attempts to render and reconstruct his sense of the impact of each play.

Knight was proposing a view of a Shakespeare play in which its effect as a symbolic whole was greater than the sum of its parts. Michael Black has likened this approach to Wagner's theories of a 'music drama':

Wilson Knight presents the poetic drama almost as *Gesamtkunstwerk*. That seems just: if a profound sense of the potentialities of poetic drama underlies Wagner's criticism and practice, it is only sensible to reflect him back on poetic drama. The seamless structure of themes, symphonically elaborated; the over-all unity to which all elements are subordinated; the idea of a tonality or characteristic atmosphere pervading a whole drama; the idea of the relationship between single dramas; the idea that the characters are, as it were, constellated, that they 'refer' to each other — in a word, the organic form: these concepts were effectively brought back into English Shakespeare criticism by Wilson Knight.[43]

The notion of poetic drama as a form of music came easily to Knight: he had no need for verisimilitude when in search of patterns[44] rather than plots, texture rather than characters. *Othello* immediately loses its terrestrial domesticity in a chapter uncompromisingly labelled 'The *Othello* Music', but it loses much of its particularity as well, those individual touches of behaviour and characterization which have always sparked Shakespeare to life on any stage. Fellow critics were quick to attack Knight's inclination to move immediately into a world of metaphorical abstractions. Stoll found that this kind of criticism, like Bradley's, was an elaborate game of second-guessing the playwright's intentions. In *Shakespearian Tragedy* (1948), H.B. Charlton challenged the assumption that the critic must 'cut below the crust' to arrive at the meaning of a play: he questioned whether 'the crust has not itself some meaning'. As with Bradley, it was all too easy to argue from one's own responses, themselves formed according to one's own ethic, and not from the play itself. Both Bradley and Knight were guilty of this kind of sentimentality, and in committing this sin both were also guilty of bleeding Shakespeare's drama of its characteristically direct and particular human interest, the very quality which made it stageworthy.

The stage-study paradox showed itself from the start. What Knight called his 'manifesto' appeared in 1928 as an essay entitled 'The Principles of Shakespeare Interpretation',[45] in which he argued that all the elements of a Shakespeare play were controlled by its central 'vision':

It will be found that each play thus expresses a particular and peculiar vision of human existence, and that this vision determines not alone the choice of the main plot, but the selection or invention of subsidiary scenes and characters, the matters brought up for discussion within the scenes, and the very fibre of the language.[46]

He was making a plea for the understanding of the total work and its source of inspiration as drama, and he called, not for criticism, but for 'interpretation'. Soon after (1929) came another short study, *Myth and Miracle: An Essay on the Symbolism of Shakespeare*, which discussed the final plays. The experience of these plays, he believed, denied the reader or playgoer any simple interest in character or plot, but pointed to a profound spiritual revelation of life's values. And the following year his best-known book, *The Wheel of Fire*, offered an initial chapter, 'On the Principles of Shakespeare Interpretation', which re-stated the position that although Shakespeare worked within the dramatic form and needed the stage, the student must go beyond them:

Nor will a sound knowledge of the stage and the especial theatrical technique of Shakespeare's work render up its imaginative secret. True, the plays were written as plays, and meant to be acted. But that tells us nothing relevant to our purpose. . . . Shakespeare wrote in terms of drama, as he wrote in English. In the grammar of dramatic structure he expresses his vision: without that, or some other, structure he could not have expressed himself . . . but a true philosophic and imaginative interpretation will aim at cutting below the surface to reveal that burning core of mental or spiritual reality from which each play derives its nature and meaning.[47]

Knight was well aware of the paradox, and in a prefatory note to *The Wheel of Fire* in 1947 he wrote,

My own major interest has always been Shakespeare in the theatre; and to that

176

my written work has been, in my own mind, subsidiary. But my experience as actor, producer and play-goer leaves me uncompromising in my assertion that the literary analysis of great drama in terms of theatrical technique accomplishes singularly little. Such technicalities should be confined to the theatre from which their terms are drawn. The proper thing to do about a play's dramatic quality is to produce it, to act in it, to attend performances; but the penetration of its deeper meanings is a different matter, and such a study, though the commentator should certainly be dramatically aware, and even wary, will not itself speak in theatrical terms. There is, of course, an all-important relation (which I discuss fully in my *Principles of Shakespearian Production*); and indeed the present standard of Shakespearian production appears to me inadequate precisely because these deeper meanings have not been exploited. The play's surface has been merely translated from book to stage, it has not been re-created from within; and that is why our productions remain inorganic.[48]

The 'organic' production of Shakespeare was yet possibly to appear at the hands of Tyrone Guthrie and Peter Brook.

Knight wrote voluminous commentaries on the plays. Yet his notion of interpretation curiously echoes the kind of full experience of Shakespeare one can have in the theatre, as Knight himself indicated:

We should not, in fact, think critically at all: we should interpret our original imaginative experience into the slower consciousness of logic and intellect, preserving something of that child-like faith which we possess, or should possess, in the theatre.[49]

The playgoer receives the poet's vision uncritically and passively if he goes to the theatre for enjoyment, and in talking about the experience afterwards, he will 'interpret' it in his own, non-dramatic, terms. It is this sense of an imaginative experience that led Knight to speak of poetic drama's being set *spatially* as well as temporally in the mind, its parts relating to each other independently of the time-sequence of the plot, determining its 'atmosphere'. As we appreciate the play more deeply, there is a continual widening of vision until we 'own' the play with our mind more surely. We seek the 'reality' of the play, which is omnipresent in the movement of its space and time pattern. Its manner is therefore essentially non-illusory (in the way that this term has been used in this book), and a character does not have to be discovered through motive as in real life, nor judged by ethical values as if he were actually alive. Interpretation is thus 'metaphysical', attempting to recreate the visionary whole through its qualities of poetic symbolism.

We should not look for perfect verisimilitude to life, but rather see each play as an expanded metaphor, by means of which the original vision has been projected into forms roughly correspondent with actuality, conforming thereto with greater or less exactitude according to the demands of its own nature.[50]

The originality of Knight's thinking seemed grandiose to many, and fraught with the danger of having the critic superimpose his own ideas upon those of the playwright; but Knight claimed no more than that this was what interpretation amounted to, in or out of the theatre.

Knight's approach would have seemed even more perilous, if he had not grounded his thinking in the practical experience of the theatre itself. He constantly challenged his own views by returning the play to the theatre: this is part of the paradox. He directed and acted in the great tragedies at Hart House Theatre, Toronto, while serving as Chancellor's Professor of English at Trinity College between 1931 and 1940, and he also directed *Hamlet* at the Rudolf Steiner Theatre, London, in 1935. He recognized, both in writing and performance, the status of *Timon of Athens* as one of the central dramatic statements of Shakespeare's career, finding in Timon 'Promethean radiations'. He was thus from the beginning prepared to pursue his theories on the stage itself, and in the midst of his quite prolific sequence of critical studies, he wrote two books on the production of Shakespeare.

The first of these, *Principles of Shakespearian Production*, appeared in 1936, and was an apt complement to his previous manifestoes for Shakespeare criticism. Where in his criticism he stressed the rhythmic structure of a play, he also urged this upon the director:

The Shakespearian movement, whether of a whole play, or a scene, or a speech, undulates: it shows a rhythmic rise and fall. There are vast waves of action, and, within each, subtler minute crests and cusps, a ceaseless rippling variation.[51]

Knight illustrated his point by tracing the action in *Hamlet*. He was aware of the effects of pace, and of the dramatic juxtaposition of scenes. He emphasized the sensory quality of Shakespeare's 'symbolic solidity', citing the apparitions which crystallized the main action in *Macbeth*, the handkerchief in *Othello* and the caskets in *The Merchant of Venice*. He was sharply aware of the aural music of the lines, with the effect, too, of a sudden colloquialism cutting into the poetry, and he acknowledged the profound impact of music in the plays. Above all, he insisted that the director interpret the elusive 'spatial and temporal' sense of a Shakespeare play by the use of 'a properly conventionalized stage area' which would 'fuse' the mixture of particular and universal qualities found in Shakespeare's peculiar kind of poetic drama.

If all this seemed to be a counsel of perfection for the floundering director, Knight's same book gave him the following staggering advice:

He has to get the play from the text on to the living stage. It is rather like moving a delicate piece of furniture or machinery. Carry it bodily across and bits will be broken off. It must be carefully taken to pieces and rebuilt. The producer should be able to hold the play in jig-saw bits in his mind, to sort them all out, to build with them and re-create the whole from understanding of its nature. Such understanding gives him full powers to cut, adapt, even, on rare occasions, transpose, according to circumstances; he has to consider his stage, his company, his audience. The feeling that cutting is sacrilegious derives from a totally false reasoning. The producer's business is not translation, but re-creation.[52]

No one dared cry blasphemy to the man who had written *The Wheel of Fire*, *The Imperial Theme* and *The Shakespearian Tempest*.

The apparent contradiction between Knight's call for recognition of Shakespeare's symbolic qualities and for their representation, their 'interpretation', on the stage is well in accord with a recent article by Knight on 'Symbolism',[53] in which he reiterated that Shakespeare's symbolic meaning must be read with 'a stage eye': we should mend our partial understanding of Shakespeare's complexities and seek the total experience, by allowing the theatre to do its own kind of work upon us 'as drama'. The new authenticity had nothing to do with Elizabethan playhouse reconstructions or an adherence to the exact text, but the grand purpose was to reveal in a new medium the central idea of the original. Writing in 1955, Alfred Harbage declared that Knight might 'stand as spokesman for the *interpretive* producer' and found him a 'truly formidable' influence.[54] The paradox was complete. It remained to be seen whether a director would yet emerge who could re-create Knight's ideas on the professional stage. Today, in a review of modern Shakespeare criticism, Stanley Wells can say with modest caution, but with fair assurance, that 'criticism based on a strong sense of the play as something that is *incomplete* until it is performed seems likely to grow in importance'.[55]

10

Guthrie and the open stage

Sir Tyrone Guthrie's place in this story may not be underestimated. Historians of our understanding of Shakespeare will remember him for the enthusiasm and authority he brought to the building of new playhouses for Shakespeare, structures which he tested in the only way possible — by mounting plays in them himself; they will remember him, too, for his determination to return to the artifice of performance in order to restore Shakespeare to his own mode of ritual.

Guthrie was always the apparent eccentric. 'Artistic or, for that matter, administrative achievements', he declared, 'are only to be had by sticking your neck out as far as ever it will go'.[1] From the beginning he invited criticism for the business and fun he wilfully interpolated in performance, his touches of parody and pastiche.[2] When censured for his impertinence, he could respond cheekily that he had 'merely added one more comment to the vast corpus of criticism, admiration, revulsion, reverence, love and so on, with which a masterpiece of human expression is rightly surrounded'.[3] But this iconoclasm was merely a more obtrusive part of his philosophy of theatre, which insisted that the purely literary approach to drama was inadequate:

Scholars have performed service of inestimable value in the elucidation of textual difficulties and in the discussion of many problems, primarily in the literary and intellectual fields. But there are limits to the purely intellectual and literary criticism of works which are intended to be realized in theatrical drama.

One of the minor tragedies of the historical development of European culture has been the divorce between the theatrical performance and the literary study of drama.

Drama is still academically charted as a backwater in the main stream of English literature. In schools and universities the fact that Shakespeare, Ben Jonson, Congreve and Sheridan were men of the theatre is still overshadowed by their status as men of letters. And their works, as well as those of other

180

dramatists, are still studied as literature. This is, of course, a more convenient and infinitely less expensive way of studying them.[4]

Guthrie was a true student of Shakespeare, one who never ceased to worry at the issues provoked by his desire to understand, explore and enjoy him fully in performance.

He started from the position taken by most post-Barker directors of Shakespeare. He had first to size up the real achievement of his great Victorian predecessors: they had made what he called 'dramatic cathedrals' of the plays, elaborate monuments regarded with reverence. And he attributed their booming, bellowing manner of performance, commonly regarded as 'the Shakespeare tradition' and embodying a correct grandeur, to the huge theatres in which they were played. 'The subtlety, intimacy, and elaborate detail which are apparent in the study entirely disappear in the theatre.'[5] He was soon to rebel against the vast emporia of the Victorians by going into the building business himself. But along with his concern for the appropriate 'scale' for Shakespeare went his interest in the appropriate style. For Guthrie, naturalism was the paradoxical attempt to make fictitious characters seem as real as possible by means of literal imitation: this was not the purpose of the theatre. Just as the painter desired, not to imitate, but to interpret nature when he recognized that the camera could achieve a better likeness, so by looking at the cinema Guthrie began to see where the real magic of the theatre lay: 'It was, I discovered, charming, interesting and exciting not the nearer it approached "reality", but the farther it retreated into its own sort of artifice.'[6]

It may seem contradictory that Guthrie also followed the current vogue of interpreting Shakespeare's major figures by psychology. We saw in the last chapter how he doggedly pursued Ernest Jones in order to present Olivier at the Old Vic as an Oedipal Hamlet and a homosexual Iago. Unluckily for the *Othello* of 1937, Ralph Richardson as the Moor was embarrassed and inhibited by Olivier's obscure affection for him, and Guthrie admitted that the production was 'a ghastly, boring hash'. Yet to the end he insisted upon Hamlet's inner conflict, a 'love' scene between Coriolanus and Aufidius ('In a relationship somewhere between a son and a lover he throws himself on the mercy of Aufidius'[7]), that Brutus regarded Caesar as a father-figure, and that in the trial scene of *The Merchant of Venice* Portia was aware that Antonio loved Bassanio. However, this search for reality of hidden motives in Shakespeare's plays did not constitute a realism of style, any more than Sophocles himself invites a realistic performance because he was writing of Oedipus's intimate relationship with Jocasta.

Guthrie's reaction against the false realism of the proscenium arch was quite in line with the theories of Granville-Barker and William Poel, whom he had read and approved.

We would follow Poel and Barker and Shaw, make no cuts merely to suit the exigencies of stage carpenters, have no scenery except a 'structure', which would offer the facilities usually supposed to have been available in the Elizabethan theatres: stairs, leading to a balcony; underneath, a cubbyhole in which intimate scenes can occur and where, concealed by a curtain, thrones, beds and so on may be stored.

This structure would serve as a permanent background throughout the play, thereby eliminating tiresome pauses while scenery was changed, eliminating the 'front scenes' with the actors standing in a line like ornaments on a chimney-piece.[8]

Backgrounds were to make no concession to pictorial realism, and avoid at all cost 'the impertinence of parodying Shakespeare's verbal indications in canvas and paint'. During his years with the Old Vic, Guthrie recalled that there was plenty of talk about 'good clean lines', and he early reached a simple conclusion:

The ideal house for Shakespeare must be designed so that every spectator is near enough to the stage to enable the actor to use the full range of his voice from a shout to a whisper; to speak, when necessary, as fast as ever he can, and to mime the action with the subtlety and delicacy which it deserves.[9]

His success in achieving the ideal house for Shakespeare was to be determined in the years after the war when he began his experiments at Edinburgh and Stratford, Ontario.

Behind this concern with the physical conditions of performance lay far-reaching principles. Guthrie believed that the drama makes its effects, not by creating illusion, but by means of what he thought of as 'ritual', and he planned his stage upon the uncompromising theory that illusion was not the aim of performance. In particular, although Shakespeare was outstanding for 'the minute observation and precise record of individual character and mannerism', he was 'only intermittently concerned with realism'. Hence Guthrie's self-inflicted laws:

182

Actual indications of time, place, atmosphere and so on, must be avoided; as must a reduction of great tragic conceptions to life-size; or no less damaging, a reduction of romances — *The Winter's Tale*, for instance, or *As You Like It* — to make them plausible. One of the charms of a tall tale is its very tallness.[10]

This explains his delight at Gielgud's *The Merchant of Venice* at the Old Vic in 1932, which he found gay and elegant, witty and sophisticated, light as a feather: 'beside it Maugham and Coward seemed like two Nonconformist pastors from the Midlands'. It also explains his constant desire to give his audiences a good time for the price of their ticket: not only the pleasure of the play, but 'they want to feel that for a brief and glittering three hours they have bought, and therefore own, something largely, loudly, unashamedly luxurious'.[11]

Guthrie's criticism was all that of a man of practice: he judged by results. This complemented his belief that 'all performance is equally a comment upon, as well as a recreation of, the work performed.'[12] His first *Love's Labour's Lost* at the Westminster Theatre in 1932 was offered as a masque, with Navarre's court in red and the Princess and her ladies in green. Four years later at the Old Vic he presented the same play as a brisk Watteau-esque pastoral: the search was for a style and a mood to match a young comedy lightly observing the follies of young love. Writing of the play in a modest chapter subtitled 'The Story of a Conversion',[13] John Dover Wilson claimed that this production altered the whole tenor of modern criticism on this comedy. Both he and H. B. Charlton had edited the text and found it wanting: made up of so many moribund quibbles, without characterization worthy the name, based upon a patently absurd oath of celibacy. But 'we had missed the whole art and meaning of it'. Guthrie's production

revealed it as a first-rate comedy of the pattern kind — so full of fun, of *permanent* wit, of brilliant and entrancing situation, that you hardly noticed the faded jesting and allusion, as you sat spell-bound and drank it all in. It was a thrilling production, Shakespearian criticism of the best kind, because a real piece of restoration. ... Mr. Guthrie not only gave me a new play, the existence of which I had never suspected, which indeed had been veiled from men's eyes for three centuries, but he set me at a fresh standpoint of understanding and appreciation from which the whole of Shakespearian comedy might be reviewed in a new light.

Wilson, and with him his mentor A. W. Pollard, the pioneer of modern textual studies of Shakespeare, that night discovered the play's vivacity and variety, and with them the dramatic reasons for the patent absurdity of its plot and characterization and surface frivolity.

In 1933 Guthrie had begun an association with the Old Vic which lasted intermittently until 1956. He was already aware of the necessity for a stage which would better serve Shakespeare's speed and variety, and in his first season, 1933–4, he directed *Twelfth Night*, *Henry VIII*, *Measure for Measure*, *The Tempest* and *Macbeth* — an astonishing range — on its architecturally designed permanent set. Dressing this set and its actors appropriately was to be the creative exercise to reveal the distinguishing quality in each play. The results were sometimes more bizarre than revelatory. The set suited the pomp of *Henry VIII* and the castles of *Macbeth*, but reduced Prospero's island in *The Tempest* to 'a log and a few strands of seaweed'[14] and became obtrusively modern for *Twelfth Night*: 'Painted pinky-grey for *Twelfth Night*, our opening production, it completely dominated the evening and suggested not Illyria but a fancy-dress ball on a pink battleship.'[15]

The *Hamlet* of 1937 at the Old Vic culminated in a happy serendipity of far-reaching consequence for Guthrie and the development of Shakespeare production. This was the Oedipal performance, with the Olivier energy scaling and leaping the structure on the stage. Its success in London was rewarded in the spring by a visit to the original castle of Elsinore in Denmark, where the Old Vic set was built again in the cobbled courtyard. But the opening night was disastrously rained out and for the Danish royal party Guthrie bravely improvised his production in the ballroom of a nearby hotel. The need to accommodate sufficient chairs for the audience forced almost an arena performance upon the company, which found itself playing in the middle of the dance floor — with miraculous results which Guthrie could not forget. With the audience seated round the players as in a circus, the weaknesses of the proscenium stage were sharply revealed:

At its best moments that performance in the ballroom related the audience to a Shakespeare play in a different, and I thought, more logical, satisfactory and effective way than can ever be achieved in a theatre of what is still regarded as orthodox design.[16]

In fact, the Danish audience recovered its primary function, itself becoming part of the play.

Guthrie and the open stage

Back at the Old Vic for the last seasons before the war, Guthrie continued his 'naughty superfluities'. *A Midsummer Night's Dream* in 1937 was a deliberate mockery of the Victorian *Dream*, gorgeously decorated by Oliver Messel, played to the full Mendelssohn score, romantically choreographed by Ninette de Valois of Sadler's Wells, with fairies in tutus flying on wires; everything was pastiche, and seemed to add up to a final statement of Guthrie's rejection of the old ways. A modern-dress *Hamlet* and a custard-pie *Shrew* were to follow in 1938. The *Hamlet* (the Prince played by the young Alec Guinness and its most fetching scene the funeral of Ophelia watched by a sad little group of mourners huddled beneath umbrellas in the rain) provoked a lengthy correspondence in *The Times* and caused at least one school to cancel its visit to the theatre. But Guthrie was now of a mind to make a more revolutionary move.

His opportunity did not come until after the armistice, and not in a Shakespeare production, and not in London. Guthrie had become increasingly impatient with picture-frame productions, and in a radio talk before the war he declared that the Old Vic 'could not be less like an Elizabethan playhouse. The result, therefore, is a compromise.'[17] The number was growing of those who believed that true Shakespeare could be experienced only in physical conditions more like his own. A leader among the critics, Herbert Farjeon, had in 1924 associated 'Shakespeare's future' with the platform stage, urging its adoption with this wry story:

A real platform stage would confer many benefits on Shakespearean actors. Among the chief of these would be the Freedom of the Clown. The Elizabethan clown is hand-in-glove with the audience. Again and again he addresses the groundlings. At present this intimacy is severely hampered by the proscenium. The little apron at the Old Vic is a very poor apology for a platform . . . but it is better than nothing, and it was on this apron that Mr. Hay Petrie, when playing Launce in *The Two Gentlemen of Verona* a few months ago, actually had the temerity to wink at a gentleman who gave a belated laugh in a private box. This liberty on the part of Mr. Petrie — a liberty he could never have taken from the back of the stage — created a small sensation among the critics. . . . It is, indeed, the most important thing that has happened at the Old Vic during the past year.[18]

Guthrie himself had worked in Terence Gray's Cambridge Festival Theatre, producing in the late twenties and early thirties upon a stage

15 The Elizabethan Theatre, Ashland, Oregon, developed after 1935

extending the whole width of the auditorium and merging into a fan of steps leading down to the audience, 'so designed that conventional realistic production was almost impossible'.[19] The annual Shakespearean Festival at Ashland, Oregon, was founded in 1935, and there the actors learned to play on a full-scale reproduction of the Fortune Theatre platform, whose specifications closely followed those of Shakespeare's Globe (see Plate 15). In the same year San Diego, California, mounted the first of its summer productions in a reduced replica of what was taken to be the Old Globe Theatre; it arranged an annual Shakespeare Festival from 1949. In 1936 Robert Atkins adapted a boxing stadium in Blackfriars for a production of *Henry V*: he erected a façade of an Elizabethan playhouse at one end of the boxing ring, and the audience sat on three sides to enjoy the unaccustomed detail of performance at close quarters, so that Farjeon could write of 'the vivid arena that saved the actors the mortification of pumping themselves out of a picture frame'.[20] An incendiary bomb on the Harrow School Speech Room in 1940 offered Ronald Watkins and his young players 'something like the conditions of the Elizabethan theatre'[21] for a production of *Twelfth Night* done in the Elizabethan manner in 1941, the first of the School's continuing series of annual productions designed to recapture Shakespeare's original intentions. Guthrie's chance came in 1948 when he was invited to direct a play in honour of Scotland for the second year of the Edinburgh Festival.

He chose to produce a cut version of Sir David Lindsay's long ignored *Ane Pleasant Satyre of the Thrie Estaites* (c. 1540), a morality play of considerable length, with a large cast amounting to about a hundred in the event, and an essentially non-realistic content and style. When looking over the text, Guthrie realized that 'here was an opportunity to put into practice some of the theories which, through the years, I had been longing to test. Scene after scene seemed absolutely unplayable on the proscenium stage, almost meaningless in terms of "dramatic illusion"'.[22] He searched Edinburgh for a suitable building in which to mount the play, and boldly decided upon the improbable Kirk Assembly Hall, Scotland's ecclesiastical parliament. Ivor Brown described the 15-foot wide 'peninsular' platform which Guthrie built to project 25 feet into the auditorium:

It was lower than the Elizabethan platform-stage, being reached from the auditorium by a few easy steps: it was also approachable in a way that Shake-

16 Tyrone Guthrie's *The Thrie Estaites* in the Assembly Hall, Edinburgh, 1948

speare's loftier stage was not. The characters could enter down the aisles and through the rows of spectators and go off in the same way. The platform was backed by a curtained recess and a gallery very much in the Elizabethan manner.[23]

On this stage the estate of 'Spiritualitie', the Ecclesiastics, could sit in pomp high in the gallery, the Barons and the Burgesses could take the flanks of the platform, and the common people could surround them on the steps (see Plate 16). When desired, the whole cast could swarm upon the stage from eight separate entrances and become a sea of colourful movement.

This stage was a try-out on Guthrie's part, as he said, a first sketch for the sort of stage he had long hoped to establish. It supported his idea that the aim of the theatre should be to transport the audience, but not by illusion:

One of the most pleasing effects of the performance was the physical relation of the audience to the stage. The audience did not look at the actors against a background of pictorial and illusionary scenery. Seated round three sides of the stage, they focused upon the actors in the brightly lit acting area, but the background was of the dimly lit rows of people similarly focused on the actors. All the time, but unemphatically and by inference, each member of the audience was being ceaselessly reminded that he was not lost in an illusion, was not at the Court of King Humanitie in sixteenth-century Scotland, but was in fact a member of a large audience, taking part, 'assisting' as the French very properly express it, in a performance, a participant in a ritual.[24]

And Guthrie revelled in his sense of non-illusory dramatic experience, in his new-found choreographic freedom and the opportunity the Assembly Hall stage gave him to create wheeling and spinning scenes of exciting crowd action.

Unfortunately, not all the spectators shared his idea of ritual participation. T. C. Worsley, reviewing Michael Benthall's *Hamlet* on this stage in 1953, may speak for the disaffected:

What an unsuitable, impracticable, disillusioning setting is the odious Assembly Hall with its bare, open platform stage! And what a particularly Guthrie joke it is to have imposed its impossibility on all his successors. It is suitable only for the arty romp where horseplay and pageantry are the main attractions. For *Hamlet* it is quite hopelessly wrong. . . . From any seat in the house you can see and hear only one-third of the play; a scurry of characters pattering on through the audience is particularly pointless in this play; every exit is seen through the wrong end of a telescope, and every exit line has to be drawn out accordingly; it requires a hundred extras to fill out the empty spaces.[25]

A more balanced assessment came from Norman Marshall in 1957, when he compared performances of the same play done by the Old Vic company both in Edinburgh and the Waterloo Road:

The crowd scenes, the brawls, the duels, and the battles have proved to be infinitely more exciting out among the audience on the open stage. The soliloquies have been more effective at the Vic where the whole of the audience has been able to see the actor's face. Broadly humorous scenes, especially those dependent on comic business, have gone better on the open stage, but verbal humour is much less effective.[26]

In his account he described the appearance of Banquo's ghost in the banquet scene in the Edinburgh *Macbeth* as 'genuinely horrifying' for the first time in his experience: at the Old Vic the scene suggested no more than an intimate supper party, with the audience merely spectators; in the Assembly Hall the audience seemed to be among the guests, intensely experiencing the same emotions. Whatever the verdict, the search for a better relationship between stage and auditorium had begun in earnest, and no doubt Marshall was right to believe that Guthrie's was the most important experiment in the British theatre since Terence Gray built the Cambridge Festival stage.

Open staging radically assisted our notion of how Shakespeare imagined his plays when he wrote them. Insights into the rhythm and structure of the action, and the purpose of the juxtaposition of scenes, came fast with attempts at a new, overlapping continuity of playing and the contrasts of style which followed: 'fast with slow, loud with soft, grave with gay, grand with squalid'.[27] A new range of stage movement made intimate soliloquies and asides, and all forms of extra-dramatic direct address to the audience, part of the natural flow of the action. At Stratford in 1949, Guthrie directed Buckingham's speech to the crowd on his way to the Tower in *Henry VIII* as an address to the audience, but even with the enlarged forestage of the Memorial Theatre the necessary declamation of the lines and the barrier of the proscenium arch made this seem an awkward pretence at illusion. The open stage was non-illusory, and using the audience as supers was effective when the spectator already felt involved with the process of creating the play himself. In all this, Guthrie saw no need for an

17   John Cranford Adams's model of the Globe playhouse, completed in 1950

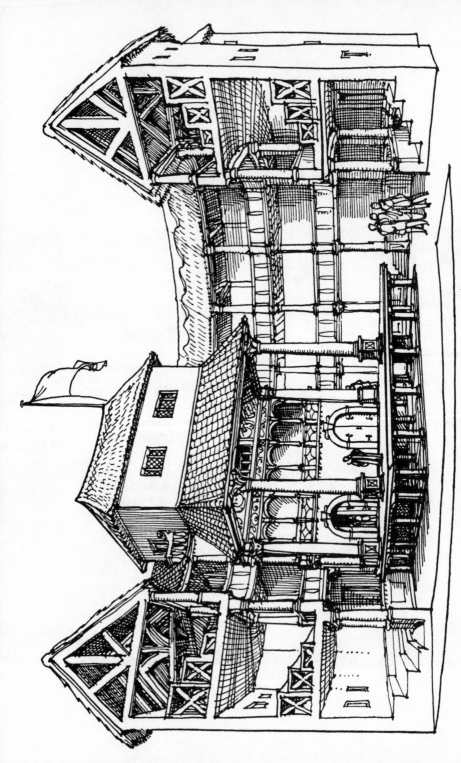

18 C. Walter Hodges's drawing of an Elizabethan playhouse, 1953

exact replica of the Globe Theatre, 'but it is essential to make the contact between players and audience as intimate as possible'.[28] In what he called his 'prentice effort'[29] in Edinburgh he accommodated a very large audience of nearly two thousand with a feeling of considerable intimacy. For Guthrie, the name of the game was how to involve the audience, since he believed that making a play a communal affair was the primary characteristic of the Elizabethan playhouse. An involved audience – Shakespeare demanded it; the picture-frame stage forbade it.

After Edinburgh, other ventures in Elizabethan playing followed quickly. At St John's Wood in 1951 for *The Tempest*, Bernard Miles built an Elizabethan stage in his garden, one with platform, balcony and 'inner stage', and called his playhouse 'The Mermaid'. For the Coronation of 1953 he set up a brilliantly decorated Elizabethan structure in the Royal Exchange, in the heart of the City itself, and there presented *As You Like It* and *Macbeth*. At Stratford in 1951 the Memorial Theatre stage was remodelled to the design of Tanya Moiseiwitsch and under the direction of Anthony Quayle: that season the company played Shakespeare's history plays in chronological order with a permanent wooden structure which served for all productions. The stage was built out beyond the line of the proscenium arch without a curtain, and steps curved up to an Elizabethan balcony which hung over a supposed Elizabethan 'inner stage'. If these features starved the scene of colour, they proved wonderfully adaptable for all the plays.

At the time scholarship on the Elizabethan playhouse had taken great steps. John Cranford Adams's elaborately detailed attempt to reconstruct the Globe from the internal evidence of the play, *The Globe Playhouse*, was published in America in 1942, and began to be known after the war. (The model of it first appeared as the frontispiece to the second edition of 1961.) It seemed to say the last word on Shakespeare's playing conditions, and everywhere the enthusiasts began to make models after Adams, complete with 'study', 'tarras', two balcony windows, pillars, a tapering platform and·so on (see Plate 17). In 1950 Hofstra College, Long Island, constructed a full-scale Adams replica in its gymnasium, and began the first of its annual spring Shakespeare festivals. C. Walter Hodges fired a counter-blast in 1953, *The Globe Restored* (see Plate 18), and there approached the problems of reconstructing the Globe with what appeared to be a good deal more practical sense of theatre. But already Leslie Hotson, accomplished literary sleuth, had begun to insinuate radical ideas about Shakespeare-in-the-round with the publication in 1954 of *The First Night of Twelfth Night,* eventually to be capped by a triumphant but outrageous battlecry of a book in 1959, *Shakespeare's Wooden O.* It was time for the bewildered student to return all this supposition to its proper testing ground, the theatre.

Luckily it again fell to Tyrone Guthrie to take the lead. Another unexpected opportunity presented itself: an invitation from the small Canadian country town of Stratford, Ontario, to initiate its Shakespearean Festival. The best of it was that this Stratford had no theatre to start with Guthrie could begin from the beginning — literally from the ground up.

One of his conditions for going was the building of a platform stage to be designed by Tanya Moiseiwitsch, and this was agreed. Working against the clock, Stratford's largely volunteer work-force succeeded in having a giant tent playhouse ready for the opening of their first six-week season in 1953. The platform was 2 feet high and, including its three steps, 30 feet wide and 39 feet deep. At the end of the season Alec Guinness is supposed to have said, 'I think you are a yard short', and the stage was subsequently enlarged. Believing in architecture before décor, Moiseiwitsch set a small jutting balcony upstage, supported on slender columns 7 feet 4½ inches high; two open staircases rose to this balcony, each with a landing and a door halfway up. A sloping amphitheatre swept 220 degrees round the platform, and two vomitories under the seats allowed actors to enter near dead-centre of the theatre (see Plate 19). Here were all the basic Elizabethan features subtly arranged in 'a large deep-dish pie, from which all but one large slice has been removed'.[30] The miracle was that although this theatre seated 1,500 in sixteen rows, no one was more than 65 feet from the stage; even so, Guthrie afterwards thought that twelve rows were enough, and that any more made the actors too remote.[31] Nevertheless, in a proscenium theatre of equal capacity, the spectators at the back would be more than twice as far away. Guthrie had achieved his three objects: a playhouse approximating the one for which Shakespeare wrote, a stage where actor and spectator could frankly accept one another for what he was, and a permanent set which prohibited the paraphernalia of scenery and illusion.

On a stage like this Guthrie could exploit his choreographic talents.

19 The Festival Theatre, Stratford, Ontario, developed after 1953.

Something more than mere showmanship and spectacle, choreography could make a dramatic statement greater than that made by scenery, and has been described as 'a subtle physical expression of the mood of each scene – indeed, a dance'.[32] Michael Langham, Guthrie's successor at the Festival, was from his directing experiences made sharply aware that 'we blind and confuse ourselves by thinking in terms of scenes'.[33] The new fluidity revealed Shakespeare's stagecraft not only as three-dimensional, but also as a rhythmic pattern of relationships between actor and actor, group and group, and stage and audience. Looking at the Folio text of *Antony and Cleopatra*, which has no scene divisions, Langham observed, 'This is a film scenario, no less, rich in cross-cuttings, dissolves, close-ups, and overlaps.'[34] Guthrie's work was thus characterized by 'stroke after stroke of magnificent insight and lightning-like illumination of great plays'.[35] More than this, his notion of theatre as 'ritual', the performance of certain prescribed actions on a stage, emerged as a new set of conventions of gesture and movement evoking something greater than themselves:

When Lady Anne moves around the bier of Henry of Lancaster, pursued by Richard of Gloucester; when the watchful soldiers close in upon the condemned Hastings; when the ghosts of his victims cluster around the sleeping Richard; when Helena dances with her suitors at the French court; when the soldiers take cover to surprise Parolles; when Helena, triumphant in yellow, takes the centre of the stage as the victorious wife — what are these and a hundred other moments in these productions but ritual? And ritual, moreover, to which we respond with eager emotion, for by their formal beauty they purge our minds of triviality, and we live for an instant at our highest imaginative peak.[36]

The Stratford stage particularly encouraged strong and significant patterns of meaning, which were 'recreated, in predetermined, ritual form by the actors for the audience every time a performance is given'.[37]

It was Guthrie's virtuosity as a choreographer which most struck the critics at the first production, *Richard III*. Brooks Atkinson found him 'infatuated' with the mechanics of his new stage, and especially remarked the fluid movement and continuous variety of the action; but he felt the play got lost with the director so busy 'summoning state processionals from the pit or setting opposing armies at each other's throats on the various stage levels'.[38] However, no one failed to be entranced when Guthrie had Alec Guinness as Richard open the play with a cheery direct address, strolling out on to the balcony and 'swinging one leg over its side like a slightly dour monkey',[39] speaking only after slowly surveying the audience and digging his dagger into the parapet to make a point. In truth, this play lent itself to scene after scene of moving 'tableaux': a winding, ghoulish procession in torchlight for the funeral of Henry VI, with the wooing of Lady Anne round and round the bier against a background of halberds and tapers (I.ii); the decline to death of Edward IV done as a religious ritual, the dying man kissing a grotesque crucifix (ii.i); the ominous arrival of the boy Prince in London (iii.i); Richard before the citizens using a prayer book so large that it needed two monks to hold it (iii.vii); the pageantry of Richard's slow ascent to the throne in a crimson robe at his coronation (iv.ii); the scene of the four queens who 'curl and writhe in an agony of hatred'[40] (iv.iv); the Ghosts rising slowly from the trap (v.iii); at the Battle of Bosworth, the eruption of Richmond's forces from all corners of the stage, the body of Richard finally rolling down the steps to the feet of the audience (v.iv). Yet the ritual impact of the production was greatly assisted by the economy of means employed: 'a handful of black-clad soldiers, a few tall banners, drums, trumpets and a tolling bell — but Mr Guthrie so disposes them in action that the scenes they create for us seem endless in their scope'.[41] And the force of this simplicity was effectively increased by the breath-taking costumes and the unashamed stylization of the make-up, with a doll-like Anne, for example, and Queen Margaret (Irene Worth) a magnificent crone.

For the birth of a new Shakespeare festival, Guthrie's second production was an unexpected and dangerous choice. *All's Well That Ends Well* was a less-known play, traditionally considered to be a commercial risk, and even stamped by one (London) critic as 'this old-fashioned prodigy of tedium'. It was as if Guthrie had set himself a challenge, and in the event exploited his own talent for comedy, rejuvenated a moribund play and further revealed the wonders of open stagecraft. Only when he translated this production to the Warwickshire Stratford in 1959 were any critics disturbed by a Falstaffian treatment of Parolles in Eighth Army battle-dress, the omission of the clown and the choice of period costume for Helena's scenes; on the Ontario stage the Edwardian 'Merry Widow' image created by Tanya Moiseiwitsch was one of light elegance exactly matching the tone of the comedy. In the judgment of the *New Statesman* critic, A. Alvarez, the period translation worked perfectly: 'Shakespeare's courtliness becomes boiled-shirt formality; the Renaissance men of honour are "gentlemen", those without it cads'.[42] The issue of modern dress need not bother us further here, for the true key to this production was the balletic quality granted by the freedom of the open platform. The sombre, processional ritual of *Richard III* had been transformed into another, in spirit that of a dance appropriate to a bitter-sweet comedy.

197

Every critic was entranced by those scenes which, by Shakespeare's rhythmic structure and sly use of rhyming couplets, lent themselves to the devices of dance. Besides controlling the tone of a scene, by these devices Guthrie could illuminate not only character attitudes and character relationships, but the whole point of the action. This intractable play found a fitting style it had not apparently achieved in its recorded history.

The magic took effect when Helena (Irene Worth) began to soothe the brows of the King of France (Alec Guinness) to the rhythm of the rhyming lines in II.i:

> Ere twice the horses of the sun shall bring
> Their fiery torcher his diurnal ring,
> Ere twice in murk and occidental damp
> Moist Hesperus hath quench'd his sleepy lamp:
> Or four and twenty times the pilot's glass
> Hath told the thievish minutes, how they pass:
> What is infirm, from your sound parts shall fly,
> Health shall live free, and sickness freely die.

Helena moved slowly behind the King's wheelchair and laid her hand on his forehead. He closed his eyes and sighed.

> Methinks in thee some blessed spirit doth speak
> His powerful sound, within an organ weak.

He touched her hand, looked at it, then slowly drew her round to face him. On her knees she made her pledge to him:

> If I break time, or flinch in property
> Of what I spoke, unpitied let me die.

And she kissed his hand and wheeled him offstage.

Such incantatory lines gave way to the new impulsion of dance in the 'recantation scene' at court (II.iii). Brooks Atkinson of *The New York Times* found that the performance 'flows without effort across the apron stage up and down the stairs, through the forest of columns and out of the ports in the pit'[43] with the elegance of ballet. First, the arena suddenly filled with courtiers from all entrances, all discussing the recovery of the King. Then the court orchestra suddenly galloped into a waltz and the King entered dancing with Helena. On the cue,

> Make choice and see,
> Who shuns thy love, shuns all his love in me,

she reviewed the eligible young officers and gentlemen to the rhythm of an elaborate dance suited to the stylized speech. Finally she concluded the dance with Bertram, and to general applause led him to the King.

> HELENA. This is the man.
> KING. Why then young Bertram take her she's thy wife.

All in a breath the choice was made and granted. But at this Bertram broke away, the music stopped and all were transfixed. When Shakespeare's rhyming ceased, it was as if reality had returned to supersede the magic (see Plate 20).

To a degree Guthrie was able to recreate these patterns on the proscenium stage in 1959. At the English Stratford he constructed entrances from the pit to match Ontario's vomitories, and the use of a rostrum and steps lent focus and variety to the crowded scene. Harold Hobson, announcing the production as 'one of the best that Stratford had ever seen', thought that Shakespeare's words had induced in the director something of 'a personal vision' and considered why he had succeeded:

The main reason is simply that Mr Guthrie's elaborate decorations of the text work with the play, and not against it. They do not assail, but reinforce the effects implicit in the words. The most striking instance of this is the scene of Bertram's rejection of his mother's ward, Helena, whom the King had promised, in return for her curing him of a serious illness, that she shall marry any man she chooses.

This scene begins with a formal dance. One by one the young eligible courtiers pass before Helena, who seems to regard most of them with an approving eye, Bertram is unperturbed; he looks upon his companions serenely; he does not realise until the last moment that there is any danger in his being the favoured man. But when the choice falls upon him he shatters the formality by rushing to the steps of the throne, and unfolding the horror by which he has been overcome. The effect is very great; the artificiality that Mr Guthrie has deliberately induced is smashed by the reality of Bertram's assertion of individual independence; and a climax is created that Shakespeare could not but have approved.[44]

The critic in *The Times* also remarked the 'half articulated suggestion that one should forget realistic motivation' while the audience res-

20 Tyrone Guthrie's *All's Well That Ends Well* at Stratford, Ontario, 1953: the 'ballroom' scene, with Alec Guinness as the King of France, Irene Worth as Helena, and Ladies and Gentlemen at the Court

ponded to 'a fairy tale magic' playing over this scene: 'Trick it may be, but we accept it as something more.'[45] Here was the true ambivalence of imaginative theatre, and in the court scenes of *All's Well* at least, Guthrie seemed to have captured for the modern stage Shakespeare's stylistic intentions.

The success of the thrust stage in Canada led to new thinking on both sides of the Atlantic, with a rapid development of playhouse design and experiment in stagecraft. Max Reinhardt's Grosses Schauspielhaus in Berlin had been built with a projecting stage in 1919, but had nothing of the influence enjoyed by the Canadian Stratford. Following the permanent erection of the Festival Theatre in Ontario in 1957, the Chichester Festival Theatre opened in 1962 with the advantage of a wider stage and a smaller auditorium, but since its platform was built into one corner of a hexagon, the actor seemed more withdrawn from the spectator. In 1962 also, the Delacorte Theatre, New York, was fitted with a 120 degree semi-arena stage projecting into the auditorium. The Tyrone Guthrie Theatre (now the Guthrie Theatre) in Minneapolis arrived in 1963 with an asymmetrical platform and the possibility of introducing scenery in the upstage area. In 1965, the Vivian Beaumont Theatre in New York's Lincoln Center cautiously provided a stage which could be adapted to either proscenium or thrust uses, but in practice found that it rarely wanted anything but the latter. The Mark Taper Forum in Los Angeles (1967) planned its thrust within a perfect circle and managed to mount scenic backgrounds as well. London's Young Vic in the Cut opened in 1970 with benches for 400 seated round a T-shaped stage. Colin George's Crucible Theatre in Sheffield (1971) decided upon a stage the same size as Ontario's, but with an intimate auditorium half its present size, seating 1,000; in addition it housed a grid over the rear stage which was capable of flying scenery (see Plate 21). Sheffield may have found all the answers; meanwhile in many colleges and universities everywhere Guthrie's presence is felt.

Guthrie's work as a director was not finished, but his central contribution to the new Shakespeare had been made. We may pass lightly over his post-war experiments with costume in comedy, a Crazy Gang *Taming of the Shrew* at Stratford, Ontario, in 1954, which modulated into a quietly romantic last scene for the surrender of Kate; back to the Renaissance for a *Merchant of Venice* in 1955, with the

21   The Crucible Theatre, Sheffield, 1971

Guthrie and the open stage

abduction of Jessica done to a masque which brought the whole theatre alive with revellers and a trial scene which had Antonio stripped and tied to a grill for Shylock's knife; but especially a 'modern-dress' *Troilus and Cressida* at the Old Vic in 1956 which made Shakespeare's anti-heroic stage images strikingly apt (see Plate 22).

Michael MacOwan had revived this play at the Westminster Theatre just after the disillusioning events at Munich in 1938, and although its scanty stage history in this century had been one of failure, Greeks and Trojans in mock-modern uniforms, with Thersites a sour correspondent from some radical paper, gave the comedy a strictly contemporary ring. Now Guthrie sought to clinch the Shakespearian argument for the post-war generation, and wickedly selected the fashions of 1913, Edwardian England and the Kaiser's Germany, to suggest that this was the last time when nations could treat war as a game. W. A. Darlington wrote of

Greeks and Trojans resplendent in uniforms which are modelled on those of the German and Austrian Emperors' armies, with the French navy thrown in for variety. And we have any amount of square bashing and saluting. The war is made to look tremendously ceremonious and abysmally silly.

It is a clever choice of period in more than one way, for it enables both Cressida and Helen to wear clothes in which no woman could be expected to behave herself.[46]

To this Kenneth Tynan was to add, 'His Trojans are glass-smashing cavalry officers who might pass for British were it not for the freedom with which they mention Helen's name in the mess'.[47] Each character was neatly nailed: Pandarus with binoculars and grey top hat was ready for Ascot, Achilles skulked in a dressing-gown, Ulysses was appropriately an admiral of the fleet, Cressida was chic in a hobble skirt and muff, Helen was 'the sort of Edwardian actress who sips champagne from her dancing shoe',[48] Thersites was a miserable Shavian radical. However, in all this Guthrie's irreverence was so overpowering that Shakespeare's serious criticism of chauvinism and its effect upon human relationships was lost in laughter: he had converted 'Cressida into a wanton and Troilus into an ass',[49] and substituted a romp for the ritual impact he had previously achieved in Canada.

Tyrone Guthrie's far-reaching influence upon the course of Shakespeare's fortunes in this century must stem from his innovations in

22 Tyrone Guthrie's *Troilus and Cressida* at the Old Vic, 1956

stage planning and his joyous use of the open stages he conceived. The latest company to heed his advocacy of open staging is none other than that of the British National Theatre, and in talking of plans for the new London home of the Royal Shakespeare Company at the Barbican, the present director, Trevor Nunn, has promised that 'the audience and the actors will share the same stage space,'[50] although this is to be accomplished by end-staging and not a thrust. St George's Church in Islington, London, is being converted into an Elizabethan theatre based upon the Globe playhouse. And the American actor and director Sam Wanamaker plans to build a replica of the second Globe in the Liberty of the Clink on the South Bank linked with a World Centre for Shakespeare Studies. But behind this concern for new stages and functional auditoria lay a greater vision. In concluding his book on William Poel in 1954, Robert Speaight knew nothing of the Canadian experiment, but could prophesy:

The theatre of tomorrow will be at once more simple and more ceremonious than the theatre of the bourgeois centuries. And in this context the multiple stage of the Elizabethans becomes an actuality instead of an anachronism.[51]

Simplicity for its directness and force, and ceremony (or Guthrie's favourite word, 'ritual') for its inclusiveness and community of experience are the Shakespearian characteristics. Nor did Guthrie believe that his own work on the open stage was more than a compromise, one in a chain of experiments, 'one of the many phases in the age-long, loving battle between Shakespeare and posterity'.[52] But he did believe that the new interpretation demanded a fresh sense of theatre as a special kind of event, one created by actor and spectator in a conscious collaboration, urging all parties to the play to acknowledge openly its processes and its ends, one confident of the multiple insights which the theatre can grant a fully involved audience.

11

Shakespeare, Peter Brook and non-illusion

Had Guthrie's work not been done, no doubt actor, audience and critic would yet have gained some sense of a new Shakespearian experience: pressures were everywhere increasing to have us re-read the plays for what they might communicate beyond realism. Michael Benthall's Stratford *Hamlet* of 1948 dressed Paul Scofield in a mid-Victorian frock-coat and set him in a candle-lit castle in order to mix realism and romance. Benthall's *Tempest* of 1951 was presented as a submarine ballet, pursuing suggestions of its allegorical and masque-like character developed by Enid Welsford's *The Court Masque* of 1927 and then G. Wilson Knight's *The Crown of Life* of 1947. Nevertheless, these pressures had not been felt radically, and in its explicitly unreal mixture of supernatural, pastoral and earthy ingredients, *A Midsummer Night's Dream* provided the perfect test case. This chapter will end with Peter Brook's quintessential *Dream* of 1970, and the sort of approach to this play characteristic of a decade or so earlier demonstrates the development.

In 1957, the Old Vic sent to New York a *Dream* smothered in its own trees and pranked up with a full corps-de-ballet for the fairies. Michael Langham's production at the Old Vic in 1960 exploited the traditional fairies and the traditional comedy at the expense of the poetry: 'Oberon seems to think of the bank "where on the wild thyme grows" in terms of a comfortable hotel near Charing Cross', complained *The Times*.[1] Tony Richardson's work at the Royal Court in 1962 — the English Stage Company's first Shakespeare production — touched the play with modern urban realism, coy little fairies and a Puck looking like an escaped convict; again the poetry evaporated, the verse going 'not on tiptoe, quivering and agleam, but uniformly flatfootedly'.[2] David William's Regent's Park performance of the same year had the fairies joylessly in masks. These productions faced in all directions, and in the 1960s it began to appear that if a director could find the right image

206

for the immortals he would also have discovered the right mode for the play.

Fresh thinking began in 1960 when Peter Hall took over the Royal Shakespeare Company at the age of 29, and worked with colleagues like Peter Brook and John Barton – 'colleagues' because the new directors of Shakespeare were no longer the actors of tradition, but college men full of ideas for experiment.[3] In the 1960s Stratford became the centre for Shakespeare studies, as it were. Unfortunately, the company was still struggling with the problems of actor–audience relationship endemic to the Memorial Theatre.

The old Memorial Theatre, built in 1879, had been destroyed by fire in 1926. The new one opened in 1932 with a 30-foot proscenium, a cyclorama, bare side walls and a great gap between the stage and the stalls. Baliol Holloway's remark was to speak for a generation of actors: 'Standing well downstage on a fine night, you can distinctly see the front row of the stalls outlined in the distance'. After the war every manager tinkered with this intractable stage. In 1951, as we saw, Anthony Quayle attacked the bare walls by extending the circle with a few boxes and built an apron over the orchestra pit. In 1960 Hall and his designer John Bury introduced a mock thrust, accentuated by a steep rake; in 1964 they had the formerly *avant-garde* cyclorama removed – it merely induced another kind of illusion and for the new Shakespeare it was self-defeating. In 1972 Trevor Nunn and his designer Christopher Morley added a new gallery of boxes to the auditorium, and two huge wing walls on the stage to disguise the proscenium further; the thrust edged out a few more feet into the stalls and a hydraulic rake could be tilted frighteningly at the audience.[4]

In his eight years with the R.S.C., Peter Hall's administrative daring transformed the established tourist and school-party character of the Stratford festivals. Ensemble playing by a permanent company made possible (in theory at least) the search for an authentic style for a contemporary Shakespeare. The Aldwych Theatre extension of the company's activities into modern drama, with experiment for a time at the Arts Theatre, training under studio conditions, improvisational approaches especially from Brook and Clifford Williams, a flirtation with the Theatre of Cruelty in 1963 and a gesture towards political theatre in 1965, seemed to guarantee that the new Shakespeare style would have some basis in current dramatic fashion. Hall began his tenure in office by stating that 'Shakespeare needs a style and tradition more than any other dramatist performed today',[5] and set about providing the means to accomplish the elusive objective. But from the beginning he had to work with 'an obstinate proscenium stage with pieces stuck on in the front', so that while he could not change the physical relationship between actor and audience as Guthrie had done, he could only adjust the decoration of the stage picture to make it as bare and functional as possible.

Hall's work with *A Midsummer Night's Dream* in 1959 was not untypical. He had evidently read Quiller-Couch's vision of an appropriate set for the play:

The set scene should represent a large Elizabethan hall, panelled, having a lofty oak-timbered roof and an enormous staircase. The cavity under the staircase, occupying in breadth two-thirds of the stage, should be fronted with folding or sliding doors, which being opened, should reveal the wood, recessed, moonlit, with its trees upon a flat arras or tapestry. On this secondary remoter stage the lovers should wander through their adventures, the fairies now conspiring in the quiet hall under the lantern, anon withdrawing into the woodland to befool the mortals straying there. Then, for the last scene and the interlude of *Pyramus and Thisbe*, the hall should be filled with lights and company. That over, the bridal couples go up the great staircase.[6]

The setting was to be in effect the 'great chamber' which Bottom anticipated for the players before the Duke. Hall's designer, Lila di Nobili, gave this a local habitation in the form of a permanent set containing a gallery reached by two great staircases upon which fairies and lovers could chase each other. No matter that this balustraded gallery remained as a rustic bridge, and even something of a stumbling block, in the wood scenes, the prenuptial court scenes acquired a special life of their own as if the play were being presented in non-illusory fashion by the members of an Elizabethan wedding party. The Elizabethan setting in turn inspired an Elizabethan form for the play, 'an aristocratic Epithalamion, not far removed from a formal masque',[7] the whole play consciously seen to be contained within an Elizabethan hall. The permanent structure on the stage also had the effect of pushing the action forward through the arch (Oberon as an Elizabethan fop spoke his line 'I am invisible' to the audience with a mocking bow), and the whole would have been more audible had the verse been better spoken.

For, unfortunately, the director had chosen to burlesque the lovers and the fairies, who in consequence seemed laboured. J. W. Lambert remarked a loutish Lysander and Demetrius, and saw Hermia as 'a whining little shrew of a maidservant' and Helena, 'constantly being made to fall with a fearful thump on her behind', by contrast as 'a sort of soppy Roedean girl, if that is not an impossibility in nature'.[8] The basic decision on the fairies was to offer them up, boys as well as girls, as 'a bunch of barefoot, wilful and childish little sprites'[9] who were being overworked by the fairy management: Titania's attendant complained wearily, 'I must go seek some dewdrops here/ And hang a pearl in *every* cowslip's ear'.[10] However, with this play Peter Hall introduced his praiseworthy policy of nursing a production from one season to another, a procedure impossible in the normal commercial theatre. The 1959 production reappeared at Stratford in 1962, and again at the Aldwych in 1963, finally having demolished those tiresome staircases and having evolved 'a richness of detail and emotional depth that force one to encounter the play as if for the first time'.[11]

A similar procedure of development by testing and experience was followed for *Troilus and Cressida*, directed by Hall in collaboration with John Barton. The production travelled from Stratford in 1960 to the Lyceum, Edinburgh, and the Aldwych in 1962. The riches of this play had found a special relevance in a sudden burst of productions since the war, but it remained one of the least hackneyed, and a true challenge to a director seeking a contemporary style for the classical repertory.

Again, a permanent and suggestive set, carefully unlocalized and non-pictorial, bare and simple, was mounted on the raked stage. It consisted of 'a sanded platform raised not more than two feet above the stage. Behind this a lurid abstract backcloth by Mr Leslie Hurry suggests restless conflict.'[12] The fine white sand on the octagonal platform was possibly prompted by Brecht's white circle of light for acting his *Antigone* in 1948. The sandpit was at once 'a parched plain outside Troy'[13] and a symbolic cockpit for making love or war. Movement on and off this area was swift and fluid, the rake tilting the actors towards the audience. Bamber Gascoigne contrasted the Old Vic's *Merchant of Venice* of that season: 'Portia and Nerissa, playing an intimate scene downstage, were lost in the open desolation behind them, in a way that could never happen with a slope tipping them into the audience's confidence.'[14] Indeed, Pandarus (Max Adrian) stole the limelight by getting into closest touch with the spectators with his obscene chuckling, and when Pandarus, Troilus and Cressida formally announced their mythological roles in III.ii, the result was 'a stunning alienation-effect'.[15] But the grossest critical confusion surrounded Dorothy Tutin's very clever Cressida. She was entirely convincing as the girl who couldn't say no: 'Her heroine emerges as a girl of the highest motives and sensibilities, whose sexuality is awakened by her true love and thereafter betrays her', wrote Clifford Hanley, 'and whether or not that's what Shakespeare meant, it was good enough for me'.[16] It was not, of course, what Shakespeare meant, and Tutin's success in realistic character-consistency pointed to the director's unwillingness to go all the way into role-playing and non-illusory theatre.

The most notable collaboration of Hall and Barton at Stratford, and their best testimony to the possibilities of a single set,[17] was a trilogy arrangement of the early history plays in 1963 under the banner *The Wars of the Roses*. These were Barton's adaptation of the three parts of *Henry VI* plus *Richard III* done in essentially realistic style. Attention here, however, must shift to a less conspicuous production during this season: Clifford Williams's *The Comedy of Errors*. This was first put together in five weeks as a stop-gap at the end of Stratford's 1962 season, transferred to the Aldwych in December, then back to Stratford again in 1963, then back to the Aldwych. The same production travelled to America in 1964. Finally it was actually revived in 1972, ten years later.

This curious history is to be explained not only by the commercial popularity of the play, but also by Williams's strikingly apt style of presentation, foreshadowing things to come. No matter that its restless invention overstressed farcical pantomime at the expense of the play's pathetic elements and to the extent of turning the old father Aegeon into a clown, it was the production's frank creation of a play-world which won its audiences. Yet this was done simply. The whole cast entered in black sweaters to the quick music of flute and tabor, on a symmetrical set of wooden rostra performed a mechanical 'ballet' after the manner of a *commedia* troupe. This was the first of many symmetrical patterns matching the verse and the plot. The prompt-book hardly suggests that these were hastily conceived. At the beginning, to every sixth beat the company faced first right, then upstage, then left, then to the front; the next three bars followed thus:

Shakespeare, Peter Brook and non-illusion

Bar 14: 3 steps D/S. Check and turn C/S with
Bar 15: PS people U/S arm to front D/S arm to back
          U/S leg to back D:S leg to front
Bar 16: Arm and leg down and turn into new direction

And so on. The Dromios who end the play upon the couplet

> We came into the world like brother and brother:
> And now let's go hand in hand, not one before another.

made their exit to another pattern as each other's mirror image. Here
are the last twelve lines of the play as recorded in the prompt-book:

Both Drs move D/S to either D/S corner ros.1
Both X to meet D/S c/ros.1 facing each other
Both turn to face front
Dr of Es jams his rt hand to Dr of S's left hand
Both turn to face U/S and run to
EXIT U/S c

In retrospect there was nothing particularly sophisticated about this
choreography in itself, but for a comedy of improbable coincidences it
made an irresistible visual assertion that ritual and convention had
gripped the stage.

Peter Brook's contribution to the sequence of developments at
Stratford in the sixties was, however, the most far-seeing. The fullest
statement of his ideas appeared in a slim volume published in 1968,
The Empty Space, although the thinking here had been initiated twenty
years earlier in a notable essay, 'Style in Shakespearean Production'.[18]
From the first, his sense of theatre was ritualistic. Audiences still un-
spoiled by the pedantic accretions of tradition, he argued, willingly
accepted the flights and suggestions, the basic inconsistencies and
anachronisms, of the stage, and he believed that a revitalized drama
always returned to its popular source: 'I can take any empty space and
call it a bare stage. A man walks across this empty space whilst someone else is watching him, and this is all that is needed for an act of
theatre to be engaged.'[19] Thus Brook began his book. The Elizabethan
theatre was born of a violent, vital, pioneering age, and it was 'just a
place with some doors —and so it enabled the dramatist effortlessly to
whip the spectator through an unlimited succession of illusions. . . .
This theatre not only allowed the playwright to roam the world, it also

allowed him free passage from the world of action to the world of inner impressions'.[20] Shakespeare was 'experimental, popular, revolutionary'[21] and productions of his plays in England at least had been influenced by the discovery that they

> were written to be performed continuously, that their cinematic structure of alternating short scenes, plot intercut with subplot, were all part of a total shape. This shape is only revealed dynamically, that is, in the uninterrupted sequence of these scenes.[22]

The task was to recreate Shakespeare's theatrical meaning for today's audiences.

The way was to be that of non-illusion. Brook's programme note to his production of *A Midsummer Night's Dream* in 1970 was the simple statement which concluded his chapter on 'The Rough Theatre', the popular category in which he placed Shakespeare in his book: 'We must open our empty hands and show that really there is nothing up our sleeves. Only then can we begin.' Anything more pictorial – a touch of period in the décor of the stage, a suggestion of day or night in the lighting – and the audience had at once surrendered its imagination into the director's hands. The theory had been set out twenty years before:

> When an audience enters a theatre, its imagination is completely open. If . . . it finds the curtain up, the stage bare, then the initial anti-pictorial gesture of the production makes it clear that no picture is going to be presented, and that the proscenium is merely an arch over a square of boards on which the actors will seek to create an illusion. Thus in the opening gambit the conventions are established, and the audience's imagination is liberated, leaving it both ready and capable of creating its own pictures.[23]

In one way this was a restatement of the old notion that Shakespeare's poetry should do the painting, but in another it was the most absolute assertion of the primacy of the theatrical over the literary experience of drama.

It was none other than Barry Jackson who in 1946 had introduced Peter Brook to Stratford audiences at the age of 21. Brook made a challenging and risky choice in *Love's Labour's Lost*, which he had seen that spring in Paris spoken in a French which reminded him of Molière, Marivaux and Musset. Faced with a stage from which 'actors and audience seem to be staring at each other rather pathetically through the wrong end of a pair of opera glasses',[24] he decided to try to capture the conceited style of this comedy by pictorial means. He turned to Watteau, 'because the style of his dresses, with its broad, undecorated expanses of billowing satin seemed the ideal visual correlative of the essential sweet-sad mood of this play'.[25] In the set and costumes, the designer, Reginald Leefe, sought a pastoral chastity which was matched by Brook's delicate groupings and 'puff-ball lightness'[26] of movement. Exquisite grace on the part of the lovers was balanced by the touch of harlequinade for the comics: Costard was a Pierrot dressed after Watteau, Constable Dull a doll policeman in pale blue Victorian uniform, Holofernes in mortar board with silver stencil and silver tassel. Yet in this context Marcade's black entrance in v.ii,

> MARCADE. The King your father —
> PRINCESS. Dead for my life.
> MARCADE. Even so: my tale is told.
> BEROWNE. Worthies away, the scene begins to cloud.

fell aptly, in Trewin's phrase like 'frost in the summer night'. The scribbles on the text of the prompt-copy convey nothing of this achievement in style: everything lay in the directing.

Brook's hunt for the 'inner vision' of a play was on. In 1947, Stratford presented his very youthful *Romeo and Juliet* (Daphne Slater was 19, Laurence Payne was 27) encircled by a stylized decoration of toy crenellated walls against a deep blue sky. In 1950, his choice was *Measure for Measure*. Awkward in the study, traditionally criticized for a disjointed structure, an uncertain 'problem comedy' as to mood, ranging in characterization, this play needed a production which would fuse its parts and prove its coherence. Brook sought the sources of its energy and compulsion as drama. He recognized the common soil which nourished at once the depravity and dark sexuality of the city, and the zealous purity of Isabella. Without being realistic, the action was rooted in 'a very real world':

This is the disgusting, stinking world of medieval Vienna. The darkness of this world is absolutely necessary to the meaning of the play: Isabella's plea for grace has far more meaning in this Dostoevskian setting than it would in lyrical comedy's never-never land. When this play is prettily staged it is meaningless — it demands an absolutely convincing roughness and dirt.[27]

213

23   Peter Brook's *Measure for Measure* at the Shakespeare Memorial Theatre, Stratford-upon-Avon, 1950

He found what Robert Speaight called the play's 'interior fire' especially in the street and prison scenes.

Brook designed his own permanent set of stone pillars and arches which could be backed and touched with suggestive detail of palace or street, convent or prison, and in spite of this semi-pictorial bent, the action could be swift and various and played out to the audience. But the set was less important than the costumes, in which several critics felt the grotesque spirit of Breughel and Bosch. The vigour of the crowded streets of dissolute Vienna is well conveyed by the prompt-book notes for i.iii:

Crowd noise and entrance immediately lights fade
6 peasants, 1 beggar, 2 whores, 3 cripples
Barrel, table, jug and mugs, bagpiper
Squabbling, hubbub, drum-roll
To see Claudio, one jumps on to back
Mistress Overdone, Pompey exeunt L then peer round door, re-enter as prison-
    ers appear
Provost leads procession on OP with drummer
Tableau and jeering
At sign from Provost, 2 take Juliet's arms and turn half circle with her,
    showing her to crowd. Jeering
Gaoler enters through soldiers with pikes, points stick at Juliet
Juliet rushes to Claudio, embraces him
2 seize Claudio, pull him back to sign from Provost
Crowd yells
Exit Claudio, jeering rising to a roar
Crowd follows jeering (see Plate 23).

For the prison, grilles and bars were set in the doors and arches, and the grim procession of prisoners themselves created the setting throughout the scene, as the prompt-book indicates:

Prisoners take positions in silence; moan, clank chains, move uneasily at entrances and exits of Pompey, Overdone. Also, when Isabella comes out of cell, and before and after final soliloquy. Otherwise quiet throughout.

It is these prisoners whom Pompey in stocks greets in iv.iii ('I am as well acquainted here, as I was in our house of profession'), but Brook missed the opportunity for the pimp/clown to embrace the house with the ironic naming of his clients. The stage was dotted with gruesome items — a block, a wheel, a weapons rack, a torture machine: T. C.

Worsley commented that this production had gone 'beyond our usual Dickensian or eighteenth-century stage prisons to the wheels, the fires, the whips and the racks of a still cruder epoch'.[28] And the orchestra pit became an extension of the stage when Barnardine was hauled up from his straw by a rope.

In such a world, Isabella's unnatural preference for her chastity before her brother's life seemed more probable. But then the temptation scenes (ii.ii, iv) were strongly physical, with Angelo grasping Isabella's arms, holding her against a table, squeezing her wrist, so that when the climax of the play came, it came with a most memorable pause. In v.i, Brook asked Barbara Jefford as Isabella to pause before she knelt for Angelo's life, and to hold it until she felt the audience could take it no longer, a lapse of time lasting as much as two minutes. Richard David reported,

'He dies for Claudio.' The pause that followed must have been among the longest in theatre history. Then hesitantly, still silent, Isabella moved across the stage and knelt before the Duke. Her words came quiet and level, and as their full impact of mercy reached Angelo, a sob broke from him. It was perfectly calculated and perfectly timed; and the whole perilous manoeuvre had been triumphantly brought off.[29]

The pause was not memorable merely for its length, but because it accurately caught the implications of all the elements built into the production, cruel and Christian, death-bringing or life-giving. Brook described the device as a 'voodoo pole': 'a silence in which the abstract notion of mercy became concrete for that moment to those present'.[30] In a motionless tableau it perhaps encapsulated something of the play's inner vision.

In 1955, Brook reclaimed *Titus Andronicus* by judicious cutting and a formalized treatment designed to emphasize the tragedy's 'ritual of bloodshed'. Again he had sensed an appropriate style for an uncommon play. He was less successful in releasing Shakespeare's ritualistic energy in his first encounter in 1957 with another intractable play, *The Tempest*. It was a fussy production of transformation scenes using gauzes and traps, and accompanied by Brook's own *musique concrète* (Kenneth Tynan conjectured 'a combination of glockenspiel, thunder-sheet, Malayan nose-flute and discreetly tortured Sistine choirboy'[31]). Not much better was the 1963 revival of *The Tempest* in collaboration with Clifford Williams. The fantasy of the play was perhaps made more obvious by a magic mirror setting in perspex, and a note by Williams in the programme hinted at the direction the R.S.C. was taking:

At one time we thought of lifting all the scenery away at the end (as happens in one of Roland Petit's ballets), or of putting all the characters of the finale in clown's costumes, to underline the derisory nature of the play's resolution.

And in 1968 Brook took what now seems the inevitable step with *The Tempest* to meet the demands of his own creative imagination.

At the instigation of Jean-Louis Barrault and sponsored by the Théâtre des Nations, Brook produced *The Tempest* for a third time in the Round House, London. The set had become a gymnasium of high scaffolding under a tent roof. The actors wore work clothes and were accompanied by percussion instruments. The intention was not a literal interpretation of the play, but 'abstractions, essences, and possible contradictions embedded in the text. The plot is shattered, condensed, deverbalized; time is discontinuous, shifting. Action merges into collage'.[32] Ariel evoked the storm by voice and gesture, while the cast enacted both the crew and the sinking ship. Miranda and Ferdinand met, touched and made love, while Ariel and Caliban mimicked them. Caliban emerged from between the legs of a giantess Sycorax standing at the top of the scaffolding, and evil was born. He raped Miranda and became master of the island in a sexual orgy. So the play's submerged ideas were dragged to the surface, improvised and explored in terms of such clues as Shakespeare had provided. The result was mutilated Shakespeare, but original Brook: in their time colleagues had said as much of G. Wilson Knight's symbolic commentaries.

While still tussling with *The Tempest*, Brook mounted his most far-reaching assault on a Shakespeare tragedy, this time on a play which was perhaps the greatest challenge the stage could accept. In early 1962 he had read in French Jan Kott's highly charged and idiosyncratic judgments in *Shakespeare Our Contemporary*, and discussed with him the unheroic, existentialist view of *King Lear* as 'a great ritual poem on evanescence and mortality, on man's loneliness in a storm-tossed universe'.[33] Kott's chapter on *Lear* had been entitled 'King Lear or Endgame': from his experience of the horrors of war in Poland, Kott thought he recognized in the play a familiar violence to humanity, and placed the King in company with the despairing anti-heroes of Samuel

Beckett, Vladimir and Estragon, Hamm and Clov. There followed the rare case of a major production directly inspired by the opinions of a literary critic.[34] Kott's assertion was that Shakespeare was like the world, in which every age found what it was looking for; it 'cannot do otherwise'. With this a director like Brook could only agree: to set any play upon a stage was to offer an interpretation for the contemporary audience. Robert Weimann reminded readers of *Shakespeare Survey* that the reason why teddy boys appeared in *Romeo and Juliet*, why a Roman mob could be presented as revolutionaries, Hamlet shown as an angry young man, Brutus presented as an existentialist, Macbeth as a Fascist ruler or *King Lear* as an absurdist play, was that '*any* Shakespeare staging has to come to terms with the tension between Renaissance values and modern evaluations'.[35]

However, in the process of coming to such contrived terms, primary Shakespearian values may be lost. Patrick Cruttwell was one of many who found Kott's thinking misbegotten and over-simplifying, and in a well-labelled article, 'Shakespeare Is Not Our Contemporary', he pointed out that 'if you ask Shakespeare the answers to the problems, you ask him the problems you yourself are obsessed with and you find the answers you yourself have already found'.[36] Jan Kott's world was bitter, brutal and erotic, and he found these qualities wherever he looked in Shakespeare, in tragedy and comedy alike. Writing of 'The Sad Case of Professor Kott', Michael MacOwan argued that 'to sustain this misguided endeavour to cut the mind of Shakespeare to the measure of the mind of Kott, the methods of argument used are, necessarily, disingenuous and unscholarly'.[37] Comedy for this contemporary lay in the outrageous plotting, but it was also coloured by his unwillingness to see the joke; tragedy lay only in the suffering of the hero, not in his nobility of mind or sacrifice. Yet the Kott/Brook *King Lear* was received with unusual enthusiasm – in London as in Prague[38] – much to the embarrassment of teachers: scholarly criticism was at odds with aesthetic acclaim.

The Kott/Brook *Lear* at Stratford in 1962 seemed to assert its artistic independence of scholarship and tradition by many felicities, but also by many deliberate distortions. Brook saw the play as a metaphysical farce about the blindness of man in an environment of savage cruelty. Accordingly the set and costumes were created in order to suggest a primitive mood of menace:

The set consists of geometrical sheets of metal which are ginger with rust and corrosion. The costumes, dominantly leather, have been textured to suggest long and hard wear. The knights' tabards are peeling with long use; Lear's cape and coat are creased and blackened with time and weather. The furniture is rough wood, once sturdy but now decaying back into its hard, brown grain. Apart from the rust, the leather and the old wood, there is nothing but space — giant white flats opening on to a blank cyclorama.[39]

The play began with slow deliberation and great formality of entrance and greeting, except that Lear (Paul Scofield) arrived unexpectedly from a side entrance, cutting through protocol. The declarations of the daughters were made with much ceremony and emphasized by the royal orb, as the prompt-book records:

Goneril rise X CS. Curtsey, Take orb from Kent. Move DSOP corner throne ros. Extend orb. Goneril return orb to Kent. Kent bow. X CS. Curtsey. X sit DSPS. Regan repeats business.

Meanwhile Lear sat with grizzled head erect, eyes narrowed dangerously and a cause for fear. He was described by J. C. Trewin as 'a figure of cold arrogance, set in tarnished gold, his hands clenched upon the arms of a crudely fashioned throne'.[40]

The first innovation was a hunting scene of rowdy knights, following Goneril's admonishment of her father. Charles Marowitz noted:

Incensed by her words, Lear overturns the dinner-table and storms out. This is the cue for general pandemonium as the knights, following their master's example, tip chairs, throw plates and generally demolish the chamber.[41]

He recorded that in rehearsal the stage 'exploded' in the improvisation, tankards flying through the air, hitting actors, ricocheting off the stage. The scene remained dangerously unpredictable in performance. This Lear, according to Harold Hobson, was not a myth, but 'a man capable of tramping twenty miles in a day over sodden fells, and arriving home at nightfall properly tired and in a filthy temper'. And Hobson added, 'In his rage he throws over his daughter's dinner table, and in its enormous revenge the universe overthrows his reason'.[42] All this had the perverse effect of diminishing sympathy with Lear and increasing it with Goneril at the very moment when Shakespeare wishes to modify our first-act revulsion against him. However, not everyone found the King's capriciousness inappropriate, and Kenneth Tynan thought the effect 'revolutionary':

Instead of assuming that Lear is right, and therefore pitiable, we are forced to make judgments — to decide between his claims and those of his kin. And the balance, in this uniquely magnanimous production, is almost even. . . . He is wilfully arrogant, and deserves much of what he gets.

Conversely, his daughters are not fiends. Goneril is genuinely upset by her father's irrational behaviour, and nobody could fault her for carping at Lear's knights, who are here presented as a rabble of bellicose tipplers. After all, what use has a self-deposed monarch for a hundred armed men? Wouldn't twenty-five be enough? We begin to understand Regan's weary inquiry: 'What need one?'[43]

It also followed that the beloved Kent of tradition became no less than a bully when he tripped poor Oswald. Tynan argued that these were correct alienation effects, making the familiar strange. But doesn't Shakespeare supply a full charge of alienation effects of his own when the King and his company are thrust upon the enigmatic heath?

Non-illusion dominated the scenes of storm on the heath. Marowitz reported that the rusted thunder-sheets had been fitted with motors which made them vibrate, and the actors mimed the storm to their orchestration.[44] J. C. Trewin wrote,

Brook always asks for our imagination. Consider the storm scene: a bare stage, the slow descent of what resemble three bleak rusted metal banners that aid the thunder's reverberation, the appearance of men crouching and huddling against the storm, and the sight of Paul Scofield's Lear striding and lunging on through the gale. Then he defies the elements with a mighty and sustained cry of 'Blow winds'.[45]

As these scenes moved to their crisis of madness, only the metallic screens were left on stage with the two pitiful figures of Gloucester and Lear. The descent of the thunder-sheets coincided exactly 'with a stylistic change in performance': the acting became 'starkly non-naturalistic'.[46] Kent and the Gentleman of iii.i ('Who's there besides foul weather?') staggered, fell, ducked and crouched beneath these sheets, and the prompt-book made a careful notation of Lear's voice and the sound effects:

Blow winds, and crack your cheeks (*short*) rage, blow (*longish*).
You cataracts, and hurricanoes spout,
Till you have drench'd our steeples, drown'd the cocks (*short*).
You sulphurous and thought-executing fires,
Vaunt-couriers of oak-cleaving thunderbolts,

220

Singe my white head (*short*). And thou all-shaking thunder,
Strike flat the thick rotundity o' th' world,
Crack Nature's moulds (*short*), all germens spill at once
That makes ingrateful man (*longish + watch Scofield gesture*).

At this point Scofield, hands to his head, staggered back a pace. These sounds seemed to speak to Lear like a supernatural voice rather than be a general background of noisy opposition, and it was this storm that was heard rumbling a further threat at the fall of the curtain.

Rehearsal and performance suffered somewhat from Brook's mistaken urge to see the Fool and Edgar as fully rounded, motivated characters rather than functional role-players. Marowitz reported an actual improvisation designed to establish the Fool's 'offstage character', no less. He was to explore an affectionate relationship with Cordelia, and behind his mask be 'a worried man and terribly tired of all the desperate foolery that he has to carry on all day long'.[47] In performance, the Fool (Alec McCowen) was treated brutally by Lear, and when the storm broke he chose not to huddle under the King's robes, but crouched apart upstage. The role of Edgar puzzled the director, who found it hard to make consistent a character who had to change his job so frequently: Brook had not yet grasped the full implications of non-illusory theatre.

The most heated criticism was prompted by Brook's treatment of Gloucester in the scene of his blinding (III.vii) (see Plate 24). Robert Speaight had properly condemned Kott for ignoring the play's great redemptive moments: 'It is easy to present Lear as a tragedy of absurdity and despair if in forty pages you leave out any mention of Cordelia.'[48] Brook was likewise determined to create a cruel and hostile world for Lear by cutting what signs of pity and hope he dared. Thus, Cornwall's servants were omitted, and with them their balancing compassion for a Gloucester who had been blinded first with Cornwall's golden spur, then with his fingers ('out vile jelly'). Instead, a cold Brechtian light came up and the audience was given the unforgettable visual image of 'a hunched Gloucester, his eyes just out and a ragged cloth thrown over his head, trying to find his way off the stage among the servants who are clearing the set'.[49] One actor was instructed to be sick, presumably to encourage the audience, who were denied 'all possibility of aesthetic shelter' and forced to 'take stock of the scene

24 Peter Brook's *King Lear* at the Royal Shakespeare Theatre, Stratford-upon-Avon, 1962: the scene of Gloucester's blinding

before being engulfed in automatic applause'.[50] By the same impulse the harmonious music Shakespeare called for to wake Lear from his madness ('louder the music there', iv.vii) was made harsh upon the ear:[51] the prompt-book has 'horns off'. And the dying Edmund was not permitted to try to save the royal prisoners at the end ('some good I mean to do/Despite of mine own nature', v.iii); instead, he died on stage and was dragged off ignominiously by Edgar.

These flaws notwithstanding, highly respected critics joined in a chorus of praise. Thinking perhaps of the ancient belief that *Lear* was unactable, Tynan wrote of 'this incomparable production'; Philip Hope-Wallace found it 'the most moving production of the play' he had seen since the war; and W. A. Darlington thought it would go into theatrical history 'as the best all-round performance of this tremendous play in modern times'. But perhaps the most acute comment came from an American scholar, Michael Goldman, who observed that all the alienation finally made the play less painful and more manageable: 'It succeeded in giving us the impression of going through a great deal of horror without having to digest it'; but with a nicely balanced judgment he conceded that Peter Brook 'shows us more of Shakespeare's meaning when he is wrong about it than most of us do when we are right'.[52]

All-white sets of plain curtains or flats date back to J. B. Fagan in the' twenties. They encouraged a non-realistic image for Shakespeare, but the tired eyes of the spectator inhibited attention as well as illusion. The practice matured somewhat with the three-sided white box design, lit harshly from above, conceived by Christopher Morley for Trevor Nunn's Stratford season of 1969, particularly for *Pericles* and *The Winter's Tale*. Nunn's professed purpose was to focus upon the actors and their relationships in 'a kind of chamber architecture'[53] which must have made the open stagers shake their heads. In *The Winter's Tale*, the set served to symbolize a white nursery world of innocence as well as to mark reality from illusion by a lighting change from yellow to blue for Leontes's first-act asides, unhappily suggesting that in his jealousy he was also subject to schizophrenic hallucinations. Peter Brook had moved in a similar direction, notably with his violently Artaudian production of Peter Weiss's *Marat/Sade* (1964), where his plain cold set was planned primarily to achieve a Brechtian effect of alienation. The ultimate setting of this kind was demonstrated by Sally Jacobs for

Brook's Stratford production of *A Midsummer Night's Dream* in 1970.

After Kott's essay, 'Titania and the Ass's Head', erotic versions of *The Dream* had proliferated, the most notable example being John Hirsch's production at Stratford, Ontario in 1968. Brook, however, did not seek the key to the play in its sexual theme, but in its element of magic. In his *Orpheus* essay of 1948 he had long before attacked the tradition of 'gauzes, ballets and Mendelssohn' associated with this play, and by coincidence a Regent's Park Open Air Theatre production in the summer of 1970 had disproved the idea that a pastoral setting provided a fitting background: 'The main casualty, of course, is magic. You cannot have magic in an environment loud with passing aircraft and where actors are obliged to trumpet their lines to reach the back row.'[54] Brook sought the magic not in the fairies, who could as well be stage hands as ballet dancers, but in the play itself, as Helen Dawson observed:

The key to this production comes when Theseus rebukes Hermia for refusing to marry Demetrius. 'Take time to pause', he tells her, and in the pause before the new moon, the play (the dream, the magic) takes place, peopled by the subconscious personalities of Theseus and Hippolyta before their wedding; of Hermia, Lysander, Demetrius and Helena before they finalise their love.[55]

Brook's problem was to find the appropriate substitutes for gauzes and ballets in all the visual and aural elements of his stage, and in the total style of performance. The result? 'The traditions of a lifetime have been torpedoed into infinity! Every accepted canon of stage-mounting has been thrown to the winds. And for what! The quaint simplicity of a child's Christmas toy-box.' But this was the response of *The Stage* to Granville-Barker's *Twelfth Night* in 1912.[56]

Sally Jacobs's set was variously seen as a three-sided white box with white carpet, a squash court, a clinic, a scientific research station, an operating theatre, a gymnasium and a big top. Two doors were cut in the back wall, two slits in the sides, two ladders set at the downstage edges, and a gallery or catwalk round its top allowed the musicians and fairies to gaze down at the players fifteen feet below in the box. Dawson found it to be 'not only a valid device, but one which bursts with invention', and Irving Wardle thought it 'removes the sense of being earthbound: it is natural here for characters to fly'.[57] Into this space the immortals could indeed descend on trapezes or manipulate flexible metal coils on the end of rods to suggest trees. For John Russell Brown, 'this was a machine for acting in',[58] and at the same time the actors acting in it were the visible puppets of the machine.

The box was lit with a fierce white light, and when drums rolled the whole company swooped into the arena in long white capes: not unlike the actors in Williams's *The Comedy of Errors*, their entrance bluntly declared that they were performers, and that thereafter the audience would be participants in their game. Capes flung off, the actors suddenly became characters in primary colours, Theseus in purple, Hippolyta in green, Egeus in blue, Philostrate in black with a tall cap, the lovers mostly in white. Philostrate later became Puck in billowing yellow silk breeches and a little blue cap, while the fairies were less than characters in their baggy grey judo pyjamas. With a great scarlet feather hammock hanging high above them, awaiting an occupant, the purple and yellow figures swung loosely on trapezes in their white open space.

The audience was to look into this magic box, not only to see the magic, but also to be shown what was up the magician's sleeve. Brook explained,

Today we have no symbols that can conjure up fairyland and magic for a modern audience. On the other hand there are a number of actions that a performer can execute that are quite breathtaking. So we went to the art of the circus and the acrobat because they both make purely theatrical statements.[59]

For a month Brook had made the actors practise their tricks in improvisation and rehearsal, and in this setting the audience willingly accepted any invention of the company. The show was indeed breathtaking. The purple flower became a twirling plate on a juggler's wand, passed spinning from Puck to Oberon, a magic image in itself (II.i). 'L'imagination n'a pas de forme', Brook stated in an interview with Guy Dumur for *Le Nouvel Observateur*:

Doit-on montrer une fleur plus extraordinaire qu'une autre, comme on le ferait dans la vitrine d'une boutique de modes? Non, la magie, c'est agir sur un être, opérer un changement. Aussi ai-je choisi de montrer l'opération magique par une scène d'acrobatie qui, jouée avec humour et virtuosité, prend la forme de quelque chose que tout le monde peut voir — un dépassement.[60]

'The plate does not *become* the flower', Peter Thomson commented; 'instead the act of passing it becomes the *magic* of the flower.' Thus, for her nightmare, Hermia was shown frantic in a jungle of the coiled wire (ii.ii). For his assignation with Titania, Bottom was carried to her scarlet bower of feathers in a shower of streamers and paper-plate confetti, backed by the blare of Mendelssohn's Wedding March as Oberon swung across the stage on a rope (iii.i).

The lovers were more athletes and tumblers than dancers, chasing up and down the ladders and round the gallery. On Lysander's 'Withdraw and prove it too' to Demetrius, Hermia threw herself sideways across a door to prevent his going, and as if by a miracle he saved her from falling to the floor. Thereupon he hung her on a trapeze and her 'O me! You juggler! You canker-blossom!' was screamed to Helena as she dangled and kicked the air helplessly (iii.ii). At the end of this scene, Puck's teasing of Lysander and Demetrius in the wood had them chasing in confusion round the legs of giant stilts, on which Puck seemed to have a supernatural power to control their movements. In an interview with Ronald Hayman for *The Times*, Brook made this point: 'Where someone in a library uses intellectual and analytical methods to try to discover what a play is about, actors try to discover through the voice, through the body, through experiment in action.'[61]

Through all this, the players who were not on stage watched those below, on occasion shooting blue and silver darts across the space and making sounds with musical saws and plastic tubes. Richard Peaslee's two small percussion groups provided an intermittent accompaniment of music from bongo-drums, guitar, autoharp or zither, bed-springs and tubular bells. Frequently the verse lines shifted into mock-operatic arias, as for Lysander and Hermia on 'Fair love, you faint with wandering in the wood' (ii.ii), Demetrius's 'So sorrow's heaviness doth heavier grow', Puck's 'Up and down' and Helena's 'O weary night' (iii.ii), and 'Sixpence a day' by the mechanicals (iv.ii). One would think that in all this the lines would be drowned. True, the text was often at variance with the action,[62] but J. W. Lambert was not alone in reporting a 'subtle sculpting of phrase'[63] and J. C. Trewin decided that 'the more closely we watched the actors' unexpected virtuosity, the more we heard of the play, better spoken than most people had ever known'.[64]

The fairies were no longer thought of as decorative, but as functional. They appeared as hefty circus hands when they swept up the

25   Peter Brook's *A Midsummer Night's Dream* at the Royal Shakespeare
Theatre, Stratford-upon-Avon, 1970

confetti,[65] as familiar spirits when they physically controlled the movements of the lovers and demoniacally trapped them in their steel forest, and as amoral trolls when they stripped Snug of his trousers and created an obscene phallus for Bottom. Yet throughout the proceedings and all their busy interventions they remained calm and casual as puppet-masters should.

The mechanicals were very sober workmen, no longer the butts of the play, but keen amateur actors whose play was important to to them. The customary laughs were missing, and Quince's tears of joy when Bottom returned in time to play Pyramus were genuinely moving. For his ass's head, Bottom wore no smothering fur, but a button nose, ear muffs and clogs, so that while he looked like a circus clown his facial expressions remained realistic to a degree: at least in this respect, the imagination was not free to run riot (see Plate 25). Quince's men were treated as individuals, not stereotypes, so that their rehearsals were afforded an unusual dignity. Consequently, the play scene was unfunny, and Snug's lion really did alarm the ladies. Miriam Gilbert carefully noted the effect of Pyramus's dying speech:

Pyramus's death speech is fairly sincere. When Theseus says, 'This passion, and the death of a dear friend, would go near to make a man look sad', he looks across at Hippolyta, as if he's testing her. And she responds, as I think he wants her to, with 'Beshrew my heart, but I pity the man'. Theseus smiles. After Pyramus dies, there are again flip remarks, but Theseus remembers something else as he says, 'With the help of a surgeon, he might yet prove an ass', and the second half of the speech is directed out to the audience, slowly, musingly, challenging us to remember that Pyramus is Bottom who was an ass in the forest.[66]

When in earnest Bottom spoke his line, 'No, I assure you, the wall is down that parted their fathers' (v.i), it was as if he were speaking the solemn moral of the piece for the benefit of all the lovers on the stage. So much sobriety among so much revelry seemed a curious contradiction, but the integration was strongly assisted by a controlling device of the director's. In *The Merry Conceited Humours of Bottom the Weaver* (1646), the pre-Restoration droll derived from *A Midsummer Night's Dream*, Theseus had doubled with Oberon and Hippolyta with Titania; it is probable that this was also the practice of the Lord Chamberlain's Men in the first production (c. 1595), since perforce they regularly doubled the roles in a play whose characters exceeded their number.[67]

Shakespeare, Peter Brook and non-illusion

Although Benedict Nightingale declared that the doubling in Brook's production was done 'for no clear reason except economy',[68] it was apparent to many that his intention was to suggest that the dream in the wood near Athens was a premarital fantasy of the Duke and his bride. The result was that the different groups within the play, the lovers, the fairies and the mechanicals, whose activities are usually set in contrast with one another, seemed more of a kind. The idea of the doubling was made neatly theatrical: Theseus and Hippolyta simply shed their white cloaks at 'dusk', and assumed them again at 'daybreak', by standing in each door to be dressed. Philostrate, Theseus's master of the revels, also became Puck, master of Oberon's magic.[69] The device was made visible: the audience was to participate as omniscient observers.

The new unity of the court and the wood scenes in addition introduced an unaccustomed and darker mood into the comedy. The high spirits of the dream were constantly undercut by the memory of the real problems facing the mortal lovers. Thus, Oberon's desire to punish, even degrade, the Titania he loved became a sobering issue. And Helen Dawson was careful to report that the wood scenes were 'not all fun':

As in a dream — and in a circus — there are moments of stark terror, at times reminiscent of Brook's *Marat/Sade*, when the tent turns into the high walls of an institution, when characters scuttle in fear through Puck's grotesque stilt legs. The fairies are streaked through with cruelty; an uneasily ambiguous bunch who seem to be warning, 'Don't meddle in illusion'.[70]

Theseus's melancholy extended to the last act, when his grave tone underscored the central concept of the imagination which 'bodies forth/The form of things unknown'. Dawson considered that Brook's interpretive idea cut through the play like a laser: 'In this extra-terrestrial world we meet that part of ourselves which we bury under social convention', and upon Theseus's rebuke to Hermia, 'Take time to pause', all parties to the play were submitted to Shakespeare's idiom of the supernatural.[71]

Needless to say, opinions about Brook's *Dream* were radically divided. Those who disliked it could not see past the surface of the production, Kenneth Hurren finding it 'a tiresomely self-indulgent display of directorial gimmickry'[72] and J. W. Lambert was troubled that the director's 'commentary' on the play 'though often stimulating and enriching, may swamp its subject'.[73] David Selbourne, who watched rehearsals, summarized this position when he argued that the production was 'technically brilliant', but a 'director-shaped commodity'.[74] However, a leader in *The Times* sought to resolve the contradiction between the eccentric setting and performance, and the shrewd and thought-provoking ideas many spectators perceived. The article asked the question, 'How, beyond an identity of text, is Mr Brook's production related to William Shakespeare's play?', and answered,

This is not the kind of production that seeks to reconstruct the performance that Shakespeare and his company are most likely to have devised. There have been such essays in theatrical scholarship. Being original, the Stratford production is not one of them. Being also appropriate, it is not at the opposite pole either, where the play is treated as if it were no more than an idea, or a structure, or a source of invention, rather in the way Joyce or Sartre has made use of Greek myth. In versions of that kind the producer does not respect the natural limits imposed by the text. He feels free to contrive situations and to characterize the *dramatis personae* as he fancies. Being appropriate, the Stratford production is not of that kind either. . . .

A good Shakespeare production is true to the original in a sense other than textual accuracy or resemblance to how it might have been at the Globe. One begins to see why Plato needed his doctrine of Forms. The question is easily resolved if one is allowed to have a Form of the *Dream* laid up in heaven. Productions of the play to be good would have to resemble the Form of it, the resemblance being not one of copying but of congruence. So it would come about that for all the trapezes, juggling, helical wire trees, and general non-Elizabethanism, the Stratford production is not just good theatre but a true production of the *Dream*.[75]

Just as the poet cannot explain his meaning in terms other than those of the words of his poem, so Brook could not express his sense of a play in terms other than those of performance. The Platonic Form lay hidden there, valid and (one would think) scholarly, awaiting discovery. How close are we here to Wilson Knight's concept of 'interpretation'?

Audiences can hope to perceive the meaning of Shakespeare's *A Midsummer Night's Dream* only by allowing it to expand the mind and senses. Performance which does not close the windows of the play is the proper stimulus for such perception, and Brook's approach was to deny all stage illusion, leaving a sufficient vacuum to be filled by the imagination of the spectator. Dawson, the most enthusiastic of the critics, found that Brook made the play and its poetry 'leap into almost Oriental clarity', and that her mind began to race. The actors never hid the *fact* of performance, and although this might seem to be merely a modish alienation-effect, in practice the audience felt an inescapable demand for its collaboration in a common endeavour. Theseus and Hippolyta spoke their opening lines to the audience as they knelt ritualistically on cushions. Egeus's complaint was spoken as a challenge to the audience. Helena's first-act soliloquy, 'How happy some', was dropped in the audience's lap. In iii.ii, Hermia and Demetrius momentarily froze in front of Oberon for Puck's 'This is the woman, but not this the man' — 'a moment of stylization which reminds us once more that we are watching a play, which can be stopped, started, controlled, speeded up, slowed down, at will.'[76] Puck's 'Lord, what fools these mortals be!' was again for the audience. When the lovers greeted the dawn, they held hands in a line facing the house, sharing their wonder: 'Why then we are awake' (iv.i). Oberon's closing verses, 'Through this house each fairy stray' (v.i), embraced the whole theatre, and on Puck's 'Give me your hands, if we be friends', the whole company turned to the audience, ran up the aisles and shook hands with everyone they could.[77] It was the audience's triumph they wished to share.

12

Conclusion:
the critical revolution

If in this survey there has been more emphasis on stage production than literary criticism, it could be judged that the initiative in recovering Shakespeare has shifted to the theatre, that the biggest single advances have been made there. In 1900 readers turned to the scholar to elucidate the plays: in 1970 scholarship seems suspect and the stage seems to be more in touch with their spirit. Nevertheless, it is the contention of this book that without the rediscovery of the Elizabethan stage, the achievement of Tyrone Guthrie in recapturing the mutuality of play and audience would not have been possible, and without the sense of Shakespeare as a dealer in visions, culminating in the kind of 'interpretation' associated with the name of G. Wilson Knight, Peter Brook would probably not have found the surprisingly wide acceptance from academic critics that he has. Knight's distinction between 'criticism' and 'interpretation' is worth recalling:

The critic is, and should be, cool and urbane, seeing the poetry he discusses not with the eyes of a lover but as an object; whereas interpretation deliberately immerses itself in its theme and speaks less from the seats of judgement than from the creative centre.[1]

Accept that, and we can accept much that is unconventional and threatening in Brook.

The giant figure behind both Guthrie and Brook was Harley Granville-Barker, whose early work at the Savoy foreshadowed our notions of Shakespeare's stagecraft and thematic interpretation when neither had reached a satisfactory maturity. If all this seems tendentious — as indeed it must at this crucial point in the development of our response to the plays —what remains true is that the Shakespeare known to both critic and playgoer in late Victorian times has changed utterly after two or three generations. Criticism has shifted its position as radically as have Shakespearian acting and directing. Except in the cinema, the straining towards a psychological and pictorial realism for Shakespeare is all in the past. The half-apprehended mystery of a supremely non-illusory drama and theatre, that of Shakespeare and the Elizabethan stage, promised to open new worlds for discovery and conquest. The immense influence of Granville-Barker upon all major Shakespearians in this century might be explained on these grounds alone: his was the promise.

It follows that histories and surveys of Shakespeare criticism, which appear with desperate regularity as contributions to Shakespeare periodicals as well as in book form, cannot hereafter ignore the events and developments that are usually collected separately in 'stage histories'. Our understanding of Shakespeare today is not divisible, and any unnatural separation of reader and playgoer implied by these publications will suggest a critical inadequacy, a failure to integrate current knowledge. The factors which contribute to our changes in Shakespearian taste and sensibility now seem infinitely wide; an article here, a performance there, an interview or a broadcast, an aesthetic theory, a trend in contemporary playwriting perhaps.

On this point, it may be thought that the development of Shakespeare production and criticism towards a fuller recognition of his non-illusory assumptions suggests in the last few years the direct influence of the work of Bertolt Brecht. It is true that Brecht's theories of epic theatre and his ideas about distancing an audience have had an incalculable impact on our thinking about the basis of communication in drama, especially since the formation of the Berliner Ensemble in 1949 with its subsequent visits to other capitals. Brecht's own 'adaptations' from periods of drama carefully selected for their highly conventional manner — those of Greek tragedy, Elizabethan tragedy and eighteenth-century comedy — made their contribution to our better understanding of the kind of theatre of imaginative release which preceded the realism of Ibsen and Strindberg.

But Brecht's practice served to accentuate and demonstrate what was becoming known about Shakespeare before. Poel and Granville-Barker would have concurred with Brecht's reiterated statement about the undesirability of a theatre of hypnosis and the need for an 'epic' theatre:

The stage began to tell a story. The narrator was no longer missing, along with the fourth wall. . . . The actors too refrained from going over wholly into their role, remaining detached from the character they were playing and clearly inviting criticism of him.

The spectator was no longer in any way allowed to submit to an experience uncritically (and without practical consequences) by means of simple empathy with the characters in a play. The production took the subject-matter and the incidents shown and put them through a process of alienation: the alienation that is necessary to all understanding. When something seems 'the most obvious thing in the world' it means that any attempt to understand the world has been given up.[2]

It is also worth remembering that Guthrie's fundamental work on Elizabethan open stagecraft was done before he knew much of Brecht. Now, whether the playgoer turns to a production like John Barton's ritualistic *Richard II* at Stratford, 1973, or to Joseph Papp's seasons of free-wheeling Shakespeare in New York, past traditions of realistic presentation are being stripped away and the spirit of Elizabethan ritual and role-playing reminds him of Shakespeare's essential theatricality in a way that Brecht would fully have endorsed.

It is a sign of the times that the previously unthinkable has happened in Britain: John Russell Brown, a professor of drama, was in 1974 appointed as an associate of the National Theatre in London, just prior to the opening of the National Theatre proper on the south bank of the Thames. This followed upon the slow but steady growth of a few university drama departments in the United Kingdom. The appointment is a matter for congratulation to both the profession and to academia. However, it is ironic that in the same year Brown should publish a polemic against directors of Shakespeare.[3] This is hardly a sign of the times, and may even seem to be an unwarranted regression, since the intermittent dissatisfaction of lovers of Shakespeare with his stage representation has been common for two hundred years. Brown's attack, however, is specifically against the power of a director to dictate the Shakespeare experience and to impose his interpretation upon an audience. This charge was sufficiently answered by Guthrie in 1960[4] on behalf of all directors and actors: both actor and director regard their responsibility as one of 'interpretation' to some degree – it is what they are paid for. The analogous activity is that of the literary critic who traces themes as if the plays were labyrinthine puzzles, except that by picking about in the text he appears to show proof that he is not falsifying the evidence. The critic also regards his responsibility as one of interpretation, though he may lack the power of the stage to *test* his thesis.

Conclusion: the critical revolution

I submit that Brown's proposal to allow actors and audience to explore Shakespeare without the intervention of a director would produce no different result. Indeed, the tyranny of the actor has not been unknown in the past, and the tyranny of an audience is the worst of all worlds. But then tyrannous excess is not the mark of a good director either. Good drama, and Shakespeare in particular, expects all parties to the play to make their creative contribution, or else the dramatist would be a tyrant himself; and I cannot think of a playwright who is less of a tyrant in this way than Shakespeare.

Critical commentaries will inevitably continue to isolate themes in the plays: to recognize 'meaning' is the conceptual end-product of any reading or playgoing experience of Shakespeare. But John Russell Brown is right to insist that the play on the stage expanding before an audience is the source of all valid discovery. Shakespeare speaks, if anywhere, through his medium. The important development in Shakespeare studies in this generation had also been anticipated in Granville-Barker: the perception of the plays as blueprints for performance.[5] When Hamlet speaks his soliloquy, 'To be or not to be', it is nowadays proper to remember that this is no soliloquy at all, and that our audience's eyes will also be watching Ophelia at her orisons as well as Claudius and Polonius behind the arras: what we *perceive* is a suicide statement coloured by the piety of a religious girl and the politics of those in power in Denmark.

The text-as-score is of course only the basis and beginning of perceptual criticism. This approach also views Shakespeare as a self-conscious artist working out immediate structural problems of stage communication, in which 'each poem contains its own poetics'.[6] Each play is shaped by the need to make its statement dramatically workable as its author explores the farther reaches of his theme in the conventional terms of his art. In 1938, E. M. W. Tillyard groped for a concept to describe the operation of the symbolism in Shakespeare's last plays, plays in which he found the playwright trying to express more than ever before, and invented the slippery concept of 'planes of reality'. 'There are times', Tillyard argued, 'when in the realm of action even the simplest and most normal people find their scale of reality upset', and he went on to hail Shakespeare as the outstanding author who was 'familiar with many planes of reality and gifted incomparably with the power of passing from one to another'.[7]

Conveying the experience of different levels of perception to an audience, urging their imaginative expansion, has also been lightly investigated by S. L. Bethell, Anne Righter and a handful of others. For Bethell, the 'multi-consciousness' of the Elizabethan audience explained how it might be at once involved with an illusion and detached by a sense of its own reality. Shakespeare's drama lay between 'the two extremes of absolute conventionalism and absolute naturalism': 'His characters are not merely personified abstractions, but, on the other hand, they are not precisely like real people.' In the course of a single play, the Elizabethan playwright slips up and down the scale between convention and realism, and 'this rapidity of adjustment is a principal component in Shakespeare's remarkable subtlety'. Bethell finds this a special characteristic of his unself-conscious art, and concludes,

I believe I am justified in asserting that there *is* a popular dramatic tradition, and that its dominant characteristic is the audience's ability to respond spontaneously and unconsciously on more than one plane of attention at the same time.[8]

Shakespeare's freedom with time and place, the impersonation and presentation of character, the mixing of comedy and tragedy, and many other phenomena of the Elizabethan theatre, are now studies which await discussion and experiment. Anne Righter's seminal work on the theatrical metaphor,[9] and the degree of assumed illusion in the writing and reception of a play, must be seen in this context of conscious or unconscious stagecraft.

None of this work can now proceed far without the active assistance of the stage itself. In a recent conference on Shakespeare and the Theatre in New York, the customary controversy between traditionalists and modernists over the practising theatre's faithfulness to Shakespeare was heard again, and in a comment Louis Marder questioned whether recent eccentricities of production were helpful or harmful:

Whether it is done for shock value, for clearer interpretation, or for making Shakespeare our contemporary, one cannot help wondering whether putting characters on trapeze bars (Brook's *MND*), on hobby horses and stilts (John Barton's *R2*), in shorts or nude, with comic warriors in *Tro.* (Lincoln Center N.Y. Festival production), making Goneril and Regan super-sensual (The [British] Actors Co. in Brooklyn, N.Y.), or Orlando's tickling Charles the

Conclusion: the critical revolution

Wrestler into surrender (The National Shakespeare [touring] Company), makes any improvement in Shakespeare.[10]

And he added, 'Only the text can tell us what Shakespeare intended'. The gist of this book has been to suggest that to stop short at the text is now a kind of surrender, for the text will not tell us much until it speaks in its own medium.

If I may dare to paraphrase a passage from E. H. Gombrich's *Art and Illusion*,[11] both actor and scholar can render only what their sense of the dramatic medium will allow, for they see what they interpret before they interpret what they see. Their Shakespeare originates in the mind, in their reactions to Shakespeare rather than in Shakespeare himself. But as the style and idiom of their interpretation gain currency in each other's eyes, so they must with audiences and readers. Actor and scholar will teach each other, not what Shakespeare 'means', but what his possibilities are beyond logic. Nor will these be exhausted. The scholar will modify the actor's illumination, the actor will modify the scholar's, a process of infinite adjustment. Shakespeare remains uncharted territory waiting to be explored and articulated. But the object of all this earnest endeavour, the experience in some degree of Shakespeare's greater vision, cannot be reached without the humble services of both parties.

Notes

Introductory

1. In his English Institute paper, 'The New Theater and the Old: Reversions and Rejuvenations', Jonas Barish writes most recently, 'Thanks to the polemics and experiments of our own stage we are drawing closer than at any time since the seventeenth century to an accurate perception of the theater of the Elizabethans' (*Reinterpretations of Elizabethan Drama*, ed. N. Rabkin, New York, 1969, p. 31).
2. General Introduction to *The Players' Shakespeare* in *The Tragedie of Macbeth*, London, 1923.
3. 8 June 1896, quoted in Robert Speaight, *William Poel and the Elizabethan Revival*, London, 1954, p. 113.
4. *Shakespearian Punctuation*, Oxford, 1911.
5. *The Times Literary Supplement*, 17 February 1921.
6. 'Some Tasks for Dramatic Scholarship', read 7 June 1922, in *Essays by Divers Hands*, III, London, 1923.
7. 'Reconstruction in the Theatre', *The Times*, 20 February 1919, p. 11.
8. Dennis Bartholomeusz, *Macbeth and the Players*, Cambridge, 1969, p. 142.
9. See Tyrone Guthrie: *A Life in the Theatre*, London, 1959, p. 20.
10. In *Shakespearean Tragedy*, London, 1904.
11. *Shakespeare's Happy Comedies*, London, 1962, ch. III.
12. G. E. Bentley's argument in *Shakespeare and His Theatre*, Lincoln, Nebraska, 1964, and discussed in Stanley Wells, *Literature and Drama*, London, 1970, pp. 98 ff.
13. Moulton's *Shakespeare as a Dramatic Artist* was completed in 1892, Baker published *The Development of Shakespeare as a Dramatist* in 1907 and Q's lectures on Shakespeare were published as *Shakespeare's Workmanship* in 1918.
14. Like A. C. Sprague, *Shakespearian Players and Performances* (Cambridge, Mass., 1953); Toby Lelyveld, *Shylock on the Stage* (Cleveland, 1960); Marvin Rosenberg, *The Masks of Othello* and *The Masks of King Lear* (Berkeley, 1961 and 1972), though more concerned with character than with play; Charles Shattuck's and Blakemore Evans's work on the prompt-books; and Dennis Bartholomeusz, *Macbeth and the Players*.
15. London, 1922. The quotation is from p. 159.
16. Cambridge, 1932.

Notes

17. *ibid.*, p. 3.
18. *An Historic Account of the Rise and Progress of the English Stage, and of the Oeconomy and Usages of the Ancient Theatres in England*, London, 1792, was based on a knowledge of the Revels Accounts and Henslowe's papers.
19. *Elizabethan Stage Conditions*, pp. 4—6.
20. *ibid.*, pp. 12—14.
21. *ibid.*, p. 114.
22. *ibid.*, p. 124.
23. *The Heart of Hamlet*, New York, 1949.
24. *The Times Literary Supplement*, 26 July 1963.
25. 'English Criticism of Shakespeare Performances Today', *Deutsche Shakespeare-Gesellschaft West, Jahrbuch 1967*. ed. H. Heuer.
26. *Style in 'Hamlet'*, Princeton, 1969.
27. *Literature and Drama, with special reference to Shakespeare and his contemporaries*, London, 1970, p. 92.
28. Wells is elsewhere quick to point out instances of falsification of meaning by Bradley and Kott (pp. 93—4).
29. *ibid.*, p. 100.
30. Under the title *Reinterpretations of Elizabethan Drama*.
31. *ibid.*, p. viii.

1 Victorian Shakespeare

1. Robert Speaight, *William Poel and the Elizabethan Revival*, p. 25.
2. I owe many details in this chapter to the indispensable labours of George C. D. Odell in *Shakespeare from Betterton to Irving*, 2 vols., New York, 1920.
3. Kemble's teapot oratory, in which the actor postured with one arm like the spout of a teapot, may well have been preferable to Kean's violent explosions of feeling, Macready's grunting and groaning and the recurring image of Phelps's picking at his chest.
4. Much of this information can be drawn from John Bell's acting edition of Shakespeare, 1773—5, 'regulated from the prompt-books, by permission of the managers'. Odell remarks that this edition is the worst imaginable with which to read Shakespeare (ii, p. 16): however, it is invaluable to the student of theatre.
5. In 1700 Cibber had pasted together lines from five of the history plays to produce a thriller which Odell considered better than Shakespeare's: 'It is nervous, unified, compact, where the original is sprawling, diffuse and aimless' (ii, p. 153). 'Whatever we may think of that master-craftsman's [Cibber's] hatchet work and carpentry on several of the historical pieces, the fact remains that his *Richard III* was a magnificent bit of theatrical effectiveness' (p. 55). Shakespeare's Richard returned with Phelps in 1845.
6. London had to wait for Macready's revival of *King Lear* in 1838 to get

some sense of the original story, although the Gloucester scenes were still omitted.

7. *Shakespeare from Betterton to Irving*, II, p. 60.

8. Pepys's verdict had been, 'It is one of the best plays for a stage, and variety of dancing and musique, that ever I saw' (19 April 1667). Phelps restored *Macbeth* in 1847.

9. Under Charles Johnson's title *Love in a Forest*.

10. James Boaden in his *Life of Kemble*, which supplies these details, found the new Covent Garden without 'a particle of taste'.

11. Thus, Tree's *Dream* of 1900 had luminous pillars. By 1911, the pillars were brighter still, and the fairy garlands were strings of electric lights; even the magic flower had a small internal light (William Winter, *Shakespeare on the Stage*, New York, 1916, vol. III, pp. 259–60).

12. From *The New English Drama, with Prefatory Remarks, etc., by W. Oxberry, Comedian*, London, 1818–23.

13. *Diary and Reminiscences*, ed. F. Pollock, 2 vols., London, 1875. Audiences had to wait for Phelps at Sadlers Wells in 1845 to see a male actor as the Fool.

14. *Shakespeare from Betterton to Irving*, II, p. 196. Odell imagined the arrangement 'very effective for the stage'.

15. *ibid.*, p. 455.

16. *The Producer and the Play*, London, 1957, p. 195.

17. *The Examiner*, 18 October 1856, reprinted in *The Journal of a London Playgoer, 1851–1866*, London, 1891.

18. G. M. Lewes, *On Actors and the Art of Acting*, New York, 1880, p. 19. I owe this reference to B. G. Cross.

19. *The Examiner*, 25 October 1856.

20. 11 January 1900

21. 13 January 1900.

22. 3 March 1900. 'Benson's presentment, while making no pretence of competition, in scenic opulence, with that of Tree, concurrent at Her Majesty's, was handsome and adequate, providing a simple, charming background for the action' (William Winter, *Shakespeare on the Stage*, vol. III, p. 258).

23. Taken from Norman Marshall, *The Producer and the Play*, pp. 148–9.

24. Its supreme achievement was embodied in the work of Stanislavsky and the Moscow Art Theatre.

25. *The Shakespeare Promptbooks*, Urbana, 1965, p. 12.

26. Norman Marshall, *The Producer and the Play*, p. 145.

27. 3 March 1900.

28. *In Various Directions: a view of the theatre*, London, 1965, p. 62.

29. Writing of Irving as Richard III, William Poel reported that Irving 'appears to aim at creating an effect by working his scene up to a striking picture upon which the curtain may fall' (Robert Speaight, *William Poel and the Elizabethan Revival*, p. 32).

Notes

30. 28 September 1895.
31. 26 December 1896.
32. Remarked in Odell, II, p. 423 and in A. C. Sprague and J. C. Trewin, *Shakespeare's Plays Today*, London, 1970, p. 55. Irving knocked and waited at the door as the curtain fell, but when Tree borrowed the idea he lacked 'Irving's natural austerity of taste', as Harold Child reports: 'Tree must go in, and the light of his lantern be seen as he searched upstairs and down for his daughter. It was very picturesque, but lacking in the dramatic intensity of Irving's stillness' ('Improving on Shakespeare'. *The Listener*, London, 27 January 1937, p. 159).

2. Scholars and actors

1. 'Actors and Scholars: A View of Shakespeare in the Modern Theatre', *Shakespeare Survey 12*, ed. Allardyce Nicoll, Cambridge, 1959, p. 77.
2. Of him J. C. Trewin tells the story, 'Just as Mr Wemmick said in effect, "Halloa! Here's a church! Let's have a wedding!", so Greet would say, "Here's a lawn! Let's do the *Dream*!"' (*Shakespeare on the English Stage, 1900–1964*, London, 1964, p. 14).
3. *The Morning Post*, London, 19 August 1919.
4. *The Daily Telegraph*, London, 22 August 1919.
5. 'The Elizabethan Shakespeare', reprinted in *Aspects of Shakespeare, British Academy Lectures, 1923–31*, ed. J. W. Mackail, London and Oxford, 1933, p. 212.
6. A. C. Bradley, *Shakespearean Tragedy*, p. 240.
7. *ibid.*, p. 216. He said the same thing again a few years later: 'I don't think that scholars and editors can see Shakespeare performed too often. Certainly I never see a performance of Shakespeare, however feeble, without learning something new about the play, something I should never have guessed at by just sitting down and reading it as a book' ('Shakespeare: The Scholar's Contribution' in *The Listener*, London, 17 March 1937).
8. *The Approach to Shakespeare*, London, 1930, pp. 3, 4, 9.
9. The introduction to *Aspects of Shakespeare*, was dated December 1932.
10. 'The Study of Shakespeare', *University of Edinburgh Journal*, Summer 1936, p. 10.
11. *ibid.*, p. 11.
12. In *The Exemplary Theatre*.
13. With Arthur Quiller-Couch for the *New Cambridge Shakespeare*. It was published by Cambridge, 1923.
14. 'Shakespeare: The Scholar's Contribution', *The Listener*, 17 March 1937.
    All are Dover Wilson's italics. The matter is taken up again in a discussion on Guthrie's contribution to Shakespeare studies, Chapter 10, p. 183.

Notes

15. 'The Study and Practice of Shakespeare Production', *Shakespeare Survey 18*, ed. Allardyce Nicoll, Cambridge, 1965, p. 69.
16. 'Associating with Shakespeare' (address at King's College, London, 1931), The Shakespeare Association, London, 1932, p. 10.
17. *Morning Chronicle*, London, 14 March 1814. Reprinted in *Hazlitt on Theatre*, ed. W. Archer and R. Lowe, New York, 1957.
18. *ibid.*, 15 February 1814.
19. *The Champion*, London, 8 January 1815.
20. In discussing Hazlitt's position, I am happy to follow the argument proposed by Arthur Eastman in *A Short History of Shakespearean Criticism*, New York. 1968.
21. 'Fifty Years of Shakespearian Criticism: 1900–1950', in *Shakespeare Survey 4*, ed. Allardyce Nicoll, Cambridge, 1951, p.3.
22. *A History of Shakespearian Criticism*, Oxford, 1932, vol. II, p. 211.
23. Kenneth Muir, 'Changing Interpretations of Shakespeare' in *The Age of Shakespeare*, ed. B. Ford, Harmondsworth, 1955, p. 292.
24. *Shakespearean Tragedy*, p. 1.
25. *ibid.*, pp. 7–8.
26. *ibid.*, p. 12.
27. 'Diabolic Intellect and the Noble Hero: A Note on Othello', in *Scrutiny*, Cambridge, vol. VI, no. 3, December 1937.
28. Reprinted in *Towards Standards of Criticism*, ed. F. R. Leavis, London, 1933, pp. 29–43. I am grateful to Michael Black for drawing my attention to Rickword's contribution, and to Black's excellent discussion in 'Character in Shakespeare' in *The Critical Review* (Melbourne), no. 17, 1974.
29. 'Diabolic Intellect and the Noble Hero', pp. 259 and 260.
30. See Louis Marder, *His Exits and His Entrances: the Story of Shakespeare's Reputation*, Philadelphia, 1963, p. 26. William Dodd's *Beauties* came out in 1752 in two volumes, and ran through forty editions in 150 years.
31. As outlined by Marder, *ibid.*, p. 133.
32. Samuel Schoenbaum, *Shakespeare's Lives*, Oxford and New York, 1970, p. 420.
33. *ibid.*, p. 421.
34. The Stage of Shakespeare' published in *Shakespeare in the Theatre*, London, 1913, p. 11.
35. *ibid.*, p. 7.
36. The best representation of the nineteenth century's idea of the interior of the Globe up to this time is a water-colour by George Pycroft (see Plate 5). It is based chiefly upon the scanty evidence of the exterior view by Visscher and pictures of continental street stages: it shows the octagonal shape, a glimpse of the sky, a high platform and groundlings thronging around it; but to these it adds a Victorian gallery, a traverse curtain and some sky borders.

Notes

37. Add to these his *Dramatic Documents from the Elizabethan Playhouses* published in 2 vols. in 1931. The latest edition of *Henslowe's Diary* is by R. A. Foakes and R. T. Rickert, Cambridge, 1961.
38. 'Shakespearian Production in the Nineteenth Century' in *William Shakespeare, 1564–1964* (The Shakespeare Exhibition catalogue of 1964), p. 110.
39. Kenneth Muir, 'Fifty Years of Shakespearian Criticism: 1900–1950'.
40. *Shakespeare's Workshop*, Oxford, 1928, p. 48.
41. *Shakespeare's Lives*, p. 485.
42. 'The Plays of Shakespeare', *The Nation*, March 1912, reprinted in *Shakespeare in the Theatre*, p. 38.
43. *ibid.*, p. 150.
44. *ibid.*, p. 203–4. Written under the title 'A National Theatre' for *The New Age*, November 1910.
45. *ibid.*, p. 205.

3 Mr Poel's 'Hamlet'

1. J. C. Trewin, *Shakespeare on the English Stage, 1900–1964*, p. 47.
2. Robert Speaight, *William Poel and the Elizabethan Revival*, p. 42.
3. Letter to Robert Speaight, 12 August 1952, in *A Bridges-Adams Letter Book*, ed. Robert Speaight, Society for Theatre Research, 1971, p. 46.
4. 'Some Tasks for Dramatic Scholarship', delivered 7 June 1922 and published in *Essays by Divers Hands*, ed. F. S. Boas, vol. iii, London, 1923, pp. 30–1.
5. *In Various Directions*, p. 64.
6. 18 March 1844.
7. Granville-Barker told the amusing story of the Duchess of Gloucester pleading for her son's life in *Richard II*. Poel called for more and more hysteria until he was satisfied: 'That's the tone, keep it up'. At this, Granville-Barker had to point out that the actress had collapsed in tears on the floor and that her hysteria was real (in Speaight, *op. cit.*, p. 70).
8. William Poel, *Shakespeare in the Theatre*, pp. 5, 60, 175.
9. *ibid.*, p. 53.
10. *ibid.*, p. 61.
11. *ibid.*, p. 215.
12. Norman Marshall, *The Producer and the Play*, p. 150. In a letter to *The Times*, 31 July 1899, Sidney Lee stated that the object of the Society was 'to give occasionally dramatic representation to the masterpieces of the Elizabethan drama in a simple and dignified manner and with little or no scenic elaboration'. The Elizabethan Stage Society was formally established in 1894.
13. Poel, *op. cit.*, p. 43.

Notes

14. *ibid.*, p. 51.
15. Quoted in Poel, *ibid.*, p. 9. My italics.
16. *Shakespeare on the Stage: First Series*, New York, 1911, p. 355.
17. 30 April 1881, p. 7.
18. Letter of 1 February 1881, quoted in Speaight, *William Poel and the Elizabethan Revival*, p. 48.
19. Letter dated 20 April in *The Era*, 23 April 1881, p. 4. In 1899, Poel still believed that Q1 showed 'the development which this great drama underwent before it reached its present shape' (*The Times*, 10 July).
20. 'Mr. Furnivall's "Hamlet"', 21 April 1881. Current theory has it that some of the actors compiled the copy for Q1 from memory, naturally recalling their own parts better.
21. *The Era*, 30 April 1892.
22. Looking like 'a stout female being led to the altar', *ibid.*, 23 April 1881.
23. *ibid.*, 30 April 1892.
24. Poel's prompt-book is in the possession of the Society for Theatre Research.
25. 'Mr. Furnivall's "Hamlet"', 21 April 1881.
26. 23 April 1881.
27. *Nights at the Play II*, London, 1883, p. 314.
28. 23 April 1881. This report is discussed by A. C. Sprague, 'Shakespeare and William Poel', *University of Toronto Quarterly*, October 1947, pp. 29–37.
29. *The Era*, 14 May 1881, p. 8.
30. *William Poel and the Elizabethan Revival*, p. 57.
31. 22 February 1900.
32. *The Times*, 11 November 1893. Poel's use of a traverse curtain was adopted as a convenience for many later Shakespeare productions inside the proscenium arch.
33. Archer also damned Poel's bowdlerizing, for example, his substituting for 'He has got the wench with child', 'He will shortly be a father'. On this point, see Speaight, *op. cit.* pp. 98–101.
34. *Dramatic Values*, London, 1911, p. 244.
35. 11 November 1893.
36. *The Saturday Review*, 2 July 1896, reprinted in *Our Theatres in the Nineties*, vol. ii, London, 1932, p. 184.
37. According to the diary of John Manningham, who had been present as a bencher of the Middle Temple. The manuscript had been quoted by Halliwell-Phillipps *in extenso*.
38. See, most recently, Richard Southern, *The Staging of Plays before Shakespeare*, London, 1973.
39. 11 February 1897.
40. *Our Theatres in the Nineties*, vol. iii, p. 242. In *The Fortnightly Review* of July 1900, Beerbohm Tree and Poel debated the question of a scenic compromise, and Poel concluded: 'The illusion must be complete or it is best not attempted at all.'

Notes

41. *The Saturday Review*, 20 June 1903, p. 776, reprinted in *Around Theatres*, London, 1953, p. 258.
42. *ibid.*, p. 531.
43. 1 March 1904.
44. *Dramatic Values*, p. 244.
45. *Our Theatres in the Nineties*, vol. III, p. 242.
46. 21 April 1910.
47. *The Times*, 12 May 1913.
48. 16 July 1927, pp. 90–1.
49. In a letter to the author.
50. 18 February 1928, p. 190.
51. *A Bridges-Adams Letter Book*, ed. Robert Speaight, p. 47.

4 The advent of stage-centred criticism

1. *A Life in the Theatre*, p. 76.
2. *Shakespeare on the Stage*, vol. II, New York, 1915, p. 85.
3. J. C. Trewin, *Shakespeare on the English Stage, 1900–1964*, pp. 48–9.
4. Guthrie, *op. cit.*, p. 76.
5. Gielgud reports that Granville-Barker in fact supervised several rehearsals and worked with the actors for ten days. See *Stage Directions*, London, 1963, pp. 51 ff.
6. Trewin, *op. cit.*, p. 216.
7. Norman Marshall describes this growth in ch. VI of *The Other Theatre*, London, 1947.
8. In a letter to the author.
9. Introduction, p. 15.
10. P. v. Nicoll's italics.
11. His Majesty's Stationery Office. Edmund Chambers was an official of the Board of Education until 1926, and John Dover Wilson had been an inspector for the Board for eleven years before becoming Professor of Education at King's College, London, in 1924.
12. *The Stage*, 15 July 1926.
13. 'The Universities and the Stage', *The Stage*, 17 June 1926.
14. Dover Wilson made the point that the standard editions printed *Hamlet*'s first court scene with the characters listed in order of rank, but the Second Quarto, nearer to the actors' script, put Hamlet last, thus suggesting his striking first entrance not only in black but also trailing ('Shakespeare: The Scholar's Contribution', *The Listener*, 17 March 1937). This kind of minor, but important, detail was to be discovered again and again when the scholar saw with playhouse eyes.
15. G. E. Bentley's seven-volume *The Jacobean and Caroline Stage*, Oxford, 1941–68, continued Chambers's work on the theatrical records after 1616.

Notes

16. Other important collections are: *Pre-Restoration Stage Studies* (1927), *Shakespeare's Workshop* (1928) and *Those Nut-Cracking Elizabethans* (1935).
17. John Cranford Adams was to lean heavily upon Lawrence's assumptions for his speculative study *The Globe Playhouse* (1942).
18. See Robert Speaight, *William Poel and the Elizabethan Revival*, pp. 84 ff.
19. Letter to Lawrence of 15 January 1914, quoted in Speaight, *ibid.*, p. 107.
20. *Review of English Studies*, vol. 4, no. 14, April 1928, pp. 229–37.
21. An appellation suggested by Arthur Eastman in *A Short History of Shakespearean Criticism*, p. 325.
22. Quiller-Couch, *op. cit.*, Cambridge Pocket Edition, 1931, p. 4. Granville-Barker reported that Q had stage-managed *The Merchant of Venice* and had confessed to him that he had 'learned a lot about the play in the process' ('From *Henry V* to *Hamlet*', *Proceedings of the British Academy* 1924–5, xi).
23. *Shakespeare in the Theatre*, p. 55, reprinted from *The Nation*, March 1912.
24. *ibid.*, p. 122.
25. Read at the meeting of the New Shakspere Society, 12 April 1889, reprinted in *ibid.*, pp. 133 ff.
26. *The New Age*, September 1909.
27. *ibid.*, August 1912.
28. Translated and published in London in 1922.
29. Schücking, *op. cit.*, p. 26.
30. *ibid.*, pp. 29 ff.
31. *ibid.*, p. 109.
32. *ibid.*, p. 221.
33. The passage in which Schücking found Ariel embodying qualities 'ideally feminine' dated him exactly. The best analysis of the shortcomings of his book is in M. C. Bradbrook's *Elizabethan Stage Conditions*, pp. 84–96.
34. *Art and Artifice in Shakespeare: A Study in Dramatic Contrast and Illusion*, Cambridge, 1933, develops and organizes his thinking on these and other plays.
35. *ibid.*, pp. 1 ff.
36. *The Poetics*, ch. 25.
37. *Art and Artifice in Shakespeare*, p. 22.
38. *ibid.*, p. 30.
39. *ibid.*, p. 34.
40. *ibid.*, p. 44.
41. Stoll cites *The Spanish Tragedy*, *Antonio's Revenge* and *Bussy d'Ambois*.
42. *Art and Artifice in Shakespeare*, p. 117.
43. *ibid.*, pp. 133–6.
44. Edward Craig, *Gordon Craig: The Story of his Life*, London, 1968, p. 123.
45. This review has been conveniently reprinted in Beerbohm's *More Theatres, 1898–1903*, New York, 1969.
46. William Poel, *Shakespeare in the Theatre*, p. 223.

47. *The Saturday Review*, 30 May 1903, p. 681.
48. Edward Craig, *op. cit.*, p. 123.
49. *The Saturday Review*, 30 May 1903, p. 681.
50. Edward Craig, *op. cit.*, p. 272.
51. *The Empty Space*, London, 1968, p. 68 (Brook's italics).
52. *On the Art of the Theatre*, London, 1911, p. 161 (Craig's italics).
53. *ibid.*, p. 84.
54. Marc Slonim, *Russian Theatre from the Empire to the Soviets*, London, 1963, p. 178.
55. *The Outlook*, 7 June 1919, p. 568.

5 Barker at the Savoy

1. 32 plays by 17 authors, according to the appendix to Desmond MacCarthy's *The Court Theatre*, London, 1907.
2. *The Exemplary Theatre*, p. 159.
3. *ibid.*, p. 228.
4. Letter to *Play Pictorial*, xxii, no. 126, 1912, p. iv.
5. *The New York Times*, 26 July 1914.
6. *Prefaces to Shakespeare: First Series*, London, 1927, p. xl.
7. *The New York Times*, 26 July 1914.
8. 'Fifty Years of Shakespearian Production: 1898–1948' in *Shakespeare Survey 2*, ed. Allardyce Nicoll, Cambridge, 1949, pp. 7–8.
9. *A Life in the Theatre*, p. 185.
10. Introduction to *The Players' Shakespeare*, London, 1923.
11. Norman Marshall remarks that this lighting device was the first in any theatre: *The Producer and the Play*, p. 153.
12. 'The Lost Leader', broadcast in 1953 and reprinted in *A Bridges-Adams Letter Book*, ed. Robert Speaight, p. 92.
13. *The Morning Post*, quoted in *ibid.*, p. 154.
14. *The Exemplary Theatre*, p. 225.
15. In the possession of the Library of the University of Michigan. They are written in the hand of Val Gurney.
16. 26 July 1914.
17. *The Observer*, 29 September 1912.
18. It is possible that Barker was influenced by the open stage methods of Max Reinhardt, whom he had visited in Berlin in 1910.
19. C. B. Purdom, *Harley Granville Barker*, London 1955, p. 140.
20. *The Daily Telegraph*, 23 September 1912.
21. 23 September 1912.
22. 2 October 1912.
23. *The Saturday Review*, 28 September 1912, p. 391.
24. 29 September 1912.

Notes

25. See below, Chapter 11, p. 223.
26. *The Daily Telegraph,* 23 September 1912.
27. 23 September 1912.
28. 23 September 1912. The first London Post-Impressionist exhibition had opened in 1911 with Cézanne, Gauguin and Van Gogh, and the second opened on 4 October, 1912 with Picasso, Matisse and Flandrin.
29. 23 September 1912.
30. 22 September 1912.
31. *Prefaces to Shakespeare: First Series,* pp. xv–xvi.
32. *The Saturday Review,* 28 September 1912
33. P. G. Konody again in *The Observer,* 29 September 1912.
34. 22 September 1912.
35. 23 September 1912.
36. *The Saturday Review,* 28 September 1912.
37. 27 September 1912.
38. Felix Aylmer, 'The One That Got Away', *Drama,* no. 86, Autumn 1967, pp. 32–3. Aylmer, who rehearsed with Barker that summer, reported that one of the *Macbeth* sets turned up in Birmingham as the Ogre's castle in *Puss in Boots,* which may suggest its character.
39. According to John Booth's count in *The Times Literary Supplement,* 17 April 1919, p. 212, it was exceeded in separate productions only by *Hamlet, Romeo and Juliet, The Merchant of Venice,* and *Much Ado,* in that order of popularity.
40. 16 November 1912.
41. In a letter to Barker, 26 November 1912, in C. B. Purdom, *Harley Granville Barker,* London, 1955, p. 142.
42. xxi, no. 126, 1912.
43. 17 November 1912. Orsino sported a turban.
44. 16 November, 1912.
45. 16 November 1912.
46. 'The Golden Thoughts of Granville Barker', *Play Pictorial,* xxi, no. 126, 1912, p. iv.
47. 16 November 1912.
48. *The Observer,* 17 November 1912.
49. The prompt-book, p. 69.
50. Reported in Purdom, *Harley Granville Barker,* p. 143.
51. *ibid.,* p. 146.
52. *The Saturday Review,* 23 November 1912.
53. *The Nation,* 23 November 1912, p. 351.
54. Quoted in Richard Southern, *The Seven Ages of the Theatre,* London, 1961, p. 263.
55. *Shakespeare on the Stage,* vol. III, p. 287. This was at Wallack's Theatre, New York, later demolished.

Notes

56. See M. St Clare Byrne, 'Fifty Years of Shakespearian Production: 1898–1948', pp. 8–9. Miss Byrne did not think this unity was achieved, but she judged only by the photographs.
57. 8 February 1914.
58. Where necessary, actual gold leaf was used. There are two pages of photographs of these characters in the *Illustrated London News*, 14 February 1914, pp. 248–9.
59. In Purdom's account, *Harley Granville Barker*, p. 149. They were Peas-Blossom, Cobweb, Moth and Mustardseed. In a letter to Gilbert Murray of 1917, Barker wrote that there were five.
60. *Shakespeare on the Stage*, vol. III, p. 290.
61. 14 February 1914.
62. *The Referee*, 8 February 1914.
63. 'An Ordinary Playgoer' writing to the *Daily Mail*, 10 February 1914.
64. 14 February 1914.
65. *New Statesman*, 21 February 1914.
66. 'G.M.' in the *Daily Mail*, 7 February 1914.
67. 14 February 1914.
68. *Shakespeare on the English Stage, 1900–1964*, p. 57.
69. London, 1914, the preface reprinted in *The Saturday Review*, 24 January 1914, p. 106.
70. 6 February 1914.
71. 8 February 1914.
72. *The Exemplary Theatre*, p. 211.
73. *The Saturday Review*, 14 February 1914, p. 202.
74. *Shakespeare on the Stage*, vol. III, pp. 295–6.
75. 8 February 1914.
76. *The Sunday Times*, 8 February 1914.
77. Others have observed this connection; thus J.C. Trewin:'[Granville-Barker's] *Dream* would have been as radical in its day as Peter Brook's is to the conservatives of 1971' ('Far Away and Long Ago', *Drama*, Autumn 1971, p. 48).

6. Granville-Barker's early criticism

1. After the war he hyphenated his name.
2. His hand in this is documented by John Gielgud in *Stage Directions*, ch. 5 and appendix 1.
3. *ibid.*, pp. 53–4.
4. M. St Clare Byrne, 'Fifty Years of Shakespearian Production: 1898–1948', p. 10.
5. *Elizabethan Stage Conditions*, p. 83.
6. In five volumes, London, 1927–47. A sixth volume of collected early prefaces has since been edited by E. M. Moore, 1974.

Notes

7. 'The Study of Shakespeare', *University of Edinburgh Journal, Summer 1936*, p. 10.
8. *William Poel and the Elizabethan Revival*, p. 200.
9. 'Some Tasks for Dramatic Scholarship', p. 17.
10. *ibid.*, pp. 17–18. Fifteen years later he was still pleading for the collaboration of scholar and actor in his broadcast 'The Perennial Shakespeare', *The Listener*, xviii, no. 458, 20 October 1937.
11. *ibid.*, p. 33.
12. *ibid.*, p. 24.
13. *ibid.*, p. 25.
14. *The Tragedie of Macbeth*, p. ix.
15. *ibid.*, p. xii.
16. *ibid.*, p. xiv.
17. *ibid.*, p. xvi.
18. *ibid.*, pp. xvii–xviii.
19. *ibid.*, p. xxi.
20. 'A Note upon Chapters xx and xxi of *The Elizabethan Stage*', *Review of English Studies*, vol. i. no. 1, January 1925, pp. 60–71.
21. *ibid.*, pp. 69–70.
22. 'From *Henry V* to *Hamlet*', *Proceedings of the British Academy, 1924–5*, xi, pp. 283–309, reprinted with corrections in *Aspects of Shakespeare*, ed. J.W. Mackail, London, 1933.
23. *Yale Review*, xv, New Haven, July 1926, pp. 703–24.
24. *Shakespeare and the Popular Dramatic Tradition*, London, 1944.
25. *Shakespeare and the Idea of the Play*, London, 1962.
26. 'Shakespeare and Modern Stagecraft', p. 711.
27. 'Associating with Shakespeare', address to The Shakespeare Association, 25 November 1931, The Shakespeare Association, London, 1932, p. 12.
28. *ibid.*, p. 13.
29. 'The Perennial Shakespeare', *The Listener*, xviii, no. 458, 20 October 1937.
30. *Shakespearean Tragedy*, p. 2.
31. 'Some Tasks for Dramatic Scholarship', p. 20.
32. 'From *Henry V* to *Hamlet*'.
33. *Harley Granville Barker*, pp. 218 ff.
34. *Prefaces to Shakespeare: First Series*, pp. xv–xvi.
35. *ibid.*, p. xxii.
36. *ibid.*, p. 1.
37. *ibid.*, pp. 7–8.
38. *ibid.*, p. 8.
39. *ibid.*, pp. 11–12.
40. *ibid.*, p. 14.
41. *ibid.*, p. 27.
42. *ibid.*, p. 94.
43. *New Statesman and Nation*, 25 July 1953, p. 100.

Notes

44. *Prefaces to Shakespeare: First Series,* p. 141.
45. *ibid.,* pp. 142–3.
46. *ibid.,* p. 176.
47. *ibid.,* p. 178.
48. *Prefaces to Shakespeare: Second Series,* London, 1930, p. 1.
49. *ibid.,* p. 8.
50. *ibid.,* p. 18.
51. *ibid.,* p. 67.
52. *ibid.,* p. 71.
53. *ibid.,* p. 243.
54. *ibid.,* p. 247.
55. *ibid.,* p. 111.
56. *ibid.,* pp. 116–7.
57. *ibid.,* p. 141.

7. Stylized Shakespeare and Nigel Playfair

1. J.C. Trewin, *Shakespeare on the English Stage, 1900–1964,* p. 63
2. *ibid.,* p. 80.
3. Norman Marshall, *The Producer and the Play,* p. 170.
4. Arthur Machen, *Evening News,* 12 May 1916, from Trewin, *op. cit.,* p. 80.
5. 30 October 1918.
6. 3 January 1920.
7. *A Life in the Theatre,* p. 185.
8. Norman Marshall, *The Other Theatre,* p. 94.
9. *ibid.,* p. 95.
10. *ibid.,* p. 96.
11. Nugent Monck, 'The Maddermarket Theatre and the Playing of Shakespeare' in *Shakespeare Survey 12,* ed. Allardyce Nicoll, Cambridge, 1959, p. 75.
12. Nigel Playfair, *The Story of the Lyric Theatre Hammersmith,* London, 1925, p. xvii.
13. *ibid.,* p. 8.
14. 25 April 1920.
15. 22 April 1920.
16. Playfair, *op. cit.,* p. 55.
17. *ibid.,* p. xxx.
18. Mrs Lovat Fraser made all 60 costumes herself for £150 from unbleached linen, and Playfair reports that 'every yard of it was dyed in the Frasers' bath—as indeed was their baby, who emerged from the evening tub one night with red and yellow streaks which lasted for weeks' (*ibid.,* p. 50).
19. 4 May 1919.
20. 23 April 1919.

21. 23 April 1919.
22. 25 April 1919.
23. 27 April 1919. Playfair recalled that Fraser's forest scene was one of the most successful things he did: 'He imagined his set right on the edge of the wood: as if the audience were looking from the thickets out towards a back-cloth of open country, and thus he escaped the necessity of representing the delicately graduated shades of the depth of a wood, which are beyond the power of the theatre' (Playfair, *op. cit.*, p. 50).
24. 23 April 1919.
25. *The Outlook*, 8 May 1920, p. 503. The reference is to W. Heal and Son, the great furniture and household goods store in the Tottenham Court Road, London.
26. 23 April 1919.
27. 23 April 1919.
28. 8 May 1920, p. 616.
29. 25 April 1920.
30. *The Observer*, 27 April 1919.
31. 23 April 1919.
32. 25 April 1920.
33. *The Daily Telegraph*, 23 April 1920.
34. *The Spectator*, 8 May 1920, p. 616.
35. 23 April 1919.
36. 23 April 1919.
37. 28 April 1919.
38. *The Outlook*, 8 May 1920, p. 503.
39. Playfair, *op. cit.*, p. 96.
40. *The Outlook*, 8 May 1920, p. 503.
41. 8 May 1920, p. 616.
42. 23 January 1932, in *A Bridges-Adams Letter Book*, ed. Robert Speaight, p. 32.
43. Letter to A.C. Sprague, 18 November 1952, *ibid.*, p. 49.
44. 'The Lost Leader', broadcast talk of 1953, *ibid.*, pp. 87–93.
45. *The Daily Telegraph*, 27 August 1919.
46. 15 August 1919.
47. 'The Lost Leader', p. 91.
48. 9 August 1919.
49. 8 August 1919. Bridges-Adams outlined his idea about lighting in a letter to John Moore: 'The golden rule, as you probably know, is to keep all projected and focussed lighting on the actors and off the set; this brings the actors into relief and pushes the set back. Footlights are a great help if judiciously used. But the most effective focus-lamps are what we used to call perch-limes, striking sideways and downwards from just behind the proscenium columns; they unobtrusively put an edge on the actors without hitting the scenery. Front of house lamps are bound to hit it unless they

Notes

are high up – and then, as we often see, the actor's mouth and eyes are overshadowed by his eyebrows' (31 January 1962, in *A Bridges-Adams Letter-Book*, ed. Robert Speaight, pp. 15–16).

50. *The Star*, 6 August 1919.
51. 25 April 1920.
52. Norman Marshall, *The Producer and the Play*, p. 168.
53. *Shakespeare on the English Stage, 1900–1964*, p. 110.
54. 19 September 1923.
55. *The Birmingham Post*, 29 April 1932.
56. *The Times*, 29 April 1932.
57. *The Birmingham Post, op. cit.*
58. *The Times, op. cit.*
59. In the library of The Shakespeare Centre, Stratford-upon-Avon. Stage abbreviations have been expanded for the convenience of reading.
60. Eyewitness account by William P. Halstead. Stanley Wells records that the comic business of stabbing oneself with the scabbard dates back at least to 1607, when it is mentioned as a joke in Edward Sharpham's *The Fleire*. See *A Midsummer Night's Dream* in *The New Penguin Shakespeare*, Harmondsworth, 1967, p. 162.
61. 17 April 1934.
62. *A Bridges-Adams Letter Book*, p. 17.
63. *ibid.*, p. 21.
64. *Looking at a Play*, London, 1947, p. 26.

8. Barry Jackson and dizzy modernity

1. *Explorations*, London, 1946, p. 80.
2. *On Reading Shakespeare*, London, 1933, p. 118. Smith refers here to *A Book of Homage to Shakespeare*, Oxford, 1916.
3. The British Academy Lecture of 1930.
4. This echoes the argument in Anne Righter, *Shakespeare and the Idea of the Play*, p. 141, and I owe some of these thoughts to my colleague Douglas Sprigg.
5. Cited in J.C. Trewin, *Shakespeare on the English Stage, 1900–1964*, p. 221. Trewin reports that the audience was baffled by Noguchi's unrecognizable décor: 'No revival was so calculated to withdraw the mind from the timeless, universal, and mythical quality of the narrative.'
6. *The Other Theatre*, p. 165.
7. Under Jackson between 1913 and 1919 the Birmingham Rep produced the following plays by Shakespeare: *The Taming of the Shrew, The Two Gentlemen of Verona, King John, Henry IV, Parts I and II, The Merry Wives of Windsor, As You Like It, Twelfth Night, Measure for Measure, Macbeth* and *The Tempest*.

Notes

8. R. Crompton Rhodes in a letter to *The Times Literary Supplement*, 24 April 1919, p. 225.

9. *Shakespeare on the English Stage, 1900–1964*, pp. 81–2.

10. 5 May 1919.

11. Trewin, *op. cit.*, p. 95.

12. *ibid.*

13. Sir Barry Vincent Jackson had been knighted in the Birthday Honours in the previous June.

14. *The Spectator*, 5 September 1925, p. 364.

15. *Illustrated London News* of 29 August 1925, carried two pages of illustrations (pp. 396–7).

16. *The Sunday Times*, 30 August 1925.

17. Hubert Griffith in *The Observer*, 30 August 1925.

18. 5 September 1925.

19. 26 August 1925.

20. *The Observer*, 30 August 1925.

21. *The Sunday Times*, 30 August 1925.

22. 'Fifty Years of Shakespearian Production, 1898–1948', p. 12.

23. 26 August 1925. Hobbs, later Sir Jack Hobbs, was a cricketer.

24. 5 September 1925, p. 364.

25. 5 September 1925, p. 677.

26. *The Producer and the Play*, p. 175.

27. *The Daily Telegraph*, 26 August 1925.

28. Ivor Brown in *The Saturday Review*, 29 August 1925.

29. *The Observer*, 30 August 1925.

30. *The Daily News*, 26 August 1925.

31. *The Saturday Review*, 29 August 1925.

32. *The Observer*, 30 August 1925.

33. 25 August 1925.

34. 2 December 1925, pp. 629–30.

35. *The Dial*, January 1926, p. 74. Seldes was referring to Barrymore's *Hamlet* of 1922.

36. 7 February 1928.

37. *The Saturday Review*, 11 February 1928, p. 161.

38. Louis Marder, *His Exits and His Entrances: The Story of Shakespeare's Reputation*, Philadelphia, 1963, p. 80.

39. 6 February 1928.

40. *Shakespeare on the English Stage, 1900–1964*, p. 112.

41. *The Producer and the Play*, p. 177.

42. Norman Marshall's ch. 6, 'A Break with Tradition', offers a good account of several pre-war modern-dress productions, notably, Henry Cass's Fascist Italian *Julius Caesar* (Embassy, 1939), Michael MacOwan's *Troilus and Cressida* (Westminster, 1938) at the time of Munich, and Tyrone Guthrie's

Hamlet (Old Vic, 1938) in stylish court dress. Cass's *Caesar* had followed Orson Welles's Fascist treatment of the same play by his own Mercury Theater in 1937, and Welles also directed a black *Macbeth*, set in Haiti, for the Negro People's Theater in 1936.

43. Norman Marshall, *The Other Theatre*, p. 64. Marshall, who was first Gray's stage manager, then one of his directors, provides the best existing account of the work of the Festival Theatre, Cambridge.
44. *ibid.*, p. 54.
45. *ibid.*, p. 63.
46. *ibid.*, p. 67.
47. *Shakespeare on the English Stage, 1900–1964*, p. 137.
48. 18 April 1935. This was the production in which the mock fairies appeared with their heads crowned with lighted candles like so many birthday cakes.
49. J.C. Trewin, *op. cit.*, p. 179.
50. Ronald Harwood, *Sir Donald Wolfit, C.B.E.: his life and work in the unfashionable theatre*, New York, 1971, p. 128.
51. *The Times*, 15 October 1936.
52. *Looking at a Play*, p. 26.
53. 'Hamlet in Plus Fours', *Yale Review*, xvi, New Haven, October 1926, p. 205.
54. *The Approach to Shakespeare*, 2nd ed., London, 1933, p. 13.
55. 'The Elizabethan Shakespeare', The British Academy Lecture, 1929, reprinted in *Aspects of Shakespeare*, ed. J.W. Mackail, London, 1933, p. 214.
56. *Illustrated London News*, 29 August 1925, p. 396.
57. *The Saturday Review*, 29 August 1925.
58. *The Producer and the Play*, p. 189.
59. 'Fifty Years of Shakespearian Production, 1898–1948', p. 13.
60. 30 August 1925.
61. 5 September 1925, p. 364.
62. *The Saturday Review*, 11 February 1928, p. 161.
63. 26 August 1925.

9. Criticism: retreat and advance

1. 'Trend of Shakespearean Scholarship', *Shakespeare Survey 2*, ed. Allardyce Nicoll, Cambridge, 1949, p. 112.
2. 28 February 1925, p. 319.
3. *A Short History of Shakespearean Criticism*, p. 228.
4. Introduction to *Hamlet*, in *The New Shakespeare*, Cambridge, 1934, p. xiv.
5. Cambridge, 1935. See the Preface to the third edition, 1951.
6. An observation by A.C. Sprague in A.C. Sprague and J.C. Trewin, *Shakespeare's Plays Today*, p. 19. The bed had previously appeared in productions in Prague, 1927, and Moscow, 1931. In Moscow the pair were fully cloth-

Notes

ed, but in Prague Gertrude was in nightgown and Hamlet in nightshirt and nightcap: where was his sword?

7. London, 1939.
8. *John Gielgud's Hamlet: A Record of Performance*, New York, 1937, p. 16.
9. Olivier's film of *Hamlet* (1947) also had Oedipal overtones.
10. 'The Old Vic' in *The Year's Work in the Theatre, 1949–1950*, London, 1950, p. 23.
11. Felix Barker, *The Oliviers*, London, 1953, p. 165. Marvin Rosenberg discusses this production fully in *The Masks of Othello*, ch. 12, 'The Modern Iago'.
12. Cambridge, 1932.
13. London, 1936, p. vi.
14. 'Introductory', above, p. 7.
15. Cambridge, 1935.
16. Bradbrook, *op. cit.*, p. 1.
17. The book has recently been reprinted by Octagon Books, New York, 1970.
18. *Preface to Shakespeare* (1765) in *Johnson on Shakespeare*, ed. Walter Raleigh, London, 1908, p. 26.
19. Cambridge, 1935.
20. *What Happens in Hamlet*, 2nd edition, pp. xii–xiii.
21. *ibid.*, p. 15.
22. *ibid.*, p. 92.
23. *ibid.*, p. 108.
24. *ibid.*, p. 146. In my *Shakespeare's Stagecraft*, Cambridge, 1967, p. 132, I accept that the audience needs to see the dumb show, but suggest that it also serves to start the contest of wits from the beginning.
25. 'A Letter by Mr. Harold Child on Some Recent Productions of *Hamlet*', *ibid.*, p. xviii.
26. *ibid.*, p. xx.
27. *The Problem of Style*, p. 108.
28. *Words and Poetry*, pp. 146–8.
29. *Principles of Literary Criticism*, 2nd edition, London, 1926, p. 291.
30. *New Bearings in English Poetry*, London, 1932, pp. 169 ff.
31. London, 1943, p. 121.
32. In L.C. Knights, *Explorations*, pp. 6–18.
33. In *Character and Motive in Shakespeare*, London, 1949.
34. *Education and the University*, p. 125 footnote.
35. *An Approach to Shakespeare*, 3rd edition, New York, 1969, p. ix.
36. *ibid.*, p. xvii.
37. *ibid.*, p. xviii.
38. Bonn, 1936, translated as *The Development of Shakespeare's Imagery*, London, 1951.
39. In *The Frontiers of Drama*, London, 1945, pp. 77 ff.

Notes

40. *Shakespearian Comedy*, London, 1938, p. 11, and quoted in part in Stanley Wells, 'Shakespeare Criticism since Bradley' in *A New Companion to Shakespeare Studies*, ed. K. Muir and S. Schoenbaum, Cambridge, 1971.
41. 'The Study of Shakespeare' (The Inaugural Lecture of the Chair of Rhetoric and English Literature at the University of Edinburgh, 17 January 1936), *University of Edinburgh Journal*, Summer 1936, p. 12.
42. *Shakespearean Tragedy*, London, 1904, p. 247.
43. 'Character in Shakespeare' in *The Critical Review* (Melbourne), No 17, 1974, pp. 114–15.
44. In his ultimate application of new critical method to *King Lear* in *This Great Stage: Image and Structure in King Lear*, Baton Rouge, 1948, Robert Heilman uses the word *pattern* 'to denote a combination or system of poetic and dramatic elements which can be shown to work together in encompassing a body of meaning that has a place in the over-all structure of the play' (p.24).
45. Reprinted as Appendix E in *The Sovereign Flower*, London, 1958.
46. Wilson Knight, *op. cit.*, p. 291.
47. *The Wheel of Fire*, London, 1930, pp. 13–14.
48. Wilson Knight, *op. cit.*, p. vi.
49. *ibid.*, p. 3.
50. *ibid.*, p. 15.
51. *Principles of Shakespearian Production*, Pelican Books edition, Harmondsworth, 1949, p. 20.
52. *ibid.*, p. 36.
53. In *The Reader's Encyclopedia of Shakespeare*, ed. O.J. Campbell and E.G. Quinn, New York, 1966, pp. 837–41.
54. 'The Role of the Shakespearean Producer' in *Theatre for Shakespeare*, Toronto, 1955, and reprinted in *Approaches to Shakespeare*, ed. N. Rabkin, New York, 1964, p. 329.
55. 'Shakespeare Criticism since Bradley', p. 261. My italics.

10. Guthrie and the open stage

1. *A Life in the Theatre*, p. 52.
2. 'I was, and still am, a sucker for jokes and horseplay, and for Great Moments, however corny' (*ibid.*, p. 62).
3. *ibid.*, p. 125.
4. *ibid.*, pp. 125–6.
5. *ibid.*, p. 188.
6. *ibid.*, p. 180.
7. *In Various Directions: a view of theatre*, p. 92.
8. *A Life in the Theatre*, p. 108.
9. *ibid.*, p. 189.

Notes

10. *ibid.*, pp. 183—4.
11. *ibid.*, p. 48.
12. *Renown at Stratford*, Toronto, 1953, p. 28.
13. *Shakespeare's Happy Comedies*, ch. III.
14. J.C. Trewin, *Shakespeare on the English Stage, 1900—1964*, p. 160.
15. Tyrone Guthrie, *A Life in the Theatre*, p. 108.
16. *ibid.*, p. 172.
17. 'Shakespeare on the Modern Stage', *The Listener*, 3 February 1937, pp. 207—9.
18. *The Shakespearean Scene: Dramatic Criticisms*, London, 1949, p. 183.
19. Norman Marshall, *The Other Theatre*, p. 54.
20. J.C. Trewin, *Shakespeare on the English Stage, 1900—1964*, p. 171.
21. *Moonlight at the Globe*, London, 1946, p. 110.
22. *A Life in the Theatre*, p. 275.
23. Foreword to *Ane Satyre of the Thrie Estaites*, ed. James Kinsley, London, 1954, p. 29.
24. *A Life in the Theatre*, p. 279.
25. 'Hamlet at Edinburgh', *New Statesman and Nation*, 29 August 1953, p. 232. This was the Old Vic *Hamlet* with Richard Burton as the Prince.
26. *The Producer and the Play*, p. 236.
27. Tyrone Guthrie, *In Various Directions: a view of theatre*, p. 68.
28. Address to the Shakespeare Stage Society, 24 March 1952, in Robert Speaight, *William Poel and the Elizabethan Revival*, p. 274.
29. 'On Three Productions', *The Year's Work in the Theatre, 1948—1949*, London, 1949, p. 31.
30. Robertson Davies, 'The Players' in *Renown at Stratford*, Toronto, 1953, p. 119.
31. 'First Shakespeare Festival at Stratford, Ontario', *ibid.*, p. 30.
32. Robertson Davies, *Twice Have the Trumpets Sounded*, Toronto, 1954, p. 12.
33. Letter to Tanya Moiseiwitsch in *The Stratford Scene, 1958—1968*, ed. Peter Raby, Toronto, 1968, p. 79.
34. *ibid.*
35. Robertson Davies, 'The Director' in *Renown at Stratford*, p. 39.
36. *ibid.*, p. 120.
37. Tyrone Guthrie, 'Do We Go to the Theatre for Illusion?', *The New York Times*, 16 January 1966.
38. *The New York Times*, 15 July 1953.
39. Walter Kerr, *The New York Herald Tribune*, 15 July 1953.
40. Herbert Whittaker, *The Globe and Mail*, Toronto, 14 July 1953.
41. *ibid.*
42. 25 April 1959, p. 572.
43. 16 July 1953.
44. *The Sunday Times*, 26 April, 1959.

Notes

45. 22 April 1959.
46. *The Daily Telegraph and Morning Post*, 4 April 1956.
47. *The Observer*, 8 April 1956.
48. *The Times*, 4 April 1956.
49. Brian Inglis, *The Spectator*, 13 April 1956, p. 490.
50. *The Guardian*, 2 February 1972. The announcement was first made by Peter Hall in 1966.
51. *William Poel and the Elizabethan Revival*, p. 273.
52. 'Shakespearean Production', *The Year's Work in the Theatre, 1949–1950*, p. 41.

11. Shakespeare, Peter Brook and non-illusion

1. 21 December 1960.
2. *The Times*, 25 January 1962.
3. See Peter Hall, *The Crucial Years*, R.S.C. pamphlet, 1963 and Gareth Lloyd Evans, 'Shakespeare, the Twentieth Century and "Behaviourism"' in *Shakespeare Survey 20*, ed. Kenneth Muir, Cambridge, 1967.
4. For an excellent short history of the Stratford stage see Frederick Bentham, 'Stratford Revisited', *Tabs*, vol. 30, no. 1, London, March 1972.
5. Quoted in Simon Trussler, 'Shakespeare: The Greatest Whore of Them All: Peter Hall at Stratford 1960–1968', *TDR The Drama Review*, vol. 13, no. 2, New York, Winter 1968, p. 170.
6. *Shakespeare's Workmanship*, Cambridge Pocket Edition, pp. 68–9.
7. A. Alvarez, *New Statesman and Nation*, 13 June 1959.
8. *The Sunday Times*, 7 June 1959. Roedean is a girls' public (*sc.* private) school.
9. Peter Forster, *The Spectator*, 12 June 1959, p. 855.
10. Mervyn Jones, *The Observer*, 7 June 1959.
11. *The Times*, 14 June 1963.
12. *The Times*, 27 July 1960.
13. Bamber Gascoigne, *The Spectator*, 2 November 1962, p. 681.
14. *ibid.*
15. Roger Gellert, *New Statesman and Nation*, 19 October 1962, p. 543.
16. *The Spectator*, 31 August 1962, p. 305.
17. 'The stage was bare and level, as spacious and free for movement as the stage at the Globe. But two wall-sections were placed on it that could be moved into almost any position, and so reveal the metal plates, staircases, doorways, trellises or bare boards that were their variable faces. Besides suggesting the location of each scene, these walls could confine the acting-space whenever necessary' (John Russell Brown, *Free Shakespeare*, London, 1974, p. 21).
18. In *Orpheus*, vol. 1, 1948, pp. 139–46. Reprinted in *The Modern Theatre: Readings and Documents*, ed. Daniel Seltzer, Boston, 1967.

Notes

19. *The Empty Space*, Avon Books ed., New York, 1969, p. 9.
20. *ibid.*, pp. 78–9.
21. Address at the UNESCO Shakespeare Quatercentenary, Paris, 1964, from J. C. Trewin, *Peter Brook: A Biography*, London, 1971, p. 148.
22. *The Empty Space*, p. 78.
23. 'Style in Shakespearean Production', pp. 252–3.
24. Stephen Potter, *New Statesman and Nation*, 11 May 1946, p. 336.
25. 'Style in Shakespearean Production', p. 254.
26. *The Times*, 29 April 1946.
27. Peter Brook, *The Empty Space*, p. 80.
28. *New Statesman and Nation*, 1 April 1950, p. 368.
29. 'Shakespeare's Comedies and the Modern Stage' in *Shakespeare Survey 4*, ed. Allardyce Nicoll, Cambridge, 1951, p. 137.
30. *The Empty Space*, p. 81.
31. *The Observer*, 18 August 1957.
32. Margaret Croyden, 'Peter Brook's *Tempest*', *TDR The Drama Review*, vol. 13, no. 3, New York, Spring 1969, p. 126.
33. Martin Esslin, Introduction to Jan Kott, *Shakespeare Our Contemporary*, Anchor Books edition, New York, 1966, p. xxi.
34. The Alec Guinness/Simone Signoret *Macbeth* of 1966 was founded on Kott's chapter 'Macbeth or Death-Infected'. Kott's essay 'Shakespeare's Bitter Arcadia' was possibly influential in the National Theatre's decision to produce an all-male *As You Like It* directed by Clifford Williams in 1967: 'An actor disguised as a girl plays a girl disguised as a boy. Everything is real and unreal, false and genuine at the same time' (*Shakespeare Our Contemporary*, p. 320). The chapter 'Titania and the Ass's Head', with its stress on female sexuality, has spawned several morbid *Dreams*, notably John Hancock's in San Francisco and Pittsburgh in 1966 and Theater de Lys, New York in 1967: in this the fairies were strange flitting creatures and the lovers' codpieces were luminous. Graham Murray's 69 Theatre Company at Manchester University tried out Kott's hunched and lecherous fairies.
35. 'Shakespeare on the Modern Stage: Past Significance and Present Meaning' in *Shakespeare Survey 20*, ed. Kenneth Muir, Cambridge, 1967, p. 115.
36. *Yale Review*, vol. LIX, New Haven, 1969, p. 49. See also Maynard Mack, *King Lear in Our Time*, Berkeley, 1965 for a similar attack.
37. *Drama*, no. 88, Spring 1968, p. 31.
38. See Zdeněk Stříbrný, 'Schola Ludens?', *The Times Literary Supplement*, 12 September 1968, p. 987.
39. Charles Marowitz, 'Lear Log', *Encore*, vol. 10, no. 1, January/February 1963, p. 21. Marowitz was Brook's assistant director, and his 'Log' usefully documents the details of rehearsal. It is reprinted in *Tulane Drama Review*, Winter 1963, pp. 103–21 and in *Theatre at Work*, ed. C. Marowitz and S. Trussler, London, 1967.

Notes

40. *The Birmingham Post*, 7 November 1962.
41. Marowitz, *op. cit.*, p. 28.
42. *The Sunday Times*, 11 November 1962.
43. *The Observer*, 11 November 1962.
44. 'Lear Log', p. 27.
45. *The Birmingham Post*, 7 November 1962.
46. 'Lear Log', p. 27. See also Carol Carlisle, *Shakespeare from the Greenroom*, Chapel Hill, 1969, p. 291.
47. 'Lear Log', p. 26.
48. 'Shakespeare in Britain', *Shakespeare Quarterly*, XIV, 1963, p. 421.
49. Bamber Gascoigne, *The Spectator*, 16 November 1962, p. 758.
50. Peter Brook, *The Empty Space*, p. 67.
51. See F. W. Sternfeld, 'Music in *King Lear* at the Royal Shakespeare Theatre', *Shakespeare Quarterly*, XIV, 1963, pp. 486–7.
52. *Shakespeare and the Energies of Drama*, Princeton, 1972, pp. 95–6 and footnote.
53. Interview with Margaret Tierney, *Plays and Players*, September 1972, p. 27. See also John Russell Brown, *Free Shakespeare*, pp. 23–5.
54. Irving Wardle in *The Times*, 7 June 1970.
55. *The Observer*, 30 August 1970.
56. Quoted in Norman Marshall, *The Producer and the Play*, p. 159.
57. *The Times*, 28 August 1970.
58. *Free Shakespeare*, p. 27.
59. Cited by John Barber, *The Daily Telegraph*, 14 September 1970 and by Peter Thomson, 'A Necessary Theatre: The Royal Shakespeare Season 1970 Reviewed', *Shakespeare Survey 24*, ed. Kenneth Muir, Cambridge, 1971, p. 126.
60. 18 September 1972.
61. 29 August 1970.
62. See especially John Russell Brown, *Free Shakespeare*, pp. 43–4.
63. *Drama*, Autumn 1971, p. 30.
64. *Peter Brook: a biography*, p. 184.
65. In 1968, William A. Ringler, Jr had argued that the fairies had probably been doubled with the mechanicals in Shakespeare's time ('The Number of Actors in Shakespeare's Early Plays' in G. E. Bentley (ed.), *The Seventeenth-Century Stage: A Collection of Critical Essays*, Chicago, 1968, pp. 133–4). According to K. M. Briggs, the Elizabethans thought of fairies as large and small (*The Anatomy of Puck*, London, 1959, pp. 13–16).
66. In a letter to the author after seeing performances in both New York and Chicago, 1971.
67. Frank Dunlop had also doubled these parts in a recent production at the Oxford Playhouse.
68. *New Statesman and Nation*, 4 September 1970, p. 281.

69. Egeus also became Quince, probably to give a leading actor a larger part.
70. *The Observer,* 30 August 1970.
71. 'Shakespeare ne s'est servi des fées, comme, dans d'autres oeuvres, des rois et des reines, que pour en dire davantage. Tout est langage chez lui: les fées, les rois et les reines ne sont que les signes de ce langage' (*Le Nouvel Observateur, op. cit.*).
72. *The Spectator,* 5 September 1970, p. 248.
73. *The Sunday Times,* 13 September 1970.
74. 'Brook's *Dream*' in *Culture and Agitation,* London, 1972, pp. 13–28.
75. 29 August 1970.
76. Miriam Gilbert.
77. At Stratford, the play had seemed on the point of spilling into the auditorium throughout, and in a one-night performance without set or costumes in the Round House, 1971, Brook had actually had the audience sitting on the floor, which constituted part of the acting area. Thus, the lovers and the fairies could chase and run round and through the spectators. He tried the experiment again in a Brooklyn boxing hall in New York in the same year. See Ronald Hayman, 'On Engaging the Audience', *Drama,* Winter 1971, p. 57. At the time of writing (1974) Brook has produced *Timon of Athens* in the shell of the Théatre Bouffes du Nord in Paris, the actors using the floor of the auditorium as a stage and the audience sitting intimately around on tiers of benches as in an arena.

12. Conclusion: the critical revolution

1. Prefatory Note to the third edition, *The Imperial Theme,* London, 1951, p. vi.
2. 'Theatre for Pleasure or Theatre for Instruction' in John Willett, *Brecht on Theatre,* London, 1964, p. 71. The original was written about 1936.
3. *Free Shakespeare.*
4. See Chapter 10, p. 180 above.
5. After Granville-Barker's *Prefaces to Shakespeare* (1927–1947), see especially Arthur Colby Sprague, *Shakespeare and the Actors: The Stage Business in His Plays, 1660–1905* (Cambridge, Mass., 1944), Richard Flatter, *Shakespeare's Producing Hand* (London, 1948), Ronald Watkins, *On Producing Shakespeare* (London, 1950), Rudolf Stamm, *Shakespeare's Word Scenery* (Zürich and St Gallen, 1954), John Russell Brown, *Shakespeare's Plays in Performance* (London, 1967) and J. L. Styan, *Shakespeare's Stagecraft* (Cambridge, 1967). *Shakespeare's Plays Today* (London, 1970) by A. C. Sprague and J. C. Trewin and the series *In Shakespeare's Playhouse* (London, 1974) by Ronald Watkins and Jeremy Lemmon are of recent interest.
6. See James L. Calderwood, *Shakespearean Metadrama,* Minneapolis, 1971.
7. *Shakespeare's Last Plays,* London, 1938, pp. 61, 68.
8. *Shakespeare and the Popular Dramatic Tradition,* pp. 13, 17, 29.

Notes

9. *Shakespeare and the Idea of the Play.*
10. *The Shakespeare Newsletter,* vol, XXIV, no. 1, February 1974.
11. New York, 1960, pp. 63 ff. (the A. W. Mellon Lectures in the Fine Arts, 1956).

Bibliography

Abercombie, Lascelles, 'Plea for the Liberty of Interpreting Shakespeare', *Proceedings of the British Academy*, 1930.

Adams, John Cranford, *The Globe Playhouse*, New York, 1942; 2nd ed. 1961.

Adams, Joseph Quincy, *The Dramatic Records of Sir Henry Herbert, Master of the Revels, 1623–1673*, Boston, 1917.

Shakespearean Playhouses: A History of English Theatres from the Beginnings to the Restoration, Boston, 1917.

Addenbrooke, David, *The Royal Shakespeare Company: the Peter Hall Years*, London, 1974.

Agate, James, ed., *The English Dramatic Critics, 1660–1932*, London, 1932.

Annan, Noel, 'The Marlowe Society Tradition', *Cambridge Journal*, July 1950.

Archer, William, *The Old Drama and the New*, London, 1923.

Baker, George Pierce, *The Development of Shakespeare as a Dramatist*, New York, 1907.

Barish, Jonas, 'The New Theater and the Old: Reversions and Rejuvenations' in *Reinterpretations of Elizabethan Drama*, ed. Norman Rabkin, New York, 1969.

Barker, Felix, *The Oliviers*, London, 1953.

Bartholomeusz, Dennis, *Macbeth and the Players*, Cambridge, 1969.

Beerbohm, Max, *Around Theatres*, London, 1953.

Herbert Beerbohm Tree, London, 1920.

More Theatres, 1898–1903, New York, 1969.

Benson, Frank, *My Memoirs*, London, 1930.

Bentham, Frederick, 'Stratford Revisited', *Tabs*, vol. 30, no. 1, March 1972.

Bentley, G. E., *The Jacobean and Caroline Stage*, 7 vols., Oxford, 1941–68.

Shakespeare and His Theatre, Lincoln, Nebraska, 1964.

Bethell, S. L., *Shakespeare and the Popular Dramatic Tradition*, London and New York, 1944.

Bishop, George W., *Barry Jackson and the London Theatre*, London, 1933.

Black, Michael, 'Character in Shakespeare', *The Critical Review* (Melbourne), no. 17, Melbourne, 1974.

Boaden, James, *Memoirs of the Life of John Philip Kemble*, 2 vols., London, 1825.

Bradbrook, M. C., *Elizabethan Stage Conditions: A Study of their Place in the Interpretation of Shakespeare's Plays*, Cambridge, 1932.

The Growth and Structure of Elizabethan Comedy, London, 1955.

The Rise of the Common Player: A Study of Actor and Society in Shakespeare's England, London, 1962.

Bibliography

Themes and Conventions of Elizabethan Tragedy, Cambridge, 1935.

Bradby, Anne, ed., *Shakespeare Criticism, 1919–1935*, London, 1936.

Bradley, A. C., *Shakespearean Tragedy*, London, 1904.

Bridges-Adams, W., *A Bridges-Adams Letter Book*, ed. Robert Speaight, Society for Theatre Research, 1971.

The Irresistible Theatre, London, 1957.

Looking at a Play, London, 1947.

Briggs, K. M., *The Anatomy of Puck*, London, 1959.

Brook, Peter, *The Empty Space*, London, 1968.

'Style in Shakespearean Production', *Orpheus*, vol. 1, ed. John Lehmann, 1948.

Brown, Ivor, 'The Elizabethan Shakespeare' in *Aspects of Shakespeare*, ed. J. W. Mackail, London, 1933.

'The Old Vic' in *The Year's Work in the Theatre, 1949–1950*, London, 1950.

'Salute to William Poel', *The Saturday Review*, 16 July 1927.

(with George Fearon) *This Shakespeare Industry: Amazing Monument*, London, 1939.

The Way of My World, London, 1954.

Brown, John Russell, 'English Criticism of Shakespeare Performances Today', *Deutsche Shakespeare-Gesellschaft West, Jahrbuch*, ed. H. Heuer, 1967.

Free Shakespeare, London, 1974.

Shakespeare's Plays in Performance, London, 1967.

'Three Directors: A Review of Recent Productions', *Shakespeare Survey 2*, ed. Allardyce Nicoll, Cambridge, 1949.

'The Study and Practice of Shakespeare Production', *Shakespeare Survey 18*, ed. Allardyce Nicoll, Cambridge, 1965.

Byrne, Muriel St Clare, 'Fifty Years of Shakespearian Production, 1898–1948', *Shakespeare Survey 2*, ed. Allardyce Nicoll, Cambridge, 1949.

Foreword and Notes to Harley Granville-Barker, *Prefaces to Shakespeare*, 4 vols., London, 1963 ed.

Calderwood, James L., *Shakespearean Metadrama*, Minneapolis, 1971.

Carlisle, Carol, *Shakespeare from the Greenroom*, Chapel Hill, 1969.

Casson, Lewis, 'William Poel and the Modern Theatre', *The Listener*, 10 January 1952.

Chambers, Edmund, *The Elizabethan Stage*, 4 vols., Oxford, 1923.

William Shakespeare: A Study of Facts and Problems, 2 vols., Oxford, 1930.

Charlton, H. B., *Shakespearian Comedy*, London, 1938.

Shakespearian Tragedy, London, 1948.

Charney, Maurice, *Style in 'Hamlet'*, Princeton, 1969.

Child, Harold, 'Shakespeare in the Theatre from the Restoration to the Present Time' in *A Companion to Shakespeare Studies*, ed. Harley Granville-Barker and G. B. Harrison, Cambridge, 1934.

Clemen, Wolfgang, *The Development of Shakespeare's Imagery*, London, 1951.

Cook, Dutton, *Nights at the Play II*, London, 1883.

Bibliography

Cooke, Katharine, *A. C. Bradley and his Influence in Twentieth Century Shakespeare Criticism*, London, 1972.

Craig, Edward, *Gordon Craig: The Story of his Life*, London, 1968.

Craig, Edward Gordon, *Henry Irving*, London, 1930.

Index to the Story of My Days, London, 1957.

The Mask (ed.), Florence, 1908–1928.

On the Art of the Theatre, London, 1911 and 1957.

Craig, Hardin, 'Trend of Shakespearean Scholarship', *Shakespeare Survey 2*, ed. Allardyce Nicoll, Cambridge, 1949.

Crosse, Gordon, *Shakespearean Playgoing, 1890–1952*, London, 1953.

Croyden, Margaret, 'Peter Brook's *Tempest*', *TDR The Drama Review*, vol. 13, no. 3, Spring 1969.

Cruttwell, Patrick, 'Shakespeare Is Not Our Contemporary', *Yale Review*, vol. LIX, 1969.

Darbyshire, Alfred, *The Art of the Victorian Stage*, Manchester, 1907.

Darlington, W. A., *The Actor and his Audience*, London, 1949.

Six Thousand and One Nights, London, 1960.

David, R. W., 'Actors and Scholars: A View of Shakespeare in the Modern Theatre', *Shakespeare Survey 12*, ed. Allardyce Nicoll, Cambridge, 1959.

'Shakespeare's Comedies and the Modern Stage', *Shakespeare Survey 4*, ed. Allardyce Nicoll, Cambridge, 1951.

Davies, Robertson, and Tyrone Guthrie, *Renown at Stratford*, Toronto, 1953.

Thrice the Brinded Cat Hath Mew'd, Toronto, 1955.

Twice Have the Trumpets Sounded, Toronto, 1954.

Day, M. C., and J. C., Trewin, *The Shakespeare Memorial Theatre*, London, 1932.

Dickins, Richard, *Forty Years of Shakespeare on the English Stage, 1867–1907: A Student's Memories*, London, 1907.

Dowden, Edward, *Introduction to Shakspere*, London, 1893.

Shakspere: A Critical Study of His Mind and Art, London, 1875.

Shakspere Primer, London, 1877.

Eastman, Arthur, *A Short History of Shakespearean Criticism*, New York, 1968.

Ellis, Ruth, *The Shakespeare Memorial Theatre*, London, 1948.

Ellis-Fermor, Una, *The Frontiers of Drama*, London, 1945.

Empson, William, *Seven Types of Ambiguity*, London, 1930.

Esslin, Martin, Introduction to Jan Kott, *Shakespeare Our Contemporary*, Anchor Books ed., New York, 1966.

Evans, G. Blakemore, ed., *Shakespearean Prompt-Books of the 17th Century*, 5 vols., Charlottesville, 1960–70.

Evans, Gareth Lloyd, 'Shakespeare, the Twentieth Century and "Behaviourism"', *Shakespeare Survey 20*, ed. Kenneth Muir, Cambridge, 1967.

Farjeon, Herbert, *The Shakespearean Scene: Dramatic Criticisms*, London, 1949.

Flatter, Richard, *Shakespeare's Producing Hand*, London, 1948.

Foakes, R. A. and R. T. Rickert, *Henslowe's Diary*, Cambridge, 1961.

Bibliography

Gielgud, John, *Early Stages*, London, 1939, rev. ed., 1953.

'Granville-Barker's Shakespeare', *Theatre Arts Monthly*, xxxi, October, 1947.

Stage Directions, London, 1963.

Gilder, Rosamond, *John Gielgud's Hamlet: A Record of Performance*, New York, 1937.

Goldman, Michael, *Shakespeare and the Energies of Drama*, Princeton, 1972.

Gombrich, E. H., *Art and Illusion*, New York, 1960.

Granville-Barker, Harley, 'Associating with Shakespeare', The Shakespeare Association, London, 1932.

ed. (with G. B. Harrison) *A Companion to Shakespeare Studies*, Cambridge, 1934.

The Exemplary Theatre, London, 1922.

'From *Henry V* to *Hamlet*', *Proceedings of the British Academy*, 1924–25, xi, 1925. Reprinted with corrections in *Aspects of Shakespeare*, ed. J. W. Mackail, London, 1933.

'Hamlet in Plus Fours', *Yale Review*, xvi, October 1926.

'Notes on Rehearsing a Play', *Drama*, i.i, July 1919.

On Dramatic Method, London, 1931.

On Poetry in Drama, London, 1937.

'The Perennial Shakespeare', *The Listener*, xviii, no. 458, 20 October 1937.

ed., *The Players' Shakespeare*, London, 1923–1927.

Prefaces to Shakespeare, 5 vols., London, 1927–1947.

Prefaces to Shakespeare, vol. vi, ed. E. M. Moore, London, 1974.

'Shakespeare and Modern Stagecraft', *Yale Review*, xv, July 1926.

'Shakespeare's Dramatic Art' in *A Companion to Shakespeare Studies*, ed. H. Granville-Barker and G. B. Harrison, Cambridge, 1934.

'Some Tasks for Dramatic Scholarship' in *Essays by Divers Hands*, ed. F. S. Boas, iii, London, 1923.

ed., *The Tragedie of Macbeth* in *The Player's Shakespeare*, London, 1923.

The Use of the Drama, London, 1945.

Grebanier, Bernard, *The Heart of Hamlet*, New York, 1949.

Greg, W. W., ed., *Henslowe's Diary*, 2 vols., Oxford, 1904 and 1908.

ed., *Henslowe Papers*, Oxford, 1907.

ed., *Dramatic Documents from the Elizabethan Playhouses*, 2 vols., Oxford, 1931.

Guthrie, Tyrone, Foreword to *Ane Satyre of the Thrie Estaits*, ed. James Kinsley, London, 1954.

'Do We Go to the Theatre for Illusion?', *The New York Times*, 16 January 1966.

In Various Directions: a view of the theatre, London, 1965.

A Life in the Theatre, London, 1959.

'On Three Productions' in *The Year's Work in the Theatre, 1948–1949*, London, 1949.

(with Robertson Davies) *Renown at Stratford*, Toronto, 1953.

Bibliography

'Shakespeare at Stratford, Ontario', *Shakespeare Survey 8*, ed. Allardyce Nicoll, Cambridge, 1955.

'Shakespearean Production' in *The Year's Work in the Theatre, 1949—1950*, London, 1950.

'Shakespeare on the Modern Stage', *The Listener*, 3 February 1937.

Theatre Prospect, London, 1932.

Hall, Peter, *The Crucial Years*, The Royal Shakespeare Company, 1963.

Halliday, F. E., *The Cult of Shakespeare*, London, 1957.

Halliwell-Phillipps, J. O., *Illustrations of the Life of Shakespeare*, London, 1874.

Hamilton, C. and Lilian Baylis, *The Old Vic*, London, 1926.

Harbage, Alfred, *Theatre for Shakespeare*, Toronto, 1955.

Harris, Arthur J., 'William Poel's Elizabethan Stage; the First Experiment', *Theatre Notebook*, vol. xvii, no. 4, Summer, 1963.

Harrison, G. B., ed., *The Elizabethan Journals, 1591—1603*, 3 vols., London, 1929—1933.

A Jacobean Journal, 1603—1606, London, 1941.

A Second Jacobean Journal, 1607—1610, Ann Arbor, 1958.

Hartnoll, Phyllis, ed., *The Oxford Companion to the Theatre*, London, 1951.

Harwood, Ronald, *Sir Donald Wolfit, C.B.E.: his life and work in the unfashionable theatre*, New York, 1971.

Hayman, Ronald, 'On Engaging the Audience', *Drama*, Winter 1971.

Hazlitt, William, *Hazlitt on Theatre*, ed. William Archer and Robert Lowe, London, 1895.

Heilman, Robert Bechtold, *This Great Stage: Image and Structure in King Lear*, Baton Rouge, 1948.

(with Cleanth Brooks) *Understanding Drama: Twelve Plays*, New York, 1948.

His Majesty's Stationery Office, *The Drama in Adult Education*, 1926.

Hobson, Harold, *Theatre*, London, 1948.

Hodges, C. W., *The Globe Restored*, London, 1953.

Shakespeare's Second Globe: The Missing Monument, London, 1974.

Hogan, C. B., *Shakespeare in the Theatre, 1701—1800*, 2 vols., London, 1952 and 1957.

Hotson, Leslie, *Shakespeare's Wooden O*, London, 1959.

Hudson, Lynton, *The English Stage, 1850—1950*, London, 1951.

Hunt, Hugh, *The Live Theatre: An Introduction to the History and Practice of the Stage*, London, 1961.

Old Vic Prefaces, London, 1954.

Inkster, Leonard, 'Shaw and Mr. Granville Barker' in *Poetry and Drama I*, London, 1913.

Irving, Laurence, *Henry Irving: The Actor and His World*, London, 1951.

Jackson, Barry, 'Producing the Comedies', *Shakespeare Survey 8*, ed. Allardyce Nicoll, Cambridge, 1955.

James, Henry, *The Scenic Art, 1872—1901*, London, 1957.

Jones, Ernest, *Hamlet and Oedipus*, London, 1949.

Bibliography

Joseph, B. L., *The Tragic Actor*, London, 1959.

Kelly, Helen M. T., *The Granville Barker Shakespeare Productions: A Study Based on the Promptbooks*, unpublished dissertation, University of Michigan, 1965.

Kemp, T. C., 'Acting Shakespeare: Modern Tendencies in Playing and Production', *Shakespeare Survey 7*, ed. Allardyce Nicoll, Cambridge, 1954.

Birmingham Repertory Theatre: the Playhouse and the Man, Birmingham, 1943.

Knight, G. Wilson, *The Imperial Theme*, 3rd ed., London, 1951.

Myth and Miracle: An Essay on the Symbolism of Shakespeare, London, 1929.

'The Principles of Shakespeare Interpretation' in *The Sovereign Flower*, London, 1958.

Principles of Shakespearian Production, London, 1936. Reprinted by Penguin Books, 1949.

'The Producer as Hamlet', *The Times Literary Supplement*, 16 July 1974.

The Shakespearian Tempest, London, 1932.

'Symbolism' in *The Reader's Encyclopedia of Shakespeare*, ed. O. J. Campbell and E. G. Quinn, New York, 1966.

The Wheel of Fire, London, 1930.

Knights, L. C., *Explorations*, London, 1946.

'How Many Children Had Lady Macbeth?' in *Explorations*, London, 1946.

Some Shakespearian Themes, London, 1959.

Kott, Jan, *Shakespeare Our Contemporary*, trans. Boleslaw Taborski, London, 1966.

Lamb, Charles, 'On the Tragedies of Shakespeare, Considered with Reference to Their Fitness for Stage Representation', 1811.

Lawrence, W. J., *The Elizabethan Playhouse and Other Studies*, 2 vols., London, 1912 and 1913.

Old Theatre Days and Ways, London, 1935.

The Physical Conditions of the Elizabethan Public Playhouses, London, 1927.

Pre-Restoration Stage Studies, London, 1927.

Shakespeare's Workshop, Oxford, 1928.

Those Nut-Cracking Elizabethans, London, 1935.

Leavis, F. R., 'Diabolic Intellect and the Noble Hero: A Note on Othello', *Scrutiny*, vol. vi, no. 3, Cambridge, 1937.

Education and the University, London, 1943.

New Bearings in English Poetry, London, 1932.

(ed.) *Towards Standards of Criticism*, Selections from *The Calendar of Modern Letters, 1925–7*, London, 1933.

Lee, Sidney, *Shakespeare and the Modern Stage with Other Essays*, New York, 1906.

Lelyveld, Toby, *Shylock on the Stage*, Cleveland, 1960.

Lewes, G. M., *On Actors and the Art of Acting*, London, 1875.

Lieven, Peter, *The Birth of the Ballets-Russes*, trans. L. Zarine, New York, 1936.

Bibliography

MacCarthy, Desmond, *The Court Theatre, 1904–1907: A Commentary and a Criticism*, London, 1907.

Theatre, London, 1954.

Mack, Maynard, *King Lear in Our Time*, Berkeley, 1965.

Mackail, J. W., *The Approach to Shakespeare*, London, 1930. 2nd ed., 1933.

(ed.) *Aspects of Shakespeare*, London, 1933.

MacOwan, Michael, 'The Sad Case of Professor Kott', *Drama*, no. 88, Spring 1968.

Macready, Charles, *Diary and Reminiscences*, ed. F. Pollock, 2 vols., London, 1875.

Malone, Edmond, *An Historic Account of the Rise and Progress of the English Stage, and of the Oeconomy and Usages of the Ancient Theatres in England*, London, 1792.

Marder, Louis, *His Exits and His Entrances: The Story of Shakespeare's Reputation*, Philadelphia, 1963.

Marowitz, Charles, 'Lear Log', *Encore*, vol. 10, no. 1, January/February 1963.

(ed. with S. Trussler) *Theatre at Work*, London, 1967.

Marshall, Norman, *The Other Theatre*, London, 1947.

The Producer and the Play, London, 1957.

McGaw, C., 'Against the Illusionistic Approach to Directing', *Educational Theatre Journal*, vol. 1, no. 1, March 1950.

McGill, Robert E., *Stratford, 1955: The Establishment of a Convention*, unpublished dissertation, University of Michigan, 1972.

Merchant, W. Moelwyn, *Shakespeare and the Artist*, London, 1959.

Miller, Anna I., *The Independent Theatre in Europe*, New York, 1931.

Monck, Nugent, 'The Maddermarket Theatre and the Playing of Shakespeare', *Shakespeare Survey 12*, ed. Allardyce Nicoll, Cambridge, 1959.

Montague, C. E., *Dramatic Values*, London, 1911.

Morley, Henry, *The Journal of a London Playgoer, 1851–1866*, London, 1891.

Moulton, R. G., *Shakespeare as a Dramatic Artist: A Popular Illustration of Scientific Criticism*, Oxford, 1885.

Muir, Kenneth, 'Changing Interpretations of Shakespeare' in *The Age of Shakespeare*, ed. Boris Ford, Harmondsworth, 1955.

'Fifty Years of Shakespearian Criticism, 1900–1950', *Shakespeare Survey 4*, ed. Allardyce Nicoll, Cambridge 1951.

(with Samuel Schoenbaum) *A New Companion to Shakespeare Studies*, Cambridge, 1971.

Murry, J. Middleton, *Countries of the Mind, Second Series*, London, 1931.

The Problem of Style, London, 1922.

Nicoll, Allardyce, 'Shakespearian Production in the Nineteenth Century' in *William Shakespeare, 1564–1964* (the Shakespeare Exhibition catalogue), 1964.

'Studies in the Elizabethan Stage Since 1900', *Shakespeare Survey 6*, ed. Allardyce Nicoll, Cambridge, 1948.

Bibliography

Odell, George C. D., *Shakespeare from Betterton to Irving*, 2 vols., New York, 1920.

Oxberry, W., *The New English Drama*, London, 1818–1823.

Palmer John, *The Future of the Theatre*, London, 1914.

Pearson, Hesketh, *Beerbohm Tree: His Life and Laughter*, London, 1956.

The Last Actor–Managers, London, 1950.

Pepys, Samuel, *The Diary*, ed. G. Gregory Smith, London, 1935.

Playfair, Nigel, *Hammersmith Hoy*, London, 1930.

The Story of the Lyric Theatre, Hammersmith, London, 1925.

Poel, William, *Shakespeare in the Theatre*, London, 1913.

'Shakespeare's Stage and Plays', *Bulletin of the John Rylands Library*, April– September 1916.

What Is Wrong with the Stage?, London, 1920.

Price, J. G., *The Unfortunate Comedy (All's Well)*, Liverpool, 1968.

Purdom, C. B., (ed.) *Bernard Shaw's Letters to Granville Barker*, London, 1957.

Harley Granville Barker, Man of the Theatre, Dramatist and Scholar, London, 1955.

Quiller-Couch, Arthur, (with John Dover Wilson) *The New Shakespeare*, Cambridge, 1921–1965.

Shakespeare's Workmanship, London, 1918, Cambridge Pocket Edition, 1931.

Rabkin, Norman, ed., *Reinterpretations of Elizabethan Drama*, New York, 1969.

Raby, Peter, ed., *The Stratford Scene, 1958–1968*, Toronto, 1968.

Raleigh, Walter, ed., *Johnson on Shakespeare*, London, 1908.

Shakespeare, London, 1907.

Ralli, A., *A History of Shakespearian Criticism*, 2 vols., Oxford, 1932.

Reynolds, G. F., *Some Principles of Elizabethan Staging*, Chicago, 1905.

Richards, I. A., *Principles of Literary Criticism*, 2nd. ed., London, 1926.

Rickword, C. H., 'A Note on Fiction', in *Towards Standards of Criticism*, ed. F. R. Leavis, London, 1933.

Ridler, Anne, ed., *Shakespeare Criticism, 1919–1935*, Oxford, 1936.

ed., *Shakespeare Criticism, 1935–1960*, Oxford, 1963.

Righter, Anne, *Shakespeare and the Idea of the Play*, London, 1962.

Ringler, Jr, William A., 'The Number of Actors in Shakespeare's Early Plays' in G. E. Bentley (ed.), *The Seventeenth-Century Stage: A Collection of Critical Essays*, Chicago, 1968.

Robinson, Lennox, *Curtain Up*, London, 1942.

Rosenberg, Marvin, *The Masks of King Lear*, Berkeley, 1972.

The Masks of Othello, Berkeley, 1961.

Royal Society of Literature, *Essays by Divers Hands, III*, London, 1923.

Rutherston, Albert, 'Decoration in the Art of the Theatre', *Monthly Chapbook*, I, August 1919.

Sixteen Designs for the Theatre, London, 1928.

Rylands, George, *Words and Poetry*, London, 1928.

Schücking, L. L., *Character Problems in Shakespeare's Plays*, London, 1922.

271

Bibliography

Schoenbaum, Samuel, *Shakespeare's Lives*, Oxford and New York, 1970.

Selbourne, David, *Culture and Agitation*, London, 1972.

Seltzer, Daniel, ed., *The Modern Theatre: Readings and Documents*, Boston, 1967.

Sharp, Cecil James, *'A Midsummer Night's Dream' Songs and Incidental Music arranged and composed by Cecil J. Sharp for Granville Barker's Production at the Savoy Theatre, January, 1914*, London, 1914.

Shattuck, Charles H., *Mr Macready Produces As You Like It: a promptbook study*, Urbana, 1962.

The Shakespeare Promptbooks: A Descriptive Catalogue, Urbana, 1965.

Shaw, George Bernard, *Dramatic Opinions*, 2 vols., London, 1907.

Simpson, Percy, *Shakespearian Punctuation*, Oxford, 1911.

Slonim, Marc, *Russian Theatre from the Empire to the Soviets*, London, 1963.

Smith, Logan Pearsall, *On Reading Shakespeare*, London, 1933.

Southern, Richard, *The Seven Ages of the Theatre*, London, 1961.

The Staging of Plays before Shakespeare, London, 1973.

Speaight, Robert, 'The Cycle of Shakespeare Production', Theodore Spencer Lecture, Cambridge, Mass., October 1969.

'Shakespeare in Britain', *Shakespeare Quarterly*, xiv, 1963.

Shakespeare on the Stage, London, 1973.

William Poel and the Elizabethan Revival, London, 1954.

Sprague, Arthur Colby, *Shakespeare and the Actors: The Stage Business in his Plays, 1660–1905*, Cambridge, Mass., 1944.

'Shakespeare and William Poel', *University of Toronto Quarterly*, October 1947.

Shakespearian Players and Performances, Cambridge, Mass., 1953.

'Shakespeare's Plays on the English Stage' in *A New Companion to Shakespeare Studies*, ed. Kenneth Muir and Samuel Schoenbaum, Cambridge, 1971.

(with J. C. Trewin) *Shakespeare's Plays Today*, London, 1970.

Spurgeon, Caroline, 'Leading Motives in the Imagery of Shakespeare's Tragedies', *The Shakespeare Association*, 1930.

Shakespeare's Imagery and What It Tells Us, Cambridge, 1935.

Stamm, Rudolph, *Shakespeare's Word Scenery*, Zürich and St Gallen, 1954.

Stavinsky, Aron Y., *Shakespeare and the Victorians: Roots of Modern Criticism*, Norman, Okla., 1969.

Sternfeld, F. W., 'Music in *King Lear* at the Royal Shakespeare Theatre', *Shakespeare Quarterly*, xiv, 1963.

Stewart, J. I. M., *Character and Motive in Shakespeare*, London, 1949.

Stoll, E. E., *Art and Artifice in Shakespeare: A Study in Dramatic Contrast and Illusion*, Cambridge, 1933.

Stříbrný, Zdeněk, 'Schola Ludens?', *The Times Literary Supplement*, 12 September 1968.

Styan, J. L., *Drama, Stage and Audience*. Cambridge, 1975.

The Elements of Drama, Cambridge, 1960.

Bibliography

Shakespeare's Stagecraft, Cambridge, 1967.

Thomson, Peter, 'A Necessary Theatre: The Royal Shakespeare Season 1970 Reviewed', *Shakespeare Survey 24*, ed., Kenneth Muir, Cambridge, 1971.

Tillyard, E. M. W., *The Elizabethan World Picture*, London, 1943.

Shakespeare's Last Plays, London 1938.

Traversi, D. A., *An Approach to Shakespeare*, London, 1938, 3rd. ed., New York, 1969.

Tree, Beerbohm, *Thoughts and After-Thoughts*, London, 1913.

Trewin, J. C., *Benson and the Bensonians*, London, 1960.

The Birmingham Repertory Theatre, 1913–1963, London, 1963.

Peter Brook: A Biography, London, 1971.

Shakespeare on the English Stage, 1900–1964, London, 1964.

(with T. C. Kemp) *The Stratford Festival*, Birmingham, 1953.

(ed.) *The Year's Work in the Theatre*, 3 vols., London, 1948–1951.

Trussler, Simon, 'Shakespeare, the Greatest Whore of Them All: Peter Hall at Stratford, 1960–1968', *TDR The Drama Review*, vol. 13, no. 2, Winter 1968.

Walkley, A. B., *Playhouse Impressions*, London, 1892.

Watkins, Ronald, (with Jeremy Lemmon) *In Shakespeare's Playhouse*, London, 1974.

Moonlight at the Globe, London, 1946.

On Producing Shakespeare, London, 1950.

Webster, Margaret, *Shakespeare Today*, London, 1957.

Weimann, Robert, 'Shakespeare on the Modern Stage: Past Significance and Present Meaning', *Shakespeare Survey 20*, ed. Kenneth Muir, Cambridge, 1967.

Wells, Stanley, *Literature and Drama, with special reference to Shakespeare and his contemporaries*, London, 1970.

'Shakespeare Criticism Since Bradley' in *A New Companion to Shakespeare Studies*, ed. Kenneth Muir and Samuel Schoenbaum, Cambridge, 1971.

West, E. J., (ed.) *Shaw on Shakespeare*, London, 1958.

Whittaker, H., *The Stratford Festival, 1953–1957*, Toronto, 1958.

Whitworth, Geoffreý, *Harley Granville-Barker, 1877–1946*, London, 1948.

Willett, John, *Brecht on Theatre*, London, 1964.

The Theatre of Bertolt Brecht, London, 1959.

Williams, E. Harcourt, *Old Vic Saga*, London, 1949.

Wilson, A. E., *Edwardian Theatre*, London, 1951.

Wilson, Edwin, (ed.) *Shaw on Shakespeare*, London, 1962.

Wilson, John Dover, 'The Elizabethan Shakespeare' in *Aspects of Shakespeare*, British Academy Lectures, 1923–31, ed. J. W. Mackail, London and Oxford, 1933.

Introduction to *Hamlet* in *The New Shakespeare*, Cambridge, 1934.

Milestones on the Dover Road, London, 1969.

'Shakespeare: The Scholar's Contribution', *The Listener*, 17 March 1937.

Shakespeare's Happy Comedies, London, 1962.

Bibliography

'The Study of Shakespeare', *University of Edinburgh Journal*, Summer 1936.
What Happens in Hamlet, Cambridge, 1935. 2nd ed., 1937.
Winter, William, *Shakespeare on the Stage*, 3 vols., New York, 1911, 1915, 1916.

Index

Index

tone, 5; on transcendental fog, 5; *Exemplary Theatre*, 6–7; his *Midsummer Night's Dream*, 15, 64, 84, 85, 95–104, 105, 130, 249; not anticipated in nineteenth century, 28; stage ripe for, 29; presides at B.D.L. Conference, 31; *Prefaces*, 31, 78, 106–21; influence on Wilson, 31–3; on Coleridge, 34; debt to Bradley, 37; on Poel, 47, 243; anticipated by Poel, 62; plays *Richard II*, 64; his *Two Gentlemen*, 64; his *Winter's Tale*, 64, 85–90, 93, 94, 104, 108; worked with Gielgud, 64, 245; Gielgud's debt to, 64; on Lawrence, 71; debt to Poel, 73; on Russian Ballet, 81; at the Court, 82; on authenticity, 82; 'gain Shakespeare's effects', 83; his settings, 83; on illusion, 84; on verse speaking, 84; his *Twelfth Night*, 85, 90–5, 104, 224; rehearses *Macbeth*, 90, 248; on illusion at the Savoy, 103; co-produces *King Lear*, 105; his disciples, 106; projects variorum edition, 107; on *Hamlet*, 107–8, 118; *Players' Shakespeare*, 108; debt to Poel and Bradley, 111–12; on essentials of Elizabethan stage, 112; on *Love's Labour's Lost*, 113–16; on *Romeo and Juliet*, 114, 118; on *Merchant of Venice*, 114, 118, 119; on *Julius Caesar*, 115, 116; on *King Lear*, 115, 116–18; on *Cymbeline*, 118, 119–20; on *Antony and Cleopatra*, 118, 120–1; stylization, 122; influence on Fagan, 123; on Playfair, 125, 128; associated with Bridges-Adams, 132; compared with Bridges-Adams, 133, 135, 137, 138; influence on Jackson, 141, 142, 157; on modern dress, 156;

taken up by Bradbrook, 164; correspondence with Wilson on *Hamlet*, 166; co-editor with Harrison, 168; Guthrie's debt, 182; his contribution, 232–3, 235; relation to Brecht, 233; possible influence by Reinhardt, 247; volume VI of *Prefaces*, 249

Barrault, Jean-Louis, 217

Barret, Wilson, 52

Barrie, J. M., on Barker, 94–5

Barrymore, John, 149, 160, 254

Bartholomeusz, Dennis, 238

Barton, John, 207; co-produces *Troilus and Cressida*, 209; his *Wars of the Roses*, 210; his *Richard II*, 234, 236

Beckerman, Bernard, 5

Beckett, Samuel, 217–18

Beerbohm, Max, on Poel, 60–1; on Craig, 79–80

Bell, John, 239

Benn, Ernest, 31

Bennett, Arnold, 125

Benson, Frank, R., his *Midsummer Night's Dream*, 25, 240; his *Hamlet*, 27; tours Shakespeare, 69; invites Playfair, 125

Benthall, Michael, his *Hamlet*, 189, 206; his *Tempest*, 206; his *Midsummer Night's Dream*, 206

Bentham, Frederick, 259

Bentley, G. E., 5, 238, 245

Bethell, S. L., 111, 165, 236

Birmingham Repertory Theatre, 106, 141–2, 149, 253

Black, Michael, 175, 242

Blackie and Son, 67

Blackmur, R. P., 168

Bliss, Arthur, 129

Board of Education, 68, 245

Boas, F. S., 243

bowdlerizing, 67; Poel's, 244

Index

Index

1; invites Rylands and Coghill, 168; his *Merchant of Venice*, 183
Gilbert, Miriam, 228, 262
Gilder, Rosamond, 162–3
Ginn and Company, 67
Globe Theatre, 48, 65; replica at Earl's Court, 66; inner stage in, 112; 120, 124, 152; replica by Payne, 167; replica at Ashland, Oregon, 187; replica at San Diego, 187; replica on South Bank, 205; model by Adams, 191, 193; Hodges on, 193; Hotson on, 193–4; Pycroft's nineteenth-century version, 242 (*see* Plate 5, p. 42)
Goethe, on *Hamlet*, 3; on Elizabethan theatre, 34
Goldman, Michael, 223
Gollancz, Israel, 46, 110
Gombrich, E. H., 237
Gosse, Edmund, 46
Gourmont, Rémy de, 168
Granville-Barker, Harley, *see* Barker, Harley Granville
Gray, Terence, 152–3; his *Merchant of Venice, Twelfth Night, As You Like It, Romeo and Juliet, Henry VIII*, 153; Guthrie associated with, 185; Marshall on, 190, 255
Grebanier, Bernard, on *Hamlet*, 8
Greet, Ben, 31; co-produces with Poel, 64; his *Twelfth Night*, 64; his *Midsummer Night's Dream*, 241
Greg, W. W., publication of Henslowe, 4, 43; member of Mermaid Club, 66; establishes text, 69
Grein, J. T., on Barker, 87–8; 91, 93, 103–4
Griffith, Hubert, 146, 148, 254
Griggs, William, publishes *Hamlet* quartos, 52
Grosses Schauspielhaus, 201
Guiness, Alec, 185, 194, 197, 198, 260

Guthrie, Tyrone, his *Love's Labour's Lost*, 3, 33, 183; new mode of performance, 5; at Stratford, Ontario, 5–6, 194–201; on Irving, 27; on Poel, 47; on directional influence, 64; debt to Monck, 64; on Barker's curtains, 83; at Old Vic, 124, 184–5, 208; his *Hamlet*, 163, 181, 184, 185, 254; his *Othello*, 163, 101; his *Coriolanus*, 163, 181; link with Knight, 177; his philosophy, 180–1; on *Julius Caesar*, 181; on *Merchant of Venice*, 181; debt to Barker, Poel and Shaw, 182; ideal house for Shakespeare, 182; on Gielgud, 183; his *Twelfth Night*, 184; his *Henry VIII*, 184, 190; his *Measure for Measure*, 184; his *Tempest*, 184; his *Macbeth*, 184; his *Midsummer Night's Dream*, 185; his *Taming of the Shrew*, 185, 201; at Edinburgh, 187–8, 193; his *Richard III*, 196–7; his *All's Well*, 197–201; his *Merchant of Venice*, 201; his *Troilus and Cressida*, 203–4; his contribution, 205, 232; link with Brecht, 234

Hall, Peter, austerities, 1; policy with RSC, 7, 207–10, 259; his *Midsummer Night's Dream*, 208–9; co-produces *Troilus and Cressida*, 209; co-produces *Wars of the Roses*, 210
Halliwell-Phillipps, J. O., 41–3, 44, 46, 244
Halstead, W. P., 253
Hamlet, Goethe on, 3; by Irving, 3, 51; by Jackson, 6; Grebanier on, 8; Charney on, 8; at Drury Lane, 11; cutting, 11–12; nineteenth-century costume in, 16; by Benson, 27; Irving edition, 28; by

281

Index

283

Index

Index

Index

Index